conversations
with leading
educators

from EDUCATIONAL
LEADERSHIP

Edited by Ronald S. Brandt

Association for Supervision and Curriculum Development
Alexandria, Virginia

Copyright 1989 by the
Association for Supervision and Curriculum Development

ASCD stock number: 611-89127
Price: $21.95

Library of Congress Cataloging-in-Publication Data

Conversations with leading educators from Educational leadership.
    p. cm.
ISBN 0-87120-162-3
1. Teaching. 2. Education—United States—Aims and objectives.
3. Educators—United States—Interviews. I. Brandt, Ronald S.
II. Association for Supervision and Curriculum Development. III.
Educational leadership.
LB1025.2.C637 1989   89-6525
371.1′02—dc20   CIP

Introduction

One of the best parts of my job is the opportunity to talk with leading educators about their exciting ideas for improving our schools. I published my first "conversation" in 1974 when, as a member of the ASCD Publications Committee, I talked with James Block for a transcribed interview on mastery learning. In following years, I did several others, and when I joined the ASCD staff in 1978, I decided to do more. For 10 years, most issues of Educational Leadership *have had at least one "conversation."*

I like printed interviews because they permit the kind of give-and-take that ordinary magazine articles do not. And I think that the informality of spoken language helps make profound thoughts more understandable and appealing.

This book brings together some of the conversations published in Educational Leadership *between 1983 and 1988. We meet a remarkable group of people: well informed, imaginative, and courageous. Their words testify to the vitality of American education.*

Even though I spent hours polishing these pieces and therefore know them well, I enjoy reading them again and again. I hope you will feel the same way.

Ronald S. Brandt
ASCD Executive Editor

Conversations with Leading Educators from *Educational Leadership*

Educational Leadership 45 (Sept. 1987): 9-16

RON BRANDT

On Leadership and Student Achievement:

A Conversation with Richard Andrews

Gains and losses in students' test scores are directly related to teachers' perceptions of their principal's leadership.

W e've known for a long time that good schools had good principals, but we didn't know what that really meant.

And now you do?

If we define the good principal as someone who provides instructional leadership for the school, yes. One of the reasons earlier researchers didn't discover as much as they might have was that they weren't asking the ones who supposedly were being led: the teachers. Our research has focused on teachers' perceptions of the leadership of their principals—and we've found some interesting things.

But how do you know the teachers' perceptions are accurate?

Because they correlate with incremental growth in student academic achievement.

So you've got both professional judgment and data?

That's correct, and they're both valid. Researchers may mistrust perceptions, but in a sense the only reality is perceived reality—and people's perceptions of their surroundings have a powerful influence on what they do.

How does your research relate to the literature on effective schools?

The foundation of our work is Ronald Edmonds' hypothesis that school characteristics are related to student achievement and that they can be observed *ex post facto*. Ron's work, of course, was mostly observational: first locate schools with high achievement, then look to see what you find in those schools that correlates with the achievement. We've gone about it by systematically gathering data from 100 schools over a three-year period, measuring the growth in achievement of individual kids within those schools. Another difference is that Ron was oriented to the equity issue, so he focused almost exclusively on socioeconomic status. He didn't deal with black kids as such, for example.

Our research includes both the socioeconomic and the ethnic factors—but it also goes beyond them to look at the incremental growth of all kids. We certainly want traditionally underachieving kids to achieve at a faster rate than those who have traditionally achieved well, but we're also finding schools where students from *all* groups do better than they ordinarily would.

How is that related to principal leadership?

First I should explain that, based on teacher perceptions and other data, we have identified three different kinds of schools. One group, which we call "high profile" schools, have principals who in the perceptions of teachers are strong instructional leaders. According to teachers' reports, the schools are also characterized by having high expectations, frequent monitoring of student progress, a positive learning climate, and goal clarity. There's another group of schools where teachers say those things are

Photographs by Mary Levin, University of Washington, Seattle

not present. We call them "low profile" schools. The third group of schools is in between, or the average school.

When we first analyzed the achievement scores of the 100 schools, we found similar patterns in all of them. White kids were generally at about the 62nd percentile in mathematics, while on the average black kids were at about the 47th or 48th percentile. But when we analyzed their incremental growth two years later, we could see changes for students from both groups in both reading and mathematics. We plotted where each child had been in the spring of '82 and where he or she was in the spring of '84—and we've done that in two succeeding years: spring of '83, spring of '85. If a student began at the 60th percentile in mathematics and if two years later his score was still at the 60th percentile, that was zero incremental growth. If it was at the 62nd percentile, that was two percentile points of incremental growth, which divided by two is one point per

year. We did that for all kids within every ethnic and socioeconomic group in the school.

We found highly significant differences in achievement between students in high, average, and low profile schools. For example, in the high pro-

> **"We might say that where teachers have very positive perceptions of the quality of their workplace, they are more productive, so we see incremental growth in student achievement."**

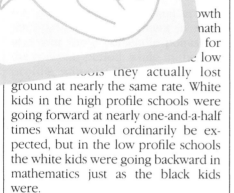

...owth ...nath ...for ...e low ...ools they actually lost ground at nearly the same rate. White kids in the high profile schools were going forward at nearly one-and-a-half times what would ordinarily be expected, but in the low profile schools the white kids were going backward in mathematics just as the black kids were.

Your design seems unusual. Haven't most researchers tended to look at group, rather than individual, growth?

In general, yes. The one segment of education that has looked at incremental growth over specific time periods is special education. For a special education student, teachers gather baseline data and compare subsequent evaluations against the baseline data. It's not a question of what other kids are doing; in a multihandicapped child it may be the flicker of an eyelid that's the first step of incremental growth. I think general education needs to learn something from that.

In fact, the schools in your study probably don't keep their records that way.

They don't. As in most districts, they get back the average level of achievement; they get the number and percentage of kids in the upper three, middle three, and lower three stanines; they get normal curve equivalent scores on each student; but they do not get *incremental* growth scores.

Let's be clear about this. You are saying that in schools with strong instructional leadership, individual student scores go up over time.

That is correct. Remember that our characterization of these schools as "high profile" is based directly on teachers' perceptions of the quality of their workplace. We might say that where teachers have very positive perceptions of the quality of their workplace, they are more productive, so we see incremental growth in student achievement.

We might think that extraneous variables, such as whether the school building is new or old, or whether the district spends $2,500 or $4,000 per pupil, would be the primary determinant. Those things may play a part, but what is far more important is the quality of the relationships with other human beings in that environment. And since the principal is in the best position to influence that, we would expect his or her leadership to be an important variable, and sure enough it is.

Would you explain how you assessed teachers' perceptions of their principals?

We began with an effective schools questionnaire that measures nine characteristics of the school. We asked collaborative teams of practicing teachers, principals, and college professors at the University of Washington to read the literature on a particular characteristic, such as strong leadership. Then we asked them, from their experience in schools and from the literature, to generate a measure; we

> **"One of the reasons earlier researchers didn't discover as much as they might have was that they weren't asking the ones who supposedly were being led: the teachers. Our research has focused on teachers' perceptions of the leadership of their principals—and we've found some interesting things."**

Ron Brandt

"Having visited all these principals, having been in their schools, I can say without qualification that whenever the spark of leadership emerges within their teachers they see it and nurture it."

didn't tell them how. We did a factor analysis on all the items they came up with. We ended up with 96 items, of which 18 measure the instructional leadership of the principal (see sidebar). We have field-tested those items in urban, suburban, and rural districts and found them to be extremely consistent and reliable. For example, with 125 teachers rating 61 principals in the spring of 1984 and then a year later, the test-retest reliability for the strong leader factor was .72, so we're dealing with very stable perceptions in the minds of teachers concerning the leadership of the principal.

What do these items deal with? What is it that teachers perceive as instructional leadership?

I can even tell you what teachers consider highest priority because we've identified 21 outstanding principals through a triangulation process—that is, they not only score high in teachers' perceptions, but they're also regarded as leaders by their peers and by their superintendents. We've then gone to the teachers who work with those principals and asked them to select from our 18 items the characteristics that are most important and state why. The results surprised me.

First is being a visible presence in the school. Now, that is contrary to what has been found in exemplary studies such as John Goodlad's Study of Schooling. The conclusion from these studies has been that in the typical school, teachers don't want their principal in the classroom. I think this shows the difference between the typical school and schools with principals who are exceptionally strong instructional leaders. In these schools, 78 percent of the teachers say they go to the principal with instructional matters or concerns. They seek these principals out; they want them in their classrooms.

The second most important thing their principals do, according to these teachers, is set a vision for the school. These principals don't sit around waiting for someone to tell them what their school is supposed to do; they have a definite idea about the purpose of their school.

And they get the resources to help their teachers deliver. Teachers tell us that when they go to their principal with an idea, he or she knows about resources, is well versed in the literature, and knows people who can provide staff assistance and development. The principal's response is, "That's a good idea. I've heard about a program," or "I know so and so. I'll put you in touch with her. We'll find a way for you to do that." One thing these principals do is arrange for their staff members to be staff developers for others in their school.

How can one individual—even the appointed leader—have so much influence? One of the criticisms of the early effective schools research was that other factors might not have been taken into consideration. Maybe in certain schools circumstances permitted the principal to be a leader while in others they did not. In other words, the school may make the leader rather than the leader making the school.

We have schools that are good even though they don't have a principal who is a strong instructional leader; however, we do not have any which have attained excellence. One school, for example, has such a strong staff that it has in the last four years spawned three principals: teachers who have gone on to become principals in other schools. And all three have come close to being strong instructional leaders in their first one or two years as principal in a new school, which is tough to attain. We're talking about a very potent group of teachers—but the school was unable to become a high profile school until it was assigned a principal whom the teachers perceived was an instructional leader.

We have some examples where a principal is regarded as a strong instructional leader, moves to another school, and in two consecutive measurements is reported as a strong instructional leader by the teachers in the new school: the school moves into the high profile category. That tells me not that the principal makes the school, but that the school was unable to achieve excellence without that kind of principal.

By "strong leader," are you implying an autocratic style?

Not at all. The leaders we're talking about know how to empower people and yell, "Charge." They are both generals and sheepherders. The ones I call sheepherders collect around them a group of people that is in some ways like a sheepherder and his dogs. I don't mean to imply that teachers are sheep or that the principal trains the dogs and calls all the shots—it's not a perfect metaphor—but there's a team that works closely together that "guides" the rest of the staff. In my analogy, the dogs do much of the work of keeping the whole group together and moving in the same direction, but the sheepherder is crucial to the process. The principal has to be the keeper of the dream and shepherd, if you will, the direction.

Now, in the case of the new principal who made such a difference, if you talk to teachers in the school, some

"We found highly significant differences in achievement between students in high, average, and low profile schools. For example, in the high profile schools the incremental growth for black kids' achievement in math was over three percentile points for the two-year period, while in the low profile schools they actually lost ground at nearly the same rate."

will say that the new principal didn't do anything; they did it all themselves. Others, though, will say they were trying to do it themselves before, but they couldn't pull it off. What was needed was for the right principal to provide that facilitative force.

Some researchers—I think of Russell Gersten and Doug Carnine—

Dimensions of Instructional Leadership

	Percentage of Teachers Who Strongly Agree or Agree		
	Strong Leader	Average Leader	Weak Leader
RESOURCE PROVIDER			
1.1 Promotes staff development activities for teachers	95%	68%	41%
1.2 Is knowledgeable about instructional resources	90%	54%	33%
1.3 Mobilizes resources and district support to help achieve academic goals	90%	52%	33%
1.4 Is considered an important instructional resource person in the school	79%	35%	8%
INSTRUCTIONAL RESOURCE			
2.1 Encourages the use of different instructional strategies	89%	78%	75%
2.2 Is sought out by teachers who have instructional concerns or problems	72%	47%	25%
2.3 Evaluation of performance helps to improve teaching	78%	46%	17%
2.4 Assists faculty in interpreting test results	54%	35%	9%
COMMUNICATOR			
3.1 Improved instructional practice results from discussion with the principal	80%	49%	25%
3.2 Leads formal discussions concerning instruction and student achievement	85%	41%	17%
3.3 Uses clearly communicated criteria for judging staff performance	90%	63%	17%
3.4 Provides a clear vision of what the school is all about	90%	49%	17%
3.5 Communicates clearly to the staff regarding instructional matters	92%	50%	17%
3.6 Provides frequent feedback to teachers regarding classroom performance	68%	29%	18%
VISIBLE PRESENCE			
4.1 Makes frequent classroom observations	72%	31%	17%
4.2 Is accessible to discuss matters dealing with instruction	94%	68%	66%
4.3 Is a "visible presence" in the building to both staff and students	93%	75%	46%
4.4 Is an active participant in staff development	97%	64%	50%

Above are 18 statements on which teachers rate their principals as instructional leaders. These statements are randomly distributed among 78 other items on the effective schools instrument used to measure teachers' perceptions of positive learning climate, staff dedication, early identification of student learning problems, frequent monitoring of student progress, high expectations, multicultural education, sex equity, and curriculum continuity.

To obtain the complete instrument, technical and administration manuals, and a sample data set, send a check for $25.00 made out to the University of Washington to Mr. Jerry Bamburg, Self-Assessment Study, M206 Miller Hall, DQ-12, University of Washington, Seattle, WA 98195.

contend that while schools do need instructional leadership, it doesn't necessarily have to be provided by the principal. Some people are good at getting others to do what they're not good at. I guess you're saying that in itself is a form of leadership?

The point is that the principal who simply sits back and says, "Okay, I'll let you do it" is not providing leadership. That's a leadership vacuum the teachers are having to fill.

How about the notion advanced by Albert Shanker and others that schools should be run by lead teachers rather than by principals?

I think that unfortunately Mr. Shanker is arguing from circumstances rather than from ideals. As near as I can determine from listening to him, his position has been arrived at strictly from a monetary standpoint. He says we can't afford to increase every teacher's salary by $10–20,000 a year, so we're going to have to increase teachers' salaries selectively. To get around the merit pay issue, he would increase the responsibility of some teachers, call them lead teachers, and pay them for the increased responsibility. Well, it's a nice idea, but if teachers' perceptions of the quality of principal leadership is the single greatest predictor of incremental growth in student achievement, that approach could depress student achievement for the sake of increasing a few teachers' salaries.

But of course you're talking about the way schools are organized now. A different model could work quite differently.

Yes, there's the hospital model, for example. You know: you have the administrator, and then you have the professionals who make the professional decisions. But in that model, there is not just a leaderless group; there is a lead doctor. Well, in most schools we already have a person who can run the building; we call that person the head secretary. So let the head secretary run the management functions of the school and have the person who sits in the principal's chair be the lead teacher. The principals we see who are strong instructional leaders are already lead teachers. They have a keen understanding of curriculum and instruction, and they are respected for their ability to communicate at three different levels: one to one, in small groups, and beyond that to the district, the public, the educational community, and so on. I see no difference between that and the lead teacher concept.

Furthermore, we run the risk of creating a more bureaucratized form of governance and organization in elementary schools. High schools already have a problem because of their bureaucratic structure: the principal, assistant principals, department heads, teachers. Appointing lead teachers in elementary schools creates similar layers of bureaucracy that will diminish productivity and inhibit change.

Are you saying you are skeptical about the whole idea of differentiated levels of responsibility within the teaching profession?

Yes. I am convinced that we have to improve teachers' perceptions of the quality of their workplace, but I'm not convinced that the solution is to create lead teachers. Instead, let's create exemplary sites staffed by highly qualified professionals where teachers and principals from other schools can go for inservice training and development—where we put future teachers, and future principals, to do their internships.

Let me ask about it a different way. Does leadership by the principal prevent teachers from being leaders?

Quite the opposite. Having visited all these principals, having been in their schools, I am quite confident that whenever the spark of leadership emerges within their teachers they see it and nurture it. Ann Lieberman calls it "expanding the leadership team." I predict that when we get more good qualitative research, we'll find that strong instructional leaders expand teachers' roles in two ways: first by

their leadership within their own classroom, which is their primary responsibility; and second, by using their creative ideas, their experience, and their enthusiasm to bring the larger organization to its ultimate level of efficacy.

Let's talk about how to use this research knowledge. Maybe we should start with how it's already being used.

One exemplary application is the Mercer Island, Washington, school district, where Wilma Smith, the superintendent, has implemented a clinical supervision model for principals. (See Smith and Andrews, pp. 34–37.) Clinical supervision of the principal means that the principal's supervisor does clinical observations of the principal in the school, the most important of which is clinically observing the principal at the same time the principal does a clinical observation of a teacher.

It sounds like an interesting program. How does it reflect your research?

The research identifies four subdimensions of leadership: principal as resource provider, instructional resource, communicator, and visible presence. The communicator category includes both creating the mission, or vision, of the school, and communicating clearly with teachers about classroom instruction. If a supervisor never observes the principal interacting at that level, the supervisor has no knowledge about the instructional leadership capability of the principal.

What are some other ways of using this research?

We're currently working with 64 school districts in the state of Washington who are using a self-study process we developed. The effective schools instruments are used to gather baseline data. Staff members at each school use these data to develop a three- to five-year school improvement plan and then use the instruments again each year to get formative information about how they're doing. The instrument includes the 18 items that mea-

> **"Frankly, I never anticipated that we would find such a powerful relationship between leadership of the principal and student outcomes. After all, the principal is one step removed from the direct instruction process. But what we found is that the teachers' perception of their work environment is so important, the power of the principal's leadership so pervasive, that it has a measurable impact on student learning."**

sure the instructional leadership of the principal.

Including perceptions of teachers?

That's right. In each of these 64 school districts the data are being fed directly back to the school. The principal sits down with the teachers to look at a profile showing the teachers' perceptions of his or her leadership, along with eight other effective schools characteristics.

That must make some principals pretty uneasy.

It does. It's interesting that many principals believe they are better instructional leaders than their followers think they are. The exciting thing for us is to see a principal—who has found out what teachers really think—get beyond that initial level of anxiety and say, "Okay, what am I gonna do?" Our first suggestion is to find out why the teachers feel that way: "They say you don't communicate criteria clearly in judging their performance. The only way to find out what that means is to go out and talk with them. If you don't want to talk with all of them, get the ones you feel most comfortable with and have a real heart-to-heart chat. When you've cataloged what they tell you, you've got your growth objectives. Later you go back and get feedback: 'How am I doing?' "

A self-help process like that isn't totally new, but it's unusual for it to be tied directly to student achievement. That's a good reason for principals to pay attention to it.

Yes, except that some are afraid that high profile schools may be preoccupied with student academic achievement: "Is it just thump, thump, thump, basic skills, basic skills?" Jerry Bamberg and I have been exploring that question, and we're finding that the answer is no. In regard to the four basic purposes of schooling, the high profile and low profile schools are much alike. They all say the first priority is basic skills; they all say the second goal is citizenship; the third is self-concept; and the fourth is meeting the individual needs of each child.

> **"We have some examples where a principal is regarded as a strong instructional leader, moves to another school, and . . . is reported as a strong instructional leader by the teachers in the new school. . . . That tells me . . . that the school was unable to achieve excellence without that principal."**

Beyond that, though, are differences in four important areas. One is higher-order thinking skills: nearly twice the number of staff members in high profile as in low profile schools say that's one of their goals. Another is learning to learn for life. And the third is academic excellence: not just recycling the basic skills but moving on to broader aspects of education. The fourth is a stronger commitment to multicultural education in high profile schools. The low profile schools are the ones preoccupied with basic skills because their students are not mastering them.

You say high profile schools want to go beyond basic skills to academic excellence, but your research is still based on standardized test scores.

That's correct.

Because you don't have any other accepted measures?

But also because we use the test scores differently. As I mentioned, we use residualized gain scores, and that's how we've found that instructional leadership is especially important for low-income and black students. If we look at students as a whole, the great-est single predictor of future achievement is prior achievement, but for black kids in our study schools the greatest predictor of future achievement is not prior achievement but strong leadership of the principal.

Suppose I'm a principal in Iowa or Arkansas. It's fine that you're doing all this in the state of Washington, but what can I do with what you've learned about leadership?

The first thing I'd suggest is to pick up the challenge that Ron Edmonds gave: disaggregate your student achievement data by ethnic group and socioeconomic status. Otherwise you can't know whether you have an effective school or not.

A second step is to start measuring incremental growth of individual students within each school, not across all schools. I don't care what measures you use. If you say, "Basic skills aren't all that important to me," how about critical thinking skills? There are measures for that—measure it!

But how about feedback? How can principals find out about teachers' perceptions of their leadership?

Our instrument is not copyrighted; it was developed with state funds and by working with the public schools, particularly, the Seattle School District, so anyone can use it. If they want us to do the statistical analysis, we offer an assessment service for what it costs us to do it. But they can hand score it, if they wish. Let's improve schools; that's our objective.

Frankly, I never anticipated that we would find such a powerful relationship between leadership of the principal and student outcomes. After all, the principal is one step removed from the direct instruction process. But what we found is that the teachers' perception of their work environment is so important, the power of the principal's leadership so pervasive, that it has a measurable impact on student learning.□

Richard L. Andrews is Chair, Policy, Governance, and Administration, University of Washington, College of Education, Seattle, WA 98195. **Ron Brandt** is ASCD's Executive Editor.

Educational Leadership 40 (Oct. 1982): 12-15

David Berliner was director of California's Beginning Teacher Evaluation Study, the prime source of today's attention to time-on-task. In this interview with Executive Editor Ron Brandt, Berliner claims there's one best way to make teachers more effective.

On Improving Teacher Effectiveness: A Conversation with David Berliner

Q What's been your experience in helping teachers use the research on teacher effectiveness?

Berliner: I've tried to disseminate knowledge by making presentations, but that seemed to have very little impact. The times I've gone into classrooms, though, what I did and said meant something to teachers and it made a difference. We could chart the changes. So my experience is simple: the research on teacher effectiveness gets used when somebody works with teachers in their classrooms. There's no substitute for what Bruce Joyce calls "coaching."

Q: What is that like? Exactly what do you do?

Berliner: Take the major variable of "engaged time." I asked teachers in a district near Tucson if we could send graduate students into their classrooms to take some records of their functioning and feed it back to them. The graduate students had learned how to code engaged time, transition time, wait time, and so on. They coded and graphed data from three, four, maybe five visits. Then they sat down with the teacher and had a conference, using some very precise consultation techniques developed by Professor John Bergan of the University of Arizona.[1] Bergan's approach is designed to elicit from the client both a statement of the problem and a statement of intent to change it.

When the teachers had defined their problems and solutions, the consultants—the graduate students—took some more measures. Five of the six classes showed remarkable change; they went from 40 or 50 percent on-

David Berliner is Professor of Educational Psychology, University of Arizona, Tucson.

task time up to whatever goals the teachers had set—70 or 80 percent. The only exception was a mathematics teacher whose time-on-task was about 40 percent. That teacher said, "Fine, that's all I want it to be." At that point, we had nothing more to do. Teachers have to make those decisions.

Q: That indirect, consultative approach seems inconsistent with the image of direct instruction.

Berliner: It's indirect in the sense that we don't tell teachers what their problem is or how to solve it. It's coercive in that we never leave an interview without a statement of the problem and either a proposed solution or the teacher's statement that he or she doesn't want to change.

Q: How does setting a goal lead to improvement?

Berliner: Let me give you an example. I might say to the teacher, "Your time-on-task in mathematics averages 43 percent over the five days we observed. How could you bring it up?" The teacher might say, "Okay, let me think. Maybe, because I'm grading papers when they're doing their math workbooks, I'm not monitoring them enough."

"Terrific. Why don't you take some breaks from your grading of papers and wander the classroom a little bit. Let's see if that has an effect."

So we collect data as the teacher increases his or her monitoring. Well, we happen to know that works. If the teacher is roaming the classroom, attending rates are higher.

Another thing the teacher might say is, "When kids are through with their assignments, I'll have other assignments ready so they'll have something to work on."

In our consultative model, the consultants learn eliciting questions like, "What can you do to accomplish that?" "Is there any other way you can use resources?"

Q: Wouldn't it be simpler just to tell a group of teachers some of the common problems and some ways to make better use of time?

Berliner: Teachers already know these things; they've heard about them in methods courses; they've been preached to. But nothing happens until someone gets the teacher to specify what he or she is going to do, and then monitors and helps the teacher look at the effects.

Q: Considering all the things teachers need to be concerned with, how important is time management?

Berliner: Probably 50 percent of all teachers don't have to worry about time *allocation*. But the other 50 percent ought to look at it. And half of them—25 percent of all teachers—are probably badly under-allocating time in some areas of the curriculum. We have evidence that the actual time available for instruction in reading and math in some elementary classrooms may total less than 100 hours. That strikes me as a gross misuse of time. So I'd say that as many as one-fourth of the teachers in this country could make marked improvements in instruction by just looking at time allocations.

Beyond that, maybe 70 percent of teachers could be helped by attending to *engaged* time—how time is used. Whenever managers in the business world do time audits, they find ways to save minutes. And that's true of teaching. For example, when the Austin, Texas, school district took this concept seriously, they found ways to save the

> **"But nothing happens until someone gets the teacher to specify what he or she is going to do, and then monitors and helps the teacher look at the effects."**

equivalent of 10–14 days of school, worth $2–3 million.

Q: Determining engaged time involves making judgments about whether students are doing what they're supposed to be doing. How can an observer tell whether students are on-task or not?

Berliner: Young kids have no guile. To observe on-task or off-task behavior in kids third grade or under is easy. You and I could sit in the back of the room, come up with some rules in about ten minutes, and show almost perfect reliability all day long. Young kids either are or are not on-task and you can tell. If they're off-task, they're dancing, tapping their pencils, chatting with friends, and so on. They're on-task if they scrunch up their faces and hold their pens and pencils tightly. You can almost see them thinking!

As students get older, you begin to see "anticipatory graduate student behavior": head-nodding, smiling, note-taking, and other signs of attending.

You may code this as on-task, but in your heart of hearts, you know the kid's not processing anything. The opposite occurs with the kid who's looking out the window: you code him off-task even though you're pretty sure he's processing everything. Because of this, we decided that with older students, individual data may be faulty, but the means for classes or groups are still valid. There are probably as many students off-task that we coded "on" as on-task that we coded "off." So once you and I agree on some coding rules, our inter-rater reliability would be about .95 at virtually any grade level.

Q: Are you suggesting that principals and central office supervisors should concentrate their staff development efforts on in-class coaching?

Berliner: I sure am. I think they should bring in fewer speakers and instead have somebody in classrooms helping teachers make changes.

Q: But that's a very time-consuming approach. With fewer people in supervisory roles can we really expect them to do coaching?

Berliner: They won't get much change unless they do. I'm convinced that the number of people who will change by exposure to books and lectures and workshops is just too small.

Q: How would someone who's already a principal or supervisor learn more about consultation skills?

Berliner: Well, Professor Bergan's model takes time to learn because it involves asking questions that do not prompt but elicit. Becoming expert requires many practice sessions, as well as analyzing transcripts of those sessions. It's extraordinarily useful, but very technical. But there are other consultation models: Meredith Gall

and Keith Acheson[2] have one, and I'm sure there are others.[3] The behavioral one appeals to me because it puts the responsibility on the person being counseled.

Q: How confident are you that this is what is implied by the term "coaching"?

Berliner: A precise definition isn't necessary. What's important is that somebody who knows the skills in question is in the classroom and provides feedback. Just as a batting coach might say, "Spread your legs a little farther apart," or "Hold the bat a little higher," a teaching coach might say, "You had the opportunity at that point to ask an analytic question and you didn't. Let's figure out why."

Q: That kind of statement is part of the consultative model?

Berliner: Not during the time of eliciting solutions. At that point you'd only say, "Here's the data. Is this what you want?" If the teacher says, "No, I want to change," you say, "Okay, how can you change?" The teacher might say, "I'm going to try to ask analytic questions." Then you can follow up by watching and saying, "Here was an opportunity to ask an analytic question. Why didn't you?"

What I exclude from coaching is walking into the classroom and saying, "You're deficient in analytic questions. I'm going to tell you how to do it." That strikes me as the wrong way to work with professionals.

Q: Must the consultant be an expert teacher?

Berliner: Coaches may not have to be

superior teachers themselves, but they must know good teaching. I'll use another analogy. We all marvel at the Olympics when somebody does a very complex dive and the judges hold up scores within three tenths of a point of one another. It happens because every one of those judges knows how to analyze a dive. Even though the dive takes only 1.8 seconds, they have coded 30 different aspects of it—entry into the water, where the legs were, whether the rollover was correct, and a lot of other things that experts know and novices don't. They're connoisseurs of diving. We need connoisseurs of teaching.

Q: What else besides time allocation, engagement rates, and time management do you watch for when you're observing classrooms?

Berliner: One thing is the match of the instructional materials to the goals of the school or district. For example, if the district says second grade kids should learn two-column addition, I look for whether there's two-column addition going on. I check the teacher-made materials to see if they're congruent with the expected goals, because lots of teachers work very hard making their own materials, some of which are good and some which are not. I've seen teachers put a lot of effort into producing units that are irrelevant to the goals of the district.

Another thing is classroom management and discipline. If the class is not learning because the teacher's time is being taken up by two or three kids, that has to be dealt with.

I also look for politeness and kindness. Classrooms should conform to a model of what a democratic workplace is like: the teacher is in charge and the kids have work to do. But they should be able to talk to each other about their assignments, there should be some choices, there should be consideration.

Q: These things you look for—are they based on research or are they simply common sense and personal values?

Berliner: They're really extrapolations from research. We don't have research that says polite classes do better, but we do have research that says observers' ratings on a scale of one to ten for "How willing would you be to send your own child to this place?" correlate pretty well with school effectiveness indicators.

It takes a connoisseur of classrooms to know what that means, just as it takes a connoisseur of wine to know a full-bodied wine. You can't define an effective classroom precisely, but I can point to some things: there's laughter and the teacher doesn't bother with it, doesn't say, "Quiet." If it goes on for ten minutes, though, the teacher does; there are limits.

Kids should learn that school is fun *and* school is work. Classes that are high on academic engaged time do better. Classes that are high on conviviality also score higher.

Q: There's no inconsistency, then, between what you like to see and what research says you should be seeing?

Berliner: No. The only time I hit an inconsistency was on the issue of success rate. I didn't believe very high success rates were necessary for kids to learn. I thought kids should be "stretched." The data changed my mind on that. It changed Barak Rosenshine's and Jere Brophy's minds, too. Now, we're all saying—especially for young kids and slow learners—that high success rate is important.

Q: You also seem to be saying that test scores aren't the only measure of teacher effectiveness.

Berliner: Effectiveness can be defined that way, but I don't think you can avoid certain moral concerns. If a school produces achievement better than other schools but its suicide rate for teenagers is higher, is that a price you're willing to pay? We have evidence that there are schools like that.

We need at least two criteria for judging schools: we have to see them as work places in which society expects certain things to be mastered. But schools are also places where young people spend important parts of their lives—so they should be enjoyable.

Q: But time-on-task research can be misused if educators aren't concerned with both criteria?

Berliner: Sure.

Q: Are you worried that some administrators may in fact be abusing the idea of time-on-task? That their singleminded devotion to improving test scores may be at the cost of other outcomes?

Berliner: I don't think so. I haven't heard of any real abuses. History may look back on these times and say there were some; I don't know. The administrators who adopted scientific management principles in the 1920s probably didn't feel foolish even though history says they did some of the stupidest things possible. I don't know what a Callahan[4] would say about the current back-to-basics movement, but my feeling is that for the most part we're reasonably well-balanced.

If American schools have gone overboard, it's in the direction of an educational smorgasbord: smatterings of knowledge and low time-on-task. We ought to take more seriously the outcomes we want.

Q: Your comments seem a bit paradoxical. You've said supervisors need to recognize that teachers have goals of their own, so they can best be approached by asking, "How can I help you accomplish your goals?" Children have goals as well, but the time-on-task researchers say effective teachers don't waste time involving students in decision making. They tell kids what the goals are and get on with teaching them.

Berliner: You've tapped right into a basic educational philosophy of mine. I believe the amount of choice you should give kids in school looks like an inverted pyramid. It should be very limited in the first few grades, but maximal in the last year or two of high school. In the early grades where basic skill acquisition is taking place, we should offer whatever opportunities for choice are reasonable—because that's the way we should treat human beings—but in fact, the expected outcomes of education are quite clear at that level; there aren't a lot of choices.

We shouldn't be hypocritical about it; kids are there to learn to read and write and do math, and a school has failed if large numbers of its kids can't do that by the end of elementary school.

But schools have also failed if that's all students can do at the end of 12 grades. Once they've acquired basic literacy, students should begin making choices about their own education.

Q: There are early childhood classrooms that are very impressive in the amount of freedom children are given and the amount of self-control they develop. In some of those classrooms the kids continue to work even when the teacher leaves the room. Yet those classrooms tend not to produce the highest standardized test scores, at least in the short run. Wouldn't it be wrong for a supervisor to come into that kind of classroom and report data about how the kids are not quite as much on-task as they would be if the teacher stood up in front and said, "Everybody listen to me"?

Berliner: If the teacher has a good system working and we're talking about a few lousy items on a standardized test, I'd leave the teacher alone. If the class is at the 20th percentile but predicted to be at the 60th, the teacher has somehow missed the boat.

The kind of classroom you've described is wonderful, but among teachers who have tried it, more have failed than succeeded. You can get teachers to succeed more easily in a direct instructional model than in an open model. So if I have to make a choice, and only 10 percent of the teachers can pull off the more open kind of classroom, while 90 percent fail—and I think the rates are pretty close to that—I'm going to try to redirect some of them into a more structured situation. That way, kids won't be cheated of their education. But for the 10 percent who can pull it off, my god, hug them. **EL**

[1] J. Bergan, *Behavioral Consultation* (Columbus, Ohio: Charles E. Merrill, 1977).

[2] Keith A. Acheson, and Meredith D. Gall, *Techniques in the Clinical Supervision of Teachers* (New York: Longman, Inc., 1980).

[3] See also David Champagne and R. Craig Hogan, *Consultant Supervision: Theory and Skill Development*, 1981, available from C. H. Publishing Company, 812 Irving St., Wheaton, IL 60187.

[4] Raymond E. Callahan, *Education and the Cult of Efficiency* (Chicago: University of Chicago Press, 1962).

Educational Leadership 43 (Sept. 1985): 33-35

On Talent Development:
A Conversation with
Benjamin Bloom

RONALD S. BRANDT

Benjamin Bloom

Respected throughout the world for his research on human growth and learning, for his conceptualization of mastery learning, and for his famous *Taxonomy of Educational Objectives*, Benjamin Bloom is one of America's most distinguished educators. In this interview, he comments on the findings of his study of the development of 120 young men and women who had reached the highest levels of accomplishment—Olympic swimmers, world-class tennis players, concert pianists, great sculptors, research mathematicians, and research neurologists—reported in his new book, *Developing Talent in Young People*.

What led you to study the development of immensely talented people?

I've been studying learning for over 40 years. My first set of studies involved differences among the states. We found that states varied enormously in the kind of learning they produced—and that the differences were quite stable. States that were low in—say—1940 were still low 40 years later.

Then we did similar studies internationally, trying to understand why students learn so much better in some countries than others. After that we studied extremes, for example, comparing learning when there was a teacher for 30 students with results when each student was tutored by a very capable teacher. In these many studies we were finding very positive effects of excellent conditions of learning in the home and the school—how teachers teach, and so on. I decided that the best way to understand the utmost limits of learning would be to study people who had continued to learn over many years and had become tops in their field. So this study of talent development is one of a long list of studies I had planned for many years.

At first impression it seems quite different from your usual focus. You have emphasized mastery learning, which is intended to *equalize* educational attainment. It would seem that it's quite a different matter to investigate the development of a small group of extremely successful people.

I firmly believe that if we could reproduce the favorable learning and support conditions that led to the development of these people, we could produce great learning almost everywhere. The basic differences among human beings are really very small. On some kinds of learning we differ very little, but in others we differ greatly—especially for the types of learning that require enormous time, motivation, and the like. For example, our pianists studied an average of 17 years to become internationally famous concert pianists. It's very rare to find anybody devoting 17 years to any kind of continuous learning.

You're not saying that given the right circumstances, just anybody could be a great pianist or neurologist, are you?

I don't really want to go that far. I would say that if the love of music is inspired in a country, then all the people in that country will learn music. For example, almost all Hungar-

13

ians learn to love the music of that country and learn to sing and play it very well. That doesn't mean that we have that many Hungarian concert pianists. In every nation and every endeavor, some excel over others because they put more of themselves into it. The point is that under favorable learning conditions most people reach a high level of excellence. What we need to consider is how to get virtually all to love music, to enjoy art, to learn mathematics, or whatever.

An unavoidable problem with the kind of retrospective research you've conducted is that there are not, and cannot be, control groups. Is it possible that other children raised in similar ways are less successful and that the people you studied actually succeeded because of some undiscovered factors?

Well, I think the study tells us some general things that apply across the board. We at one time thought that the development of a tennis player would be very different from the development of a concert pianist or a sculptor or a mathematician or neurologist. What we've found is that even though the content and the procedures may be enormously different in each field, there is a common set of characteristics in the home, the instruction, and the like. There is a very general process that seems to be central to the development of talent no matter what the field. My students at Northwestern University are now studying other talent fields such as poets, authors, and concert singers, among others, and they're finding much the same processes at work.

It is quite true that we've only studied the successful people and haven't asked much about the unsuccessful. However, we did study a small group of people who didn't quite make it to the highest level, and we found that there were a number of chance or accidental conditions that seemed to get in the way. For example, one person was as good by age 15 as the best of our tennis players, but when he chose a college he didn't inquire about the tennis coach. When he arrived at the college he was amazed to find that it did not have a good tennis coach. That sort of thing didn't happen to the extremely talented people we studied. Each new step was planned

very carefully with the help of former teachers, experts in the field, and the parents.

What I'm saying is that two individuals can be at almost the same level at age 15 but one goes on to the championship and the other doesn't because of certain learning and support conditions.

What should parents know as a result of your study? What can educators help them understand about developing talented children?

What we're finding is that parents' own interests somehow get communicated to the child. I guess it's a little like the way religious parents' interest in religion gets communicated to their children. They don't ask their 5-year-old, "Would you like to learn the various things you need to learn to be a religious person?" We don't ask a child, "What mother tongue would you like to learn?" Everybody takes it as natural that if the parents' major language is English, the children will learn to speak English. Similarly, we found that the talent which was later developed so highly—music, for example, or swimming—was something that the parents thought was "natural" for their children to learn and enjoy.

But it went beyond that. We found over and over again that the parents of the pianists would send their child to the tennis lessons but they would *take* their child to the piano lessons. And we found just the opposite for the tennis homes.

Your book also says, I think, that parents of these highly talented people had strong achievement motivation.

Yes, we found that almost all the parents embraced the work ethic. They insisted on things being done well. They expected that one should work before one plays, that one always tries to do his or her best, and that each try should be better than the one before. Virtually all these parents seemed to embrace this idea and to communicate it to their children.

Do your findings suggest ways educators can develop the talents of the children they teach?

Well, they do a very good job in sports. There's nothing we can tell coaches in high schools and colleges. But when we get beyond sports, things are sporadic, accidental. Students may

have a good teacher one year and a very poor one the next. And even in the academic subjects, all kinds of chance circumstances are at work.

For example, our mathematicians had great difficulty with teachers who insisted that they must learn math exactly as it was written in the book. A student may have been doing calculus on his own while he was expected to learn algebra by rote. Schools do not seem to have great tolerance for children who are out of phase with other students in their learning process.

Are there other things educators can gain from this knowledge of how people develop talent?

When educators try to develop talent, they often go about it by looking for the one in a hundred or the one in a thousand rather than expecting that virtually all can learn a particular talent field satisfactorily, and that the best will go even further. I think schools are wrong if they are highly selective in providing special learning experiences.

Are you saying it's not a good idea to use screening devices to identify talented students?

I am not opposed to screening devices to discover talent in order to do something about it as long as the instruments measure performance and achievement rather than particular "aptitudes." We in this country have come to believe that we can tell who is going to become a great musician by giving musical aptitude tests, who's going to be a great mathematician by giving mathematics aptitude tests. Doing that counts some people in and others out far too early.

What is a better approach?

All the children should be given opportunities to explore fields that they might be interested in. Then gradually the students can narrow their interests to particular fields, learn them to a high level, and develop a long-term commitment to one or more talent fields.

I believe your research found that those who became highly talented in a field were usually introduced to that field in a playful way. Does that suggest that children's encounters with school subjects should be playful at first?

Alfred North Whitehead wrote about that in 1929 in *The Aims of Education*, and we discovered it when we were about halfway through our study. Whitehead believed that there are rhythms of learning. For example, no matter at what age you start learning science, you should begin to learn it playfully, almost romantically, with wonderful teachers who make it exciting and interesting. Then, one moves to what Whitehead called the stage of precision, where you learn the underlying principles and develop great accuracy and skill in the field. That allows you to move to a third level, where a master teacher helps you to develop new ways of looking at the subject, new ways of participating in it, and your own unique style in the field.

Whitehead thought this had nothing to do with age; it had to do with the way you introduced a subject like mathematics to any learner. In most schools, we ignore what Whitehead was trying to tell us. We begin almost all instruction with precision and accuracy when we should begin with something more exciting, romantic, and playful.

Your study of highly successful people does help us understand, then, how all students could be more successful.

I am confident that virtually all people have enormous potential for something. The problem is to find some way of unearthing what that is and to make it possible for them to excel in the things they find most interesting.

I don't mean that all of them could or should become world-class performers in a particular field. We could, for example, produce a million great pianists—but we probably don't have a need for that many concert pianists.

Nevertheless, almost everyone can enjoy making music, and it is worth learning for its own sake. Not many people are going to become professional musicians or champion tennis players, but many more people can learn these and other valuable things if we improve the *conditions for learning.*□

Reference

Bloom, Benjamin S., ed. *Developing Talent in Young People*. New York: Ballantine Books, 1985.

Benjamin S. Bloom is Professor of Education, Northwestern University and the University of Chicago, Department of Education, 5835 Kimbard Avenue, Chicago, Illinois 60637. **Ronald S. Brandt** is Executive Editor, ASCD, 225 N. Washington Street, Alexandria, Virginia 22314.

Educational Leadership 46 (Sept. 1988): 4-9

RON BRANDT

On the High School Curriculum: A Conversation with Ernest Boyer

Photograph courtesy The Carnegie Foundation

President of The Carnegie Foundation for the Advancement of Teaching, Ernest Boyer assesses the limits of reform, phrases the substantive questions needed to move reform to a higher level, and proposes a visionary convocation of educators—a sort of "Manhattan Project"—to move American schools into true reform for the 21st century.

Your book *High School* was published five years ago, shortly after *A Nation at Risk*. How has the school curriculum changed in that time, and how have the issues changed?

Curriculum has not been at the heart of this movement. Cued by *A Nation At Risk*—and to some extent recently reinforced by William Bennett's *James Madison High School*—most improvement efforts have involved taking traditional labels and simply adding on: more history, more science, more English. I'm not against this effort since in the end we can't avoid converting our curriculum into currency for transcripts and the like, but what's missing is how the various disciplines can serve larger, more integrative ends. So we aren't helping students understand how their courses relate to the world in which they live or to the larger interdependent world they will inevitably confront.

You're saying, then, that the fundamental issues remain the same?

Yes, core curriculum, for example. I get uneasy when I hear that term, even though I use it myself, because it conjures up an image of a fixed number of units and labels. Of course, students need common understandings and common knowledge in order to read the morning paper and converse with others about important issues; but I'm much more concerned that students go beyond a study of the disci-

plines to develop an understanding of human commonalities, which could be achieved in a variety of ways. And yet I don't think we've had, during the past five years, a creative debate about how we might organize the academic fields to help students integrate knowledge and apply it to the world they will inherit.

In what high school subjects is there the most need for thorough curriculum revision, in your opinion?

Two areas come to mind. I continue to be bewildered by the teaching of

I'm concerned that students go beyond a study of the disciplines to develop an understanding of human commonalities.

An education is not simply an exercise in choice.

science; I really wonder why we can't more effectively relate scientific discoveries to the generalist in a useful way, rather than offering material intended for future scientists and engineers, which touches only a handful of our students.

How we handle technology, for example, is crucial for everyone and may determine whether we survive. We need more creative work in how to relate the science and technology curriculum to the nonspecialist, who may not be going on to further study but who must act responsibly as a concerned citizen. Asking these students to take an isolated course in biology or chemistry, without placing that study in a larger context, does not fit the bill.

You said there was another area that concerns you.

Well, I think social studies couldn't be more confused. We've completely lost our way in setting priorities among the traditional fields of history, civics, geography, economics, and the like. We need fresh, integrative thinking here. That's why I look with sadness on what happened to *Man, A Course of Study*, which came out of the Sputnik era. It wasn't necessarily the best curriculum design, but it was on the right track—an imaginative attempt to approach social studies in a powerful cross-cultural way.

Students need to see other cultures in the context of our interdependent world. I worry about Secretary Bennett's treatment of non-Western cultures because our very survival depends on how we deal with the rest of the world. We study Western civilization to understand our past; but we need to study non-Western cultures to understand our future.

You write and speak eloquently about the value of history and literature, as do Lynne Cheney, Diane Ravitch, Chester Finn, and William Bennett. They insist that a chronological approach is essential if students are to develop a sense of history, but you differ by saying these courses need not be taught chronologically. What makes you think these subjects can be taught successfully in other ways?

I'm not against chronology. But the larger issue is to help students discover that we are all products of the past and shapers of the future. In order to understand this essential fact, we must place ourselves in time and space. My suggestion is that we start, not with the past, but with the present—and then take leaps back. Several years ago the BBC had an exciting program called *Connections* that followed this procedure. For example, starting with the internal combustion engine, the narrator then traced the theories and inventions of the past that made possible this "discovery." Unfortunately, we usually start with past events and move forward chronologically; and students rarely see connections between the present and the past.

We need more creative work in how to relate the science and technology curriculum to the nonspecialist.

You don't agree with those who would eliminate "social studies" and just teach history, geography, and so on?

No, no! The term *social studies* has been used, all too often, as a whipping boy; but what critics forget is that the distinguished historian Charles Beard chose that title in a study of the schools in the mid-1920s. The aim was to go beyond the isolated subjects and to help students place the human story in larger context.

There's a related question. Conspicuously absent from most current statements about social studies is any attention to students' own personal and social development. I don't recall any references to that in your book *High School*, other than your recommendation for a new Carnegie unit. You didn't call for instruction in child

development or family living, for example. Does that mean you're skeptical about teaching those kinds of things?

I'll give two answers. First, if I were to rewrite my book, I'd put more emphasis on the physical and social dimensions of students' education. My only justification for perhaps undervaluing that was my feeling that we urgently needed a way to inform students about what I call the "commonalities" of human experience—but I should have stressed the point that birth and growth and death are, of course, at the very heart of our existence.

But, second, I would say that I remain unclear about how formal educational experience can affect students' attitudes and values. I know that "moral education" is important, but I've seen few examples of successful courses that rearrange the students' value systems. Perhaps it is here that the influence of a mentor is most consequential.

But there is growing support for sex and drug education programs.

Society, while it criticizes the schools, expects us to be Mr. Fixit for the nation. But when schools take on such assignments and there's still drug abuse, we end up being called "failures" once again. I have to tell you: I don't think educators, working in isolation, can solve the nation's drug problems, I don't think we can solve all the sex problems. That doesn't mean we shouldn't try, but—given the context in which the schools must work—I'm afraid we can only play at the margins. Still, if I were to rewrite *High School*, I'd put more emphasis on health and wellness and social development so that such topics as drugs and sex could be put in a larger context.

One of the unusual recommendations in *High School*, as I mentioned earlier, was your call for a new Carnegie unit: a requirement that all students engage in community service.

Yes. We introduced the idea of community service to make the point that there is a problem among young people—not of their making—that has to do with a sense of isolation and drift and anonymity. A high school principal on our commission told about getting angry calls from citizens who drove past his school. They complained that kids were hanging around outside the building—even though the school day had not yet begun. They didn't understand that many young people face serious difficulties at home. He pointed out the diminishing contact between the older and the young. So we suggested a service term to stress the need for students to interact with people in the community and to see connections between what they learn and how they live.

If we ignore student alienation in our reform efforts, we are kidding ourselves. There are a variety of ways to make a school a more humane place, to make students feel they belong, to overcome the sense of anonymity—but of course schools can't do it alone. Unless society is friendlier to its children, we're in trouble.

If we focus on the trivial—if we measure that which matters least—testing will suffocate school reform.

You've said you felt a sense of urgency about improving the curriculum. What efforts impress you as moving in the right direction?

I'll mention two. I've seen several examples of locally designed curriculums involving integration of two or more fields of knowledge to help students understand what I refer to as "the connectedness of things": to show relationships between the subject areas and contemporary problems or to reveal how past events relate to the future. These attempts to use the subject areas thematically help students gain perspective. They are a move in the right direction.

I believe that specialty schools are also a move in the right direction. I like the idea of having schools for the arts, schools in certain career-related fields, but only if they educate students broadly. The ideal, for some students at least, is to start with their special interest and then work in English, history, or foreign language in relation to that special field of study. What I do worry about, frankly, are specialty schools that narrow the students and don't attempt to lead to breadth as well as depth. I also worry about special schools for only "the gifted" while those students who need the most help get the least.

You have a strong commitment to general education. In fact, it was something of a shock to find that both you and John Goodlad believe that a substantial portion of a student's curriculum should be required. I had felt for years that schools needed to restrict requirements to allow as much individual choice as possible. That's because when a person has chosen to do something, he or she does it with more energy and commitment.

I'm torn in the same way. You can't deny that labeling anything "required" tends, at least at first, to dampen enthusiasm for it, especially among adolescents struggling for independence. On the other hand, I feel strongly that there are shared ideas and traditions

Man, A Course of Study was on the right track—an imaginative attempt to approach social studies in a powerful cross-cultural way.

worth knowing and that an education's not simply an exercise in choice alone.

Language is a good example: students simply must become proficient in reading and writing the English language. We can't say, "Well, if language doesn't interest you, we won't bother with it." There's no way to be a participant in society, even passively, without common knowledge; it's needed both for functional literacy and for what E. D. Hirsch calls "cultural literacy." The truth is we couldn't even be carrying on this conversation without an impressive amount of shared knowledge.

It's possible, though, that if we took a look at what's taught in high school classes, it wouldn't be a very good match for the cultural literacy most adults need on a day-to-day basis.

Oh, I don't pretend that today's curriculum comes close to what today's students need to know. Again, one of the great disappointments of the curriculum debate is the way we borrow sentiments from the past. Secretary Bennett gives us a list of traditional literary sources—but when I talk about the need for literacy, common experiences, ideas and events, I'm not referring to a list of books, I'm talking about a language that is not static, but evolving. Even though I support many of Hirsch's basic arguments, I think his list of "cultural literacy" items may have gone too far. A short, illustrative list could have made the point that while we live independent lives we are, at the same time, deeply dependent on each other and that to sustain a culture, shared experiences and traditions are required.

Your thesis is that we should require about two-thirds of the curriculum for all students. Do you really mean *all* students? We have some evidence that while the abstractness of the usual curriculum is anathema to some students, they'll respond to another kind of experience. In the right kind of alternative school these kids can succeed. Would you do away with alternative schools?

No, of course not. But an alternative school should not have a wholly different curriculum. When I say that about two-thirds of the student's program should be required, I'm not imposing any single set of courses. I only ask that the school establish what it expects of all its graduates, in terms of both basic skills to be performed and areas of general knowledge to be understood. After all, even students in alternative schools must be able to negotiate life after graduation; they need skills to get a job, they need knowledge to participate as citizens, and they need the tools and motivation to go on learning. There can be a number of ways, including electives, to get to individual goals, but I'm still convinced that there are general goals that apply to all students.

In recent years the most notable response to concerns about making the curriculum more coherent, more focused, has been action by legislatures and state boards of education to raise high school graduation requirements. That has upset educators, because they see it as interfering with local control.

You're right—in the past five years the main actors in the reform movement have been governors, school boards, and legislators. From a legal point of view, you might say that's the way it should be. Schools are, after all, creatures of the public will. But what has occurred in the name of reform has been regulatory. Now, that's not all bad. We've just surveyed some 13,500 teachers, asking them about the reform movement, and in general teachers report progress in terms of more requirements for graduation and more testing. But they also report more paperwork and more political interference in the school.

We study Western civilization to understand our past; but we need to study non-Western cultures to understand our future.

What we've seen thus far has been a mechanistic approach to school improvement—it's not what I would call true reform. The challenge now is to focus on education as a human enterprise, not as a "system" to be regulated. If that doesn't happen soon, the result will be only a modest fixing of a program designed for the present, not the future, and will be helping the "winning" students, not the least advantaged. In other words, the reform will fail at the most crucial point. Clearly the focus now must shift from regulation to renewal.

There are indications that the flood of state mandates may be slowing down.

Yes, I think regulation has about run its course. We've increased testing, tightened teacher credentialing, and added more Carnegie units, but people are now starting to ask more substantive questions: What precisely should we be teaching? How can we attract and hold outstanding teachers? How do we evaluate results? Above all, how do we deal with common expectations for a diverse student body? These four questions will endure. The second wave of reform may get us into them.

I should perhaps add that the "regulators" have been trying to do right. Mistakes were made, but the aim was to clarify goals, raise standards, and rebuild confidence in the system. And if a better direction hasn't been found, I don't blame the so-called outsiders. Education must share the responsibility too. We haven't found a way to carry reform forward to a higher level.

But if we now have a chance to catch our breaths, what should we do?

I've listed the questions we must now address. I'm probably most concerned about evaluation because, in the end, what we test will probably determine what we teach. Certainly what we test is a statement of our priorities in education. And if we focus on the trivial—if we measure that which matters least—testing will suffo-

The term *social studies* has been used as a whipping boy, but the distinguished historian Charles Beard chose that title.

cate school reform. It's easy to criticize testing; my best speeches are about why I don't like tests. But that's not going to be sufficient; we urgently need to figure out better ways to assess our students. Until we do, I suspect students and schools will continue to be held hostage by the SATs or some other inappropriate yardstick.

Getting something better won't be easy.

True. But inaction is not the answer. I wish we could create a kind of Manhattan Project for both curriculum *and* assessment. I wish we could bring together for several years classroom teachers, education association leaders, university professors—with time to really think about what to do. Indeed, I wish the next President of the United States, in his State of the Union message, would announce that the nation's top priority is education. Just as Kennedy said, "Ten years from now, we'll be on the moon," this President would say, "By the turn of the century, we're going to have the best schools in our history. We're going to create a Manhattan Project that will move education reform to a level of excellence for all."

Including extensive work on curriculum?

Yes, the heart of the effort would be a creative look at curriculum in relation to the future and not to the past. School districts could still pick and choose from several models—I do not think there's a single way.

I don't mean we'd be starting from scratch. There are many models already on the drawing board—or in practice. What is required is positive leadership. The reform movement has been seriously damaged by the failure of our national voices to inspire and lead. At no other moment in our history was this nation better poised to move ahead. Corporate leaders and governors and parents and educators

There are a variety of ways to make a school a more humane place, to make students feel they belong, to overcome the sense of anonymity.

were ready to be led. Instead, we've been given the most contentious and argumentative issues: prayer in school, cut the department, reduce Chapter I, vouchers. Most serious perhaps, educators have been presented as the problem. Simply stated, a potentially powerful movement has been squandered. What we urgently need at the federal level is high vision—not ideology. We need voices of credibility, to inspire and build consensus—leaders who see educators as the solution, not the problem.

In the meantime, though, local educators can take a hard look at their own school curriculums.

Sure. We like to look for heroic solutions, but in the end, educational renewal occurs at the local school, in a thousand classrooms, every day. Reform occurs when a principal arranges a better program or a teacher tries a new idea. We have an obligation to think things through as carefully as we can and to affirm our ideas with conviction.

Here at The Carnegie Foundation we try to help shape the debate and define priorities. But, in the end, excellence relates to what happens between the teacher and the student in the classroom. And that's where my confidence and hope are greatest. I am most discouraged when I'm talking to people who don't meet with students every day, but I'm most encouraged when I meet with teachers and students. They have a better fix on what's needed than all the experts on leave from Mt. Olympus. That's why the school-based management movement is so crucial.

Let's celebrate the gains we've made. But I'm convinced the time has come to move beyond the regulations and focus on the leadership of the principal, the renewal of the teachers, and, above all, the dignity and potential of every student.□

Ernest L. Boyer is President, The Carnegie Foundation for the Advancement of Teaching, 5 Ivy Lane, Princeton, NJ 08540. **Ron Brandt** is ASCD's Executive Editor.

Educational Leadership 43 (Feb. 1986): 13-17
RONALD S. BRANDT

On Improving Achievement of Minority Children: A Conversation with James Comer

The Yale Child Study Center in collaboration with the New Haven School System initiated a school improvement plan that addressed the negative impact of change, social stratification, and conflict and distrust between home and school. The results, documented in James P. Comer's book, *School Power* have been dramatically improved student attendance and achievement, and a new bonding between parents, teachers, and students. Comer is Maurice Falk Professor of Child Psychiatry, director of the School Development Program, and Associate Dean for Student Affairs at the Yale Medical School.

Photograph by G. Marshall Wilson, used with permission of Ebony magazine, Johnson Publishing Company, Inc.

You've been remarkably successful in improving schools for low-income, predominantly minority children. How did you do it?

Our program intervenes at the school level rather than the classroom or student level. The idea is to try to change the social system by applying the principles of behavioral and social science.

How do you do that?

A key element is to create a governance and management group that is led by the principal and includes several parents selected by parents; two or three teachers selected by teachers; and a mental health or support team person: a psychologist, social worker, or special education teacher.

This representative group addresses three things we consider critical to changing schools: climate, the academic program, and staff development. They bring together the available data and make a plan for the entire school year. Then they mobilize the resources, carry out their plan, evaluate the outcomes, and so on.

Are there other elements?

Yes, one is the mental health team, which brings together the psychologist, the social worker, and the special education teacher in the building. They sometimes work in the traditional way, focusing on a particular child, trying to provide service to that child's family, and so on, but they also work as a preventive group by trying to make sure that everything the governance and management team does is consistent with current knowledge of child development.

> ## "[The] program made the teaching of basic skills very relevant to the children; it created a very exciting school, and the achievement scores just leaped upward."

What's an example?

We had a child who had been in a classroom for eight months without ever smiling at the teacher. She was suspicious and hostile because she had had bad experiences with adults and felt she couldn't trust them. When the child smiled for the first time, the teacher was just devastated because she realized that in two more months, the child would go on to another classroom and would have to start all over with another adult.

We had a discussion, thought about discontinuity in the lives of many low-income children, and about the number of children who had problems establishing relationships with mature adults on an ongoing basis. Together we came up with the idea of keeping children with the same teacher for two years. We tried it and we had dramatic improvement in the performance of many of the children. There were some who had made no academic gains the first year but who made two years of academic gains the second year.

You've mentioned the governance group and the mental health team. Is there another ele-ment to the project?

Yes, parents participate on three levels. We have one parent per classroom, working on a parttime basis. They are paid minimum wage for ten hours of work a week, but each parent gives many more hours of volunteer time. That group of parents forms the core of a parent group because, when they invite two or three other parents to come in, you have 30–40 parents to make up the parent group in the school. That group plans, with teachers, all the assemblies and co-curricular activities. When we began using this approach, we got a great turnout from parents because the parents themselves were involved in putting the activities together, and they wanted to make them successful.

At the second level of participation, the parents in this parent group select a few of their members to serve on the governance and management group. That's a higher level of responsibility, so they're careful to select people who can work well with teachers and who have leadership skills. The third level of participation is the general turnout to the activities put on by the parent-teacher group. We went from having 15–20 people show up for activities to having 250 turn out. That increase occurred because the parents felt they had real responsibility and were really making a difference in the school.

And the effects carried over to the students' achievement?

There were a number of important effects. Having the children's own parents, or people like their parents, in the school made a big difference to the academic program. Children would hurry out of their classrooms after classes to show their papers to their parents who were in the school, and they didn't act in troublesome kinds of ways because they wanted to maintain the respect of the parents—as well as of the teachers, because parents and teachers were in agreement; they were working together. There was no way for children, as children will if they can, to play one adult authority figure against another. So we had great improvement—in academic achievement, in social behavior, and in attendance. Martin Luther King, the school we started with, has had the best attendance record in the city—ahead of all the higher socioeconomic schools—for four out of the last five years.

How do you explain that?

When you address the social climate and improve the quality of relationships among parents, teachers, administrators, and students, that reduces distrust and frees the energy that had gone into fighting each other, so that people have more time to concentrate on the academic program, to plan, and simply to manage the school better.

You described this as the intentional application of social science in education. Please say a little more about that.

One aspect of it is conceptualizing the problems of modern schools as contrasted with those of the schools of yesterday, and considering how to modify today's schools so as to support the development of children.

In the pre-1940s, the school was a natural part of the community. If after school you went to the grocery store with your parents, you would bump into your principal or your minister or your teachers. As they exchanged pleasantries and commented on how you were doing in school, you understood that these were people who knew your parents. They and your parents spoke with a common tongue about what was right or wrong, good or bad, and what they expected of you.

Since World War II, we've had high mobility. With mass communication, especially TV, children see and hear events from around the world all the time. Every half hour you can listen to the news and hear differences of opinion. Teachers live far from school, so there's both social and physical distance between them and the children they serve.

Often struggles that develop in society—between blacks and whites, or between people in middle and low income groups—create potential difficulties between home and school. Very often parents don't back up school people in the same way they did when the school was a natural part of the community. But schools continue to operate in the hierarchical authoritarian way they did in the past, ignoring the distrust and alienation between home and school. Children will act up in that kind of environment because there's confusion, and there are fewer authority figures influencing their behavior just when they need more of them. That's what I mean by understanding how social conditions affect behavior.

So understanding these conditions, we created the governance and management group I mentioned earlier, which brought parents, administrators, and teachers together in order to recreate a consensus about what was right and wrong, good and bad, and what everyone wanted the school to accomplish.

And both these things—understanding the social situation and designing a suitable response—are what you mean by the application of social science. Does your experience suggest that other schools may need to rethink these matters?

I think that many social systems serving children—recreational, even religious, institutions—must reexamine what they're trying to accomplish in the light of what we know about how children learn. School, for example, is not only about academic achievement; we are preparing young people so they can hold jobs, live in families, serve as heads of households, find satisfaction and meaning in life,

> "**W**e asked the parents, 'What do you want for your children as adults?' . . . They came up with ideas. . . . So we worked out programs that integrated the teaching of academic skills, appreciation of the arts, and specific social skills."

and be responsible citizens. You don't get all of that by simply focusing on academic content.

But across the country there is almost exclusive emphasis these days on academics.

And I'm greatly concerned about that, because most of the so-called reformers don't understand how people learn. They think of learning as a mechanical process; they don't seem to understand how much it depends on imitation, on identification with authority figures, on internalization of attitudes and values through relating emotionally to others. They do not give enough attention to the kind of climate that must be created to make that possible.

And the time and care it takes to build it.

Absolutely. When we went into King and Baldwin schools, they were 32nd and 33rd out of 33 in achievement. They had the most chaotic school climates you can imagine, with fighting, poor attendance, disrespect for authority, high turnover of staff—all the conditions you often find in such places—and all of that had to be turned around gradually.

What was your role in doing that?

Well, to help people understand the social system and to work out ways to change it.

Specifically how did you go about doing that?

The first year I spent a great deal of time in the building myself, dealing with immediate, hands-on problems along with the staff. I learned about the school, but it was important that I not be there so much, because that was a model that couldn't be replicated. So in the second year, our social worker became the person on the spot, and I became the conceptualizer, working with the social worker, the teachers, and the principal to plan the kinds of things that needed to be done. I was also the liaison to downtown. I put on a number of workshops in the behavioral sciences and child development, and I helped with the mental health team in particular, taking referrals on children with problems.

In responding to those referrals, we were able to convey a way of thinking about children and their problems: rather than thinking of them as bad children or children who weren't so smart, it was more helpful to think of them as underdeveloped, or as having developed ways of managing themselves that were troublesome to the system. We took the attitude that because they were underdeveloped, they could be given skills that would enable them to be successful.

We started out with individual teachers presenting children with problems and our mental health team responding to them. Teachers found it so helpful they began dropping in on the meetings even when they hadn't referred any of the children being discussed. After awhile we said, "Why not make this a workshop or a seminar?" They agreed, so they all started coming. We would go over what had happened, what the behavior meant, and what the teacher might do to address it. Other teachers would share their ideas about how they had handled similar problems.

How did you become involved in this project in the first place?

We were asked by the Ford Foundation. Our Center had been doing consultation in the schools on a parttime basis. The Ford people suggested that it might be more useful if we were there fulltime and if we had equal responsibility with the school for the outcomes of our suggestions.

Initially, our Center had been brought in by a progressive superintendent, but it was a very chaotic time—1968, when there was a lot of social unrest—so the superintendent left after the first year. The new superintendent was interested but caught up in his own problems and couldn't work with us. The third superintendent had much the same problems but was less supportive of our ideas and ways of working; he was a very dedicated man, but he wanted to make it happen right away. So we didn't get very much support during those first five years. We were able to bring about a change in the climate of the school, but we couldn't show academic gains. We hung on for a couple of more years and then started to leave, but the parents objected, so we decided to stay.

Then we got support for a program called "Social Skills Curriculum for Inner-City Children," because it was clear to us that helping the children develop good social skills reduced stress in the schools and made it possible for teachers and others to plan. So we decided to continue the effort to teach social skills in an even more systematic way.

We asked the parents, "What do you want for your children as adults?" Then we asked, "What do you think are the kinds of skills your children will need?" They came up with ideas in several categories: politics and government, business and economics, health and nutrition, spiritual and leisure time. So we worked out programs that integrated the teaching of academic skills, appreciation of the arts, and specific social skills.

Well, that program made the teaching of basic skills very relevant to the children. It created a very exciting school, and the achievement scores just leaped upward.

Some educators say it's a mistake to bring parents—especially low-income parents—in on school governance; that instead we should concentrate on getting parents to play a more direct role in the day-to-day learning of their own children—and that's enough.

It's not a mistake if you prepare the parents, if you genuinely respect them and assist them to participate construc-

> **"...Most of the so-called reformers . . . think of learning as a mechanical process; they don't seem to understand how much it depends on imitation, on identification with authority figures, on internalization of attitudes and values through relating emotionally to others."**

tively, and if you tap their strengths rather than their weaknesses. If we had taken low-income parents and tried to use them in the academic support area, they would have felt inadequate, defensive, and rebellious, and that would have created problems. But because we used them in the social support area, they felt they were doing something that was worthwhile and useful.

And many of them gained confidence from being in the school; in fact, at least seven of the parents we know of went back and finished high school, went on to college, and became professional people themselves. One got a master's degree; her daughter, who just finished at Yale University last year, is now in medical school.

You said the curriculum emphasized instruction in social skills. What is that like?

Well, for example, at the time we initiated a unit on politics and government, there was a mayoralty contest going on in the city. The children wrote letters asking the candidates to make presentations to them and their parents. The children were taught how to be hosts for the candidates and their parents, and how to raise questions with the candidates so as to put them on the spot without being disrespectful. After the presentations the children wrote thank you letters as part of their language arts. Parents and teach-

ers rented a bus and took the children around town to show them conditions. They discussed relationships between those conditions and politics and government, and the children came back and wrote about it for their language arts and social science lessons. To develop appreciation for the arts, the children put on a dance and drama program for their parents and the candidates.

That's a very broad interpretation of social skills. I thought it might just mean saying "please" and "thank you."

Well, it's that also, but these were more ambitious and more important social skills.

What about other aspects of the academic program?

After the climate of the school changed dramatically, there was more time and energy to identify problems and needs, and to plan. We changed the testing program so we could get the test scores back in time to identify weak areas and then have staff development for teachers to help them develop the skills necessary to improve in those areas. Teachers would identify weaknesses of the children and areas where they themselves needed more work, and we would base our staff development on our building-level goals rather than on ideas from downtown.

Your experience is certainly consistent with the principle that the individual school should be the base for school improvement activities.

Right. It's very difficult to transfer practices from one school to another because people are different, circumstances are different. Also the sense of empowerment that comes from looking at the problems of your own school and making adjustments for yourself is very important to bringing about change and improvement.

How do these ideas relate to the effective schools work of Ronald Edmonds and others?

Well, Ron and I were good friends, but we had a continuing debate. Ron believed that our approach—a comprehensive strategy that paid attention to relationship issues—was really the most desirable, but unfortunately he died before he could say so publicly. His concern about our approach was that if you told school people they had to know something about relationships and so on in order to improve schools, that would let them off the hook. They would say, "We aren't trained in that, and we can't do anything." What he did was to find schools that were readily identifiable as successful and then say to people, "This shows it can be done; you must find a way to do it."

The questionable aspect of that, as he himself was the first to admit, was that his five factors were not necessarily the cause of the success.

That's right. And what most people forget is that Ron used to say regularly that he personally never had changed a single school.

You would agree, though, that he did a great service by attracting national attention.

A tremendous service, because what he did—and this is what he insisted was necessary—was to disprove some of the dangerous notions about the inability of poor children and minority children to learn. When he first started his work, right after issuance of the Coleman Report, a lot of people were ready to write off poor kids. I think he found enough cases to clearly prove that under the right conditions, minority and poor children could succeed.

Do you see any dangers in the possible misuse of the effective schools literature?

Yes, I do—and he was concerned about that. But I think more people are beginning to understand that what he was talking about were end products, and there's a process you must go through to reach them; you can't create them instantly out of nothing. You can't demand that people have high expectations; you've got to develop a climate that allows people to have high expectations. The same teachers in our schools who, working in chaotic conditions, had low expectations for children developed high expectations when they were working in a desirable and supportive climate—and even if you start with high expectations, you can't sustain them in chaos.

> "**I**f we had taken low-income parents and tried to use them in the academic support area, they would have felt inadequate, defensive, and rebellious, and that would have created problems. But because we used them in the social support area, they felt they were doing something that was worthwhile and useful."

What's the current status of your project in New Haven?

It's now been mandated in 12 of the lowest achieving elementary schools, and we're working with the central administration to help those schools use our model.

Are you wary of having it mandated?

No, because the new superintendent did a lot of groundwork, so the key school people, as well as parents, approve the idea of creating a desirable climate in order to attain academic achievement. I think mandating only shows that the central office really supports the program.

Based on your record of successful collaboration between the Yale Child Study Center and public schools, what advice do you have for our readers?

Most of all, collaboration takes respect for other people. You know, one of the reasons universities and public schools often have trouble working together is that university people are assumed to have higher status than public school people. School people are on the front line, carrying out what is probably the most important task in our society, but they're not given the recognition. It's very important for university people to understand that these are good people doing very tough jobs.

That's why I'm so troubled by some of the studies that focus on the IQ scores of educators. That's nonsense; it's irrelevant. There's a threshold level above which people have what it takes to do the job, and there's no need to worry about exact IQ scores.

So respect is essential, plus finding the talent that's there, establishing a goal, and then working together to achieve that goal. And, of course, that involves confronting issues, not running away or hiding from them—and confronting each other in a cooperative, problem-solving way, rather than a destructive way.

A final word?

I might just add that achievement of low-income and minority children is tremendously important. A lot of people seem to think it's going to be possible to close low-income people out of the mainstream, as we did in the past; that they'll have low-level jobs, and so on. It's just not going to happen. There was a time when you could have stability in society even though many people weren't well educated, because they could go take low-level jobs in the steel mills, or a variety of other blue-collar positions, and support a family, feel good about themselves, and be good citizens as a result. Today, in order to get even the low-level service job, you need good social skills. You need to be able to interact appropriately with people in a variety of settings.

You also need to do that to be able to achieve in school, so schools are going to have to modify the way they work to make it possible for low-income kids to be successful in school. If not, the rest of us are going to be victimized by people who are frustrated, disappointed, and angry: people who have seen others on television who are actually no brighter than they are but who have had different experiences. And they're simply not going to tolerate it.

That's why I say there's probably no more important mission in our society today than educating low-income and minority children.□

James P. Comer is Maurice Falk Professor of Child Psychiatry, Yale University Child Study Center, P.O. Box 3333, New Haven, CT 06510.

Ronald S. Brandt is executive editor of the Association for Supervision and Curriculum Development, 125 N. West Street, Alexandria, VA 22314.

Educational Leadership 45 (April 1988): 10-13

RON BRANDT

On Teaching Thinking: A Conversation with Art Costa

Editor of ASCD's popular resource book *Developing Minds*, Art Costa asserts that the results are disappointing when we teach content alone in the hope that students will also learn to think. On the other hand, the teaching of thinking skills in isolation is just as unproductive. To combine these approaches, he recommends that we select content for its relationship to thought processes. Further, he observes that administrators who model intelligent behavior are effective in creating a climate for thinking in their schools.

Photographs by Gary Irwin

For several years you've been a leading advocate of teaching thinking. How would you assess what has been accomplished so far?

I think we're making great progress. There is heightened awareness of the need for teaching thinking. Large numbers of people are attending conferences on the subject. Textbook publishers and test writers are giving increased attention to the need for more thought-provoking materials. Parents are becoming interested in developing their kids' intelligence; there have been articles in popular magazines like *Woman's Day*. Teachers are feeling a new excitement about teaching for thinking. But we still have a long way to go.

Many of your speeches and articles focus on what schools and teachers can do to foster thinking in regular classes. Does that mean you're skeptical about the value of special published programs?

No, not at all. Some of the published programs have been designed by brilliant philosophers, psychologists, and researchers. They've taken years to put together, and they've been designed with great precision and creativity.

They have benefits that might not be readily apparent. For example, we think mostly of the effects of special programs on students, but one of their greatest benefits may be their effects on teachers. I am fortunate to have been trained in several published programs, and I want to tell you that it changed my thinking. It was a glorious event for me, not only because I saw what it could do for kids, but also because *I* got better. As a result of Instrumental Enrichment, I am less impulsive. As a result of CoRT, I think I consider other people's points of view more now. As a result of Tactics, I think I focus and resist distraction more. These programs can have powerful residual effects on teachers.

I do have a problem, though, with simply buying a program as an add-on. That doesn't go far enough, because then it's something the 3rd grade teacher does or the social studies teacher does. If thinking is to be a core value, all the teachers—and all of the students—must be committed to it.

Does it concern you that there isn't a lot of research evidence for the effectiveness of some of the things schools are doing: writing thinking skills into the curriculum, encouraging teacher questioning behaviors, and so on? We can't guarantee that even if schools do these things, students are going to be better thinkers.

Well, that depends on what you mean by research. If you demand statistics, they're hard to find. However, when I talk with teachers, I hear convincing evidence. Teachers say they're seeing kids in a different light; they are coming to appreciate differences in their cognitive styles. And they report that students are overcoming problems like impulsivity and lack of organization. That's the kind of evidence I find impressive; it's "harder" data than inferences drawn from multiple-choice tests.

But it's difficult to evaluate the infusion of thinking in regular classes the way you would a special program.

That's correct. A published program is designed to accomplish specific outcomes, and tests can be constructed to measure those outcomes. When teachers integrate thinking skills in with regular instruction, on the other hand, the change in student behavior is bound to be diverse and elusive. Most materials have not been designed to teach thinking.

How important is it that regular subject-matter materials have specific provisions for teaching thinking?

I would like to see more materials that have thinking skills as their central focus. For the most part they attend more to the content to be covered than to the thought processes that need to go along with it. We are entering an age, I believe, in which curriculum will be redesigned according to developmental levels. Content will be selected for what it contributes to thought processes. In history, for example, a teacher might choose a topic not only because of its historical importance, but also because it causes students to consider original sources, evaluate the adequacy of data, and distinguish fact from opinion.

That seems exactly the opposite of what people like E. D. Hirsch, Jr., and Lynne Cheney[1] say. They claim that curriculum generalists already put too much stress on process over content.

We have a lot of evidence that teaching content alone, and hoping it will cause students to learn to think, doesn't work. The teaching of content alone is not enough.

And yet those who are skeptical about teaching skills—specifically, E. D. Hirsch, Jr.—say that evidence is very strong that skills don't transfer from one content area to another.[2]

First, I doubt that most traditional school instruction pays much attention to transfer. Some of the published thinking skills programs, Instrumental Enrichment for example, include a bridging activity in every lesson.

Second, we have to look at the research methodology used to measure transfer. For example, the other day a teacher told me that she had taught her students about creativity, brainstorming, mind mapping, and so on. A few days later, a parent reported that when his daughter had a slumber party, and the kids had played all their games and got bored watching television, they started saying, "What'll we do now?" His daughter said, "I know; let's brainstorm." Well, isn't that transfer? Here was a situation completely different from the original setting, and yet this teenager used a technique she had learned in school.

I hear increasing numbers of anecdotes from teachers who say, "You know, we can be talking about something entirely new, and a kid will bring up a thinking skill we practiced earlier and apply it to the new content."

Some of the psychological research on transfer of skills is rather narrow. For example, researchers have subjects practice memorizing random digits until they get very good at it, but then they find they're no better at memorizing random letters of the alphabet than they were before. I assume that you're talking about skills that are more global and more meaningful?

Yes. And that brings up the whole matter of assessment. If we're going to adopt a goal of developing intelligent behavior, then we need a paradigm shift not only in how it's taught but in how it's measured. Most of our assessment procedures involve counting the number of answers students get right on tests. Now, when we think about intelligent behavior, we're concerned with how students behave when they *don't* know an answer. Do they persevere? Do they check for accuracy? Do they approach a problem flexibly, trying novel solutions? I don't want to throw out conventional tests, but they're not adequate for measuring intelligent behavior.

Are you primarily concerned about improving the way we assess achievement in the academic fields, or do you want to go beyond that to assess thinking as such?

Both. I'm talking about analytical behavior, about awareness of our own thought processes, of being inclined to spot problems, being able to pose questions, and so on.

But you'd also like to see changes in the way we assess achievement in mathematics and reading?

Yes. And your word *assessment* is really much better than the word *testing*, because it's broader. We've also got to look at the audience for whom the assessment is intended. Regrettably, our current testing is mostly for political purposes. I'm talking about getting feedback for teachers and other staff about the results of their efforts, so they can use it in their planning.

Do you think current testing practices are hindering the further development of teaching thinking in schools?

They certainly affect teachers' and parents' perceptions of what is important. I talk with teachers who say, "Why should I teach for thinking when I'm

being evaluated, and my students are being judged, on the basis of low-level knowledge?" I should add that when teachers do teach for thinking, their standardized test scores usually go up—but still there's a perception that teaching for thinking and the tests we use are antithetical.

That brings up the effective teaching research, which has been widely publicized in an effort to bolster achievement test scores. You've often expressed concern about use of those research findings. Are they actually incompatible with teaching thinking?

No. In fact, I try to incorporate effective teaching practices into my own teaching. What I am opposed to is translating research findings into competencies by which to measure teachers. I'm opposed to going into classrooms with checklists to see if teachers are performing those behaviors. One reason is that when you examine the effective teaching research closely, you find that some teachers don't use those behaviors but still get marvelous

results, while other teachers do all those things but get poor results. In other words, effective teaching is quite idiosyncratic.

I want research findings on effective practices to become part of the teacher's knowledge base—part of the teacher's repertoire. We should help teachers understand what is known about the effects of those behaviors on students, and teachers should decide where and when to use them depending upon the situation, the goal of their instruction, and the particular kids the teacher is dealing with.

You also advocate use of teacher behaviors that are not on most lists of "effective" teaching behaviors.

Yes, I have worked with many teachers over the years, helping them increase their repertoires of questioning strategies, of ways to organize the classroom—their range of responses to youngsters. And the results have been very positive. Teachers tell me that kids become more thoughtful, that they engage in more long-term learning rather than just "learn-it-for-now-and-forget-it-after-the-test," that classroom discussions are more intensive.

What can you say about the extent of attention to these behaviors in undergraduate teacher education?

I don't know much about that, because my field is school administration, not teacher education, but I do hope that teacher preparation institutions will focus more on teaching as thinking and teachers' ability to teach thinking. In 1984, when we were preparing *Developing Minds*,[3] we searched for a description of an undergraduate program with a well-articulated thinking skills component, but we couldn't find one. Since that time a few teacher education institutions have begun to focus on teaching thinking, but I'm not aware of much interest in that theme nationwide. I would like to see teacher education programs include a core of strategies such as how to teach a concept attainment lesson, how to teach a thinking skill directly, how to organize for cooperative learning.

You mentioned teaching a thinking skill directly. An issue dividing leaders of this movement is whether skills—reading skills, for example—should be taught explicitly rather than implicitly.

Well, explicit skill teaching can be, and often is, inappropriate. Still, in day-to-day classroom life, teachers or curriculum materials often invite particular thought processes. For example, a science book might give directions for conducting an experiment and say, "What conclusions do you draw from these data?" It seems to me that if kids are going to be asked that—and I think they should—they ought to know how to draw a conclusion. Or a teacher will say, "Let's summarize some of the things we've learned about the desert." Well, what do you do when you summarize? And when a teacher says, "Let's compare the farm decline of the '30s with the farm decline of the '80s," students should know what's supposed to go on in their heads when they compare and contrast.

I don't think these skills should be taught in isolation, but I do think we should be courteous enough to let kids know what we mean when we use such terms as *classify*, *analyze*, or *infer*.

All the examples you've given are embedded within broader academic purposes. What some observers are concerned about is the idea of teaching thinking skills unrelated to any immediate academic application.

Well, that can be like memorizing the state capitals; it goes no place. It's what David Perkins calls "inert knowledge." Teaching thinking skills in isolation, without providing for transfer, is futile.

Many administrators would probably agree with the importance of teaching in such a way that students become better thinkers, but they may be a bit frustrated because it's hard to get started when teachers are already fully occupied. What have leaders done where schools have made real progress?

> **"The reason I suggest focusing on desired student behavior first is that it can be less threatening to teachers. If you begin by focusing on the skills of teaching, some teachers will take it as criticism of the ways they have been teaching."**

Successful leaders encourage teachers to look carefully at the intelligent behavior of their own students. For example, how well do the students apply the mathematics they have learned? How well do they comprehend what they are reading? Are they impulsive? Do they follow directions well? Do they strive for accuracy? Is their language precise? Are they creative?

The next step is to talk about what we want students to do: Instead of acting impulsively, they would have a plan of action. What would it look like if they followed directions well? What kinds of problem-solving behaviors would we like to see? In other words, develop some positive visions, with indicators of what we are looking for. Then consider how to arrange the classroom, what teacher behaviors to use, and whether to purchase materials to achieve those skills.

The reason I suggest focusing on desired student behavior first is that it can be less threatening to teachers. If you begin by focusing on the skills of teaching, some teachers will take it as

criticism of the ways they have been teaching.

Another effective leadership practice is to provide for lots of teacher decision making: getting teachers to study the issues, plan their own inservice; sending them to conferences; taking time in faculty meetings for reporting back; purchasing materials for teachers to experiment with; arranging for teachers to do team planning, to share materials, to observe and coach one another; and so on.

I think administrators do best by modeling intelligent behavior themselves. As the gatekeeper of the school, the administrator is looked upon as a model and as a source of values. So if he or she spends time talking about thinking, modeling it, releasing teachers to engage in it, and purchasing materials to support it, that sends a very powerful signal to teachers about priorities and values.

Effective administrators can also bring school practices in line with thinking. For example, do report cards say anything about thinking? What about teacher evaluation and supervision? Are there provisions for engaging teachers' intellects in those procedures? What about the school's discipline code: is it behavioral, or does it appeal to students' rational processes? Administrators need to examine the policies, the organization, the practices of the school, and ask whether they support the goal of advancing thinking.□

1. E. D. Hirsch, Jr., *Cultural Literacy: What Every American Needs to Know* (Boston: Houghton Mifflin, 1987). Lynne V. Cheney, *American Memory: A Report on the Humanities in the Nation's Public Schools* (Washington, D.C.: National Endowment for the Humanities, 1987).

2. Hirsch, p. 60.

3. Arthur L. Costa, ed., *Developing Minds: A Resource Book for Teaching Thinking* (Alexandria, Va.: Association for Supervision and Curriculum Development, 1985).

Arthur L. Costa is Professor of School Administration, California State University, 6000 J St., Sacramento, CA 95819. **Ron Brandt** is ASCD's Executive Editor.

Educational Leadership 46 (Nov. 1988): 11-15, 17

ANNE MEEK

On Teaching as a Profession: A Conversation with Linda Darling-Hammond

Foremost policy watcher at the Center for the Study of Teaching, Linda Darling-Hammond analyzes the impact of state and district policies on teachers in classrooms, comes out squarely in favor of full partnership for teachers in decision making, and points out the critical necessity of the knowledge base for the professionalization of teaching.

Photographs by Dennis Johnson

Why does the RAND Corporation have a center for studying teaching?

About six or eight years ago, Art Wise and I started looking at how policies affect teachers in classrooms. It soon became clear to us that there was a choice to be made in terms of school improvement strategies between improving the capacity of teachers to do what they felt was most effective with kids, on one hand, and prescribing ever more specific and detailed prescriptions for practice, on the other. At the same time, we became aware that a shortage of teachers was building.

RAND decided that our analysis was correct, that if we wanted to improve American schools, we had to pay a lot more attention to teachers—what types of people were attracted into teaching, what they knew when they got there, and what they were able to do in classrooms. So the corporation decided to establish a Center for the

Study of the Teaching Profession, to support a long line of work about how to improve teaching.

What sorts of things do you study?

We've continued to study teaching in classrooms and what constructs and constrains that activity, including district-level policies like teacher evaluation and teacher selection, as well as instructional policies that define how teaching will take place in schools and classrooms. We've done studies of teacher supply and demand. We also look at state-level policies that determine who becomes teachers: certification, compensation, testing policies. So we've been looking at all levels of the policy system from the bottom up and the top down to better understand teaching.

How did you get to be a policy watcher?

I don't know! I started out in education as a teacher; I still consider myself a teacher. I've taught at every level, and I love teaching. At some point, however, I felt I could not be professionally accountable for my students in the way I wanted to be, given the constraints I operated under. And that propelled me to graduate school. And I became involved in research, and taught at Temple University, and went to the National Urban Coalition to try to figure out how to bring equity into schools, because I always taught in urban settings, and the results of inequity were obvious.

Then I began to realize that once you got the finances straight, and if you could manage to desegregate schools, there were still questions about how to improve what goes on in classrooms. So my work has come around to focus on teaching again. I've come back to my roots.

How would you summarize the status of teachers in America today?

I think America is ambivalent about teachers. There is some evidence that the public is willing to support teachers in terms of greater compensation, and there are efforts to improve con-

Teachers work directly with children, yet they are still not perceived as the most knowledgeable and important members of the education community.

ditions for teaching. There is dialogue about improving teachers' status, responsibility, and autonomy. But, at the same time, teachers continue to be treated as second-class citizens—in education the greatest status accrues to those who work least closely with children. Teachers work directly with children, yet they are still not perceived as the most knowledgeable and important members of the education community. They are not well represented in decision making about curriculums, testing policies, grouping and promotion policies, textbook adoption, and the like.

What are the major factors affecting changes in the profession?

Although I don't want to paint education as a purely economic activity, the changing economic status of America has a profound effect on education and on teaching. As a country we cannot expect to maintain, or regain,

economic and political status in the world while allowing our human capital to fall out however it may. We're in a situation where we simply cannot allow children to fail.

This reality requires teachers who are highly trained and sensitive to what the child brings to the learning experience and what he or she needs, rather than someone who can simply stand up and give a lecture in hopes that the kids will understand it but who has no tools for dealing with a child who doesn't.

So the work of teachers requires more than a prescription of methods?

Certainly. The need to ensure that students don't fail pushes us toward a conception of teaching that requires a lot of pedagogical knowledge—a lot of knowledge about children—a conception that is oriented toward the needs of the client, that in fact is a professional conception.

How will we know when teaching has finally attained the status of a profession?

On the day when parents can expect any teacher to whom their child is assigned to know whatever the profession has decided is most important, then we'll know. We'll have professional accountability in education when every client can expect that every professional will know certain things in order to have been allowed to practice.

So you would say that the crucial hallmark of a profession is its application of knowledge in the service of its clients.

Exactly. As the role of knowledge in responsible service has become recognized, there's been an inexorable march toward professionalization, not only in teaching but in a number of occupations. These are fields where we've accumulated knowledge, and we expect those who practice in those areas to use that knowledge. And that is what has impelled so many fields toward a professional structure.

Yet a great many critics of teaching have called for less in the way of pedagogy and more in the way of content. How will these two kinds of knowledge balance out in teacher preparation programs?

In some states there has been increased emphasis on pedagogical preparation, in others, decreased emphasis. Some critics have advanced the bizarre argument that teacher preparation institutions are not very good and therefore we will get better teachers by avoiding these institutions. This argument ignores the question of whether there are things these talented college graduates ought to know about teaching. It also ignores the choice of improving teacher education institutions as a deliberate strategy. Instead, it substitutes the Bright Person myth of teaching. This myth is that simply by being smart in an area, having gotten a degree in it, one has the tools to convey that knowledge to other people so that it becomes their own. Now, if teaching were only a matter of giving an elegant, well-crafted lecture, we could sit the kids down in front of big videoscreens where performers or other bright people deliver elegant, well-crafted lectures, have them do that six hours a day, and send them home with assignments.

> **If teaching were only a matter of giving an elegant, well-crafted lecture, we could sit the kids down in front of big videoscreens.**

Good point.

But that's not all there is to teaching. The situation in teaching is analogous to what was happening in medicine at the end of the 19th century, when the occupation was trying to band together to change the caliber of medical training, and legislators continued to allow irregular practitioners to practice. Their contention was, well, you don't learn much in these terrible medical schools anyway, so go follow somebody around on a buggy, and you can be a doctor. These assertions were made at Harvard and other universities: you don't learn to practice medicine, you're either born with a healing talent, or you're not.

Teachers are born, not made.

That's right. And if the born-to-be-a-doctor philosophy had won out, the quality of medical care, health, and life expectancy in this country would be much lower than it is today. So the fact that some teacher education institutions have been disappointing to the people who've gone through them, as well as to the policymakers who oversee them, is not an argument for doing away with teacher preparation. We have a substantial amount of knowledge that teachers need to know in order to teach effectively. We know a lot about how children learn. We know a lot about how children can be both helped and harmed. And if we don't transmit that knowledge, we are being irresponsible.

Educators are experimenting with various methods of acquiring that knowledge: five-year programs, alternative certification, and the like. In theory, at least, it would seem preferable to emphasize what a person knows in giving that person access to credentials, rather than how many credits a person has in this course and how many credits in that.

Most other professions don't license on the basis of courses taken. They license on the basis of the bar examination or the architectural registration exam or whatever. Of course, those tests often determine what courses people will take. You would be foolish to take the bar if you had not had good courses in torts, contracts, constitutional law—

There aren't very many Abe Lincolns studying in front of the fireplace any more to become lawyers—

Right. In most states you have to be a graduate of an accredited institution, professionally accredited, in order to sit for the bar. But no state agency dictates to the law school the courses it must offer in order to be approved or certifies graduates based on the courses they have taken. So law schools can figure out the best way to convey their body of knowledge. This freedom allows the field to grow in terms of the knowledge base and how it is transmitted.

However, teacher education institutions have a lot of constraints on how they can configure their programs. And part of the reason is that we still have questions about how to regulate this quasi-profession. It's being regulated now by state agencies rather than by professional bodies. As licensure tests are increasingly used, the requirements for particular courses for program approval and certification should be eliminated. That's a reasonable trade-off to expect.

Other professions have a different structure; for example, state standards boards composed of members of the profession that determine how the profession will be regulated. The state legislature delegates authority to this body. But right now everybody seems to be trying to regulate teaching.

The Carnegie Foundation, the Holmes Group, and others are in the process of developing national standards. What's your prediction as to whether these efforts will succeed?

It's too soon to know exactly how the National Board for Professional Teaching Standards is going to influence the field. It will perform a great service in articulating for the profession what teachers ought to know and be able to do. It is the first established

That's right. The stage of collective bargaining that we still see in most places is adversarial, it's viewed as a win-lose situation, and it's very rule-oriented. And in places where that approach is clung to, we'll find it very hard to professionalize.

This adversarial stage seems to be a function of the fight over the territory of decision making, not an assessment of direction or movement, just arm wrestling.

Oh, yes, we certainly have turf battles going on. But we do see places like Dade County and Rochester where a win-win philosophy has been adopted by the board and the union. Columbus, Cincinnati, Toledo—it's happening in a lot of the middle-sized cities that were the most destitute 10 years ago. These were the places that had teacher strikes, financial crises, desegregation crises, you name it. And out of the ashes in those places the phoenix is rising. It'll be interesting to see whether others follow suit.

Female-dominated occupations have had a hard time achieving the status of professions. How have efforts to professionalize been affected by the preponderance of women in teaching?

Any occupation that has been female-dominated *has* had a hard time professionalizing. Nursing is a very close analog. There are aspects of role, allocations of authority, and salary considerations that go along with gender. In the last 15 years, however, we've seen a change in women's career opportunities. And this change means teaching must compete with other careers, not only in terms of compensation but also in terms of the authority and responsibility and status associated with the occupation. Michael Sedlak and Steve Schlossman (1986) conducted a historical analysis of teaching; they concluded that the women's movement is probably the most important change of any in the 20th century to affect the structure of teaching. They think it will be the major impetus for the professionalization of teaching.

professional structure outside the subject area organizations that will have some authority to anoint members of the profession in some way. That's very important. You have to have a professional structure before you can have anything else in terms of self-governance in a profession.

The Holmes Group is also an important historical event. I don't know if there's ever been a time when the education deans in this country have come together to try to think with one head about what teacher preparation ought to be. It's too soon to see exactly what the outcomes will be—but that's an important activity that is bound to have some effect on how teachers get prepared. And the fact that it is an effort toward unity among teacher educators is again a statement of professionalism—because the profession is the collective.

What about the influence of the unions? Historically and currently, what part have they played in the effort to professionalize teaching?

At this moment, the unions are part of the vanguard for professionalization. Mitchell and Kirschner, who have studied labor unions for a long time, have hypothesized a theory of maturation of collective bargaining. It goes through stages: first, just getting the right to bargain, then bargaining on bread-and-butter issues, and ultimately negotiating policies. Well, I think there's a fourth stage beyond those, which is negotiating responsibility.

Now we are beginning to see in contracts, particularly where unions have been strongest in the past, a move toward negotiated responsibility. In places like Dade County and Rochester and Salt Lake, the contract doesn't specify how something shall be done; the contract says everyone agrees to a process by which teachers and administrators and members of the community will make certain decisions in certain ways. So they're negotiating who makes decisions about what and by what process, but they're not saying what the decisions themselves will be. And that's been the basis for creating shared governance structures and new professional obligations in the last couple of years.

It would be hard for people who have been adversaries all these years to start seeing it that way.

Are there assumptions, expectations, customs among teachers themselves as a group that hinder further professionalizing teaching?

Teachers have been socialized into the system as it is now. Those who found it hard to be socialized either have become the local renegades and mavericks or have left teaching. The ranks of ex-teachers are filled with those who found it difficult to adapt to a situation in which they were not expected to use their knowledge on behalf of children. Nevertheless, we have a very well-educated teaching force at this moment, as well educated as it's ever been, and perhaps as well educated as it will ever be, depending on how things work out in the next few years.

But we have a closed-door ethic in schools. The notion of collegial consultation and decision making is alien in most schools and will be resisted by some teachers. Of course, other teachers are embracing these ideas and working very hard to find ways to make practices like peer review and collaborative decision making real in schools.

Sedlak and Schlossman think the women's movement will be the major impetus for the professionalization of teaching.

And these activities are central to professions because they ensure that there is, not an idiosyncratic piece of knowledge in each practitioner, but a shared body of knowledge.

There is probably some ambivalence in the teaching force about the role of knowledge in practice, about the extent to which research and other forms of collective knowledge have anything to offer "me in my classroom with my students." Again, that's because there has not been a form of preparation and socialization that particularly legitimizes and makes useful that kind of knowledge.

If you were in charge of a district, how would you process teachers into the profession, from preservice preparation into teaching?

I'd start with a theory that the caliber of the people is the most important thing you have to work with, not the procedures or handbooks or regulations or curriculum guides. I would emphasize selection, recruitment, and evaluation; and I'd pay much less attention to creating a new curriculum every year, for example, because I would have to make trade-offs, monetarily. I would reduce the size of the curriculum development office and allocate resources to finding, getting, keeping, and supporting good people.

I would look for teachers who were well prepared, with a strong grounding in child psychology, that is to say developmental psychology, cognitive science, learning theory—teachers with strong pedagogical training as well as good subject matter backgrounds.

Suppose you had secured a pool of well-trained applicants. How would you choose your new teachers from among them?

I would put in place a selection process in which teachers in the local school were actively involved—faculties, including the principal, of course—in selecting their colleagues, after the East Williston model in New York (see Wise et al. 1987). This kind of process forces people to talk about good teaching—it's one of the ways in

We have a very well-educated teaching force at this moment, as well educated as it's ever been.

which people talk about what their shared knowledge base is and their shared values are—and once you've selected somebody, you're much more inclined to support that person as a member of the faculty.

You would involve the principal in this process?

Yes, because the principal is also a colleague, but ultimately because I wouldn't want a principal to be able to escape responsibility for any of his or her staff by saying, "I didn't pick this person; you sent him to me." If the principal helps make the decision, you begin to get accountability in the school system. Of course, some centralization of the selection process is necessary to make sure that people get equitably selected and placed, but accountability begins at the school site.

How would you introduce these peer-selected teachers to their work?

I would place beginning teachers in a professional development school. This school would be overstaffed—it would have more than the usual ratio of faculty to students. The teachers would be master teachers, that is, expert veterans, who were interested in and capable of inducting new entrants as well as teaching kids very well. Beginning teachers would be assigned to work in teams with master teachers to learn how to put theory into practice, how to become good clinical teachers.

In a large urban district, I would create such a school in the central city; and I'd see to it that the kids got a state-of-the-art education, because the school would have to be an exemplar of good practice. I would also use that kind of setting—not necessarily just one, perhaps more than one—as a way to provide sabbaticals to veteran teachers. They could take a year's assignment, or a semester's, in the professional development school to rejuvenate, to experience the exhilaration of seeing what's new under the sun and of working with the young teachers coming through. A school like that would encourage professional growth across the district.

Of course, day-to-day support for teachers would be part of your plan, too?

In my schools I would expect shared governance: governance shared between faculty, administrators, and parents like the Salt Lake City model (see Wise et al. 1984). The school decision-making councils worked so effectively that the stakeholders in the process not only *felt* the education process was effective, but all indicators showed that in fact it was.

Faculties would meet at least two hours a week in their departments or in grade-level teams to talk to each other about how they were doing their work, why they were doing it in this way, and how well it was working. They would determine what kinds of staff development they wanted to purchase or acquire for themselves as a faculty.

And I'd emphasize evaluation for beginning teachers prior to tenure to ensure that once they got tenure, we didn't have to check on them once a year for competence. We could then go on and do more useful things on their behalf and on behalf of the kids. And then I would put in place peer review of practice, much more than peer review of practitioners, where peers in fact review the practices in their schools.

> **The caliber of the people is the most important thing you have to work with, not the procedures or handbooks or regulations or curriculum guides.**

It's going to take some time and some work, but these are the practices I see as the most promising for turning teaching into a true profession.

What are the effects of recent state policies on teaching, on teachers, and on the prospects for making teaching a profession?

Some of the reform activity has been encouraging to teachers, particularly in those states where teachers have been taken seriously as partners in the reforms and where the act of teaching has not been treated in a trivial, simplistic manner. But there's a lot of cynicism among teachers who have been reformed many times and are tired of it.

So the reform movement has been a mixed blessing for teachers; and it's been a mixed blessing for kids, as well. The idea that education can be improved by mandating annual testing of kids and 822 curriculum objectives for each grade level and a new management scheme with a little merit pay sprinkled in—it's an impoverished idea. And when you see what's happening now—for example, Georgia and some other places that are testing kindergartners now for

promotion—you know that there are policies being enacted that all of our professional knowledge tells us are irresponsible means of educating or treating children.

Now, either our professional voice will become much stronger, or such well-intentioned but misguided ideas are going to hurt children. In the next decade 30 percent or more of the school population will include categories of kids who have traditionally been underserved: minority and low-income children and recent immigrants. If we persist in policies that track them, that convey to them from kindergarten on that they cannot succeed, that deliver dumbed-down textbooks to them and lists of curriculum objectives totally divorced from either real life or meaningful schoolwork—those policies are going to destroy a cohort of kids in our schools. And we'll see unbelievable dropout rates and failure rates . . . prescribed by policy.

The outcome depends on whether our professional voice becomes sufficiently strong to convey what we know about the proper education of children to the people who create the policies. It is the policies that will determine what schools and classrooms look like in the 21st century.□

References

Sedlak, M., and S. Schlossman. (November 1986). *Who Will Teach? Historical Perspective on the Changing Appeal of Teaching as a Profession.* Santa Monica, Calif.: The RAND Corporation, R-3472.

Wise, A.E., L. Darling-Hammond, M.W. McLaughlin, and H.T. Bernstein. (June 1984). *Teacher Evaluation: A Study of Effective Practices.* Santa Monica, Calif.: The RAND Corporation.

Wise, A.E., L. Darling-Hammond, and B. Berry. (January 1987). *Effective Teacher Selection: From Recruitment to Retention.* Santa Monica, Calif.: The RAND Corporation, R-3462.

Linda Darling-Hammond is Director, Education and Human Resources Program, The RAND Corporation, 2100 M St., N.W., Washington, DC 20037-1270. **Anne Meek** is Managing Editor, *Educational Leadership.*

RONALD S. BRANDT   *Educational Leadership* 44 (Nov. 1986): 28-30

On Early Education:
A Conversation with Barbara Day

Former ASCD president Barbara Day is a nationally recognized author and consultant on early education. She knows the pressures that lead educators to establish transition rooms, junior kindergartens, and similar special programs, but she recommends a different way of providing for "not ready" students.

Photographs by Larry Childress

You see educators all over the country who are concerned about early education. What are some of the issues they're wrestling with?

One of the largest issues is whether to begin offering programs for younger children in the public schools. This, of course, is a societal issue as well as an educational one. A second is whether kindergarten programs should be full-day, half-day, or alternate days.

Related to that is, if children don't do well in kindergarten, should they move into a regular first grade or into a transitional classroom? If by the end of kindergarten a child hasn't completed the requirements for that age group, the child must either go into regular first grade anyway, repeat kindergarten, or move into a transitional classroom. A pattern emerging in some areas of the country is the transitional classroom, which means that developmentally delayed children are placed in a homogeneous group. Now, I am opposed to that. I don't want

four-, five-, and six-year-old children categorized as failures.

But there must be an argument for it if it's being done more widely?

The argument goes something like this. Picture a child—very often a little boy—who is small in stature, emotionally insecure, and who—perhaps because of his home situation—is simply not a social little being; he doesn't have a lot of verbal and social skills. As a consultant, I'm often asked what I would recommend: should a child like that move on to a first grade classroom where, in this particular instance, instruction is very formal and where that child is going to be absolutely frustrated, or should the child be placed in a setting where he is developmentally capable of happy, successful learning? That's a hard question to answer.

Now, the problem is not where the child is developmentally; it's perfectly appropriate that a child should be at this particular stage in his or her life. Our challenge as educators is to pro-

vide a program based on the child's needs and in tune with his or her individual development. So I say there are some alternatives, such as a total, child-centered early childhood program, meaning birth through about age nine. It should be ungraded, experiential, and developmental in nature. In such a program, children work at whatever developmental level they are capable of, and we simply do not say that every child must pass through neat packages of graded subject matter whether he or she is ready or not.

A second thing I recommend to school districts is—and we're having problems with this due to funding—instead of segregating these children who are so-called "developmentally delayed" or "presumed unable to meet the competencies of a particular grade," give them more opportunities for growth. I'm recommending that school systems assess these children and set up an eight-week summer school at the beginning of kindergarten or a program for four-year-old children if one is available, and that they do this every summer thereafter for the next several years. My hypothesis is that by about third grade, those children will have caught up. They simply need a little more time to grow, physically and socially as well as cognitively.

They would be with other children during the regular school year, but in a special program during the summer when the other children don't attend school?

Well, they might be, but—because I'm an advocate of quality care for children of all developmental levels—I believe strongly that schools should be open in the summer to all children

37

who want to attend enrichment classes. So the children who are developmentally delayed would have time to work on the kinds of remedial skills that they need, but they would also be involved with the other children in the enrichment activities. I wouldn't want this summer program to be a burden and categorized as remedial only; I'd want it to be something that children look forward to attending. Art, dramatic play, dance, and language development opportunities should be provided; that's the way school should be for young children all the time. Specific skills in reading, writing, and math should be integrated throughout the day and approached from a child-centered view.

From an administrator's standpoint there are lots of problems to getting a program like that. Funding, organization, training.

There are, but creative administrators can do it. Chapter 1 funds can be used for the children who need them, additional scholarships should be available, and many working mothers and fathers will pay whatever is necessary for children to attend enrichment programs during the summer.

Does what you're describing actually exist anywhere?

Well, Chapel Hill is an example. I chair the advisory council for the Chapel Hill Community Schools that plans all the enrichment activities for children in the regular school year and during the summer. My daughter, Susan, can leave her elementary school on Thursday afternoon, ride the school bus to another school in the same town, and attend violin classes. Other children can leave their elementary schools and go to classes on poetry, storytelling, bread-making, math games, and so on.

That's what I want to be happening in the summer. In North Carolina we have new legislation providing that, beginning with second grade and designated grades thereafter, any child who falls below a certain level on standardized achievement tests must go to summer school. I think that's wonderful; those children should have those kinds of opportunities; but I don't want children who go to school in the summer branded as "You've got to go to summer school because

you've failed." I want to see the schools offer enrichment classes so other children are involved as well. For example, this last summer my daughter went to a public school in Chapel Hill for five weeks of special art activities. Other elementary children attended classes in theatre, dance, computers, and so on.

You don't have research evidence at this point that the kind of program you recommend would produce the results you predict?

No, but I do have an "educated opinion" based on several years of research on young children. It would make a wonderful research project.

Let's talk about a different use of screening tests. We hear a lot about tests being used to find out whether children are ready to attend school. If they can't pass the "entrance exam," their parents are encouraged to keep them home another year. Is very much of that going on?

That is a very questionable practice, and, yes, there is some of it going on. I have to present both sides of the issue. First of all, I believe in evaluating children to see where they are developmentally. The real concern is what we do with that information. I believe it should be considered a diagnostic process, not an entrance exam.

But let me represent the other side of the issue. I've had teachers say to me about a given child, "But Professor Day, I can assure you that if that child comes into my classroom as he is right now, he will not be able to meet the minimum competencies of the kindergarten." And that prediction might be very accurate. So which is better? For that child to go to kindergarten and fail, or to say to the parent, "I think your child needs one more year to grow and develop."

Of course, neither of these answers, in my opinion, is the right one. The right answer is that child absolutely *should* come into kindergarten and have a wonderful developmental program. A child like that needs the program more than a five-year-old who might be able to read on a third- or fourth-grade level.

I am also very concerned about the impact it has on a child to be brought to a testing situation knowing he or

she might not be able to enter school if he or she doesn't do well. That's very wrong.

What's the alternative?

Good teachers, psychologists, and other evaluators are developing testing situations that make it a lot of fun for children. The Chapel Hill schools spend the first three days of the school year in this kind of testing for kindergarten children. Except for the time they are being evaluated, the children don't even come to school for the first three days. Now some people question that technique, but I favor it more and more because it permits a very intensive look at a child's developmental level. The children have a great time. The kindergarten teachers who do the testing interact with the children in a very warm, supportive, encouraging way: it's like, "Here you're in school for the first time, and I'm one of the teachers; I might just be your teacher." It's never with the notion that, "Depending on how you score on that test, it will determine whether or not you come to kindergarten." Instead, it's, "We're going to play these games and have lots of fun."

Another issue you've said is a concern is full-day versus half-day kindergarten. Is that really a legitimate question?

Yes, although it's not simply a question of which produces higher achievement. We have plenty of research showing that children in full-day kindergarten have higher test scores, but we also have data showing no significant difference over time. There is more research favoring full-day, but we have evidence on both sides. So let's check that one off and move to other concerns. There are at least two.

The main reason I favor the full-day kindergarten is that in my observation all over the country, I note that children in full-day kindergartens are less hurried. There's no need to rush and have the language development group right this minute. There's no need to keep children from going to the block center because if they do we won't have time for our colors, our numbers, and letter recognition. In the full-day program it's perfectly fine for Sylvia to go to the block center; it's okay for children to go to the art center every day; it's wonderful if children want to go to the housekeeping center and involve themselves in dramatic play. So a full-day program allows time for the kinds of activities that are so important in the development of children of this age.

The second reason I believe that full-day is needed is a controversial one; it involves the need for quality care as well as quality education. I believe that many children today need a safe, secure, happy environment, and that the public schools should provide it.

Some educators don't like to hear that kind of talk because we feel we're professionals; we're responsible for education. The fact that society has a need is not necessarily our problem; that should be somebody else's problem.

I understand, but I don't feel that way at all. Caring for children's physical, social, and mental needs is all part of quality care and education. If we support a child development approach, then we understand that a child's social, emotional, and physical needs are just as important as cognitive needs and, in fact, all are dependent on each other. Good quality care as well as quality education for our young children will offer the potential for long-term effects on positive social behaviors and intellectual achievement.

To help administrators know what kind of vision they might be working toward, will you describe how a developmental program operates?

Children in the programs that I've worked with spend about a third of their time on teacher-directed activities, small group or large group. Another third of the time they work on activities assigned to them by the teacher, and then work independently or in small groups with other children. The remaining third of the time they work on activities of their choice. Now, to organize a program like this you've got to believe that children are naturally motivated to learn, and that they learn best when they're able to select and initiate some of their own activities. This internal motivator is encouraged by basing activities on

children's own interests—by allowing children to make choices among activities that are clearly useful and meaningful to them. The curriculum in such a developmental program focuses on exploration, discovery, and experimentation with hands-on materials.

Don't a lot of educators feel that the idea popular in the '60s of having children make their own decisions may have been unwise, and that teacher-directed instruction is really more efficient?

Yes, there's definitely a move away from student decision making, and for a very good reason: many teachers tried this approach without incorporating the appropriate amount of structure that is required. I say that an experiential, child-centered learning environment must be very structured, meaning very organized. Teachers must know what they're doing, and children must know what they're *supposed* to be doing: when and where and how. Unless you have a management system that they clearly understand, children will not learn the basic skills, will not learn to move from one activity to another smoothly, will not learn to be responsible and independent.

Let's say a principal or superintendent believes that the kind of program you describe is desir-

able. How can he or she go about getting it? How open are most teachers to these ideas?

I find that most teachers are very open to doing whatever they think will be helpful for the children in their classrooms. Most teachers really do trust and respect children; they support a child-centered philosophy that stresses peer interaction, learning by doing, and positive self-concept development. The problem comes with the support they need, financial and moral. To have a developmental classroom, you must have a wide variety of concrete and sensory materials. The classroom needs to be organized with experiential learning centers that allow for differences in learning styles, that encourage children to explore a variety of materials and make decisions. In addition to learning centers, the curriculum in a developmental classroom is integrated and uses a unit approach to teaching and learning. It uses hands-on experiences and integrates math skills in areas such as cooking and science. It emphasizes language development. The program must be flexible enough to help each child learn according to individual needs, interests, and abilities.

A principal or administrator must believe that this kind of experiential learning is the way children grow, and must reward teachers through his or her comments, through his or her endorsement of materials they need and want, and through saying to the community, "We have a fine program here."

You make it sound as though all an administrator has to do is give adequate support and it will happen. Is that your experience?

Well, the support of an administrator is absolutely essential. We do have some strong teachers who are capable of moving ahead on their own, but there is a tremendous difference when that instructional leader is involved and supports the program.☐

Barbara Day is a Professor and Chair of the Department of Teaching and Learning, School of Education, University of North Carolina at Chapel Hill, Chapel Hill, NC 27514. **Ronald S. Brandt** is Executive Editor of ASCD.

Educational Leadership 45 (Dec. 1987/Jan. 1988): 30-34

RON BRANDT

On Assessment in the Arts: A Conversation with Howard Gardner

The author of *Frames of Mind: A Theory of Multiple Intelligences,* Howard Gardner has spent years investigating issues of creativity, intelligence, and the artistic process. Here he explains the endeavors of Project Zero to develop assessment techniques for the arts. He contends that "making art" is central to artistic learning and that perception and reflection activities must be linked directly to student production of art.

You and your colleagues at Harvard Project Zero are working with Educational Testing Service and the Pittsburgh schools to develop ways to assess student achievement in the arts. Why?

We want to know whether individuals involved in the arts are getting something out of their experiences, and whether those results can be documented. I see school as a place to develop the different components of the mind. Artistic thinking—thinking in artistic symbols—is a distinctive way of using the mind, but one usually downplayed in school. For example, we use the mind in a certain way in creating or listening to music. You could work with mathematics or language for the rest of your life, and it would not affect your ability to deal with music. By the same token, the abilities involved in dealing with the visual arts—with sculpture or painting, with dance, mime, use of the body, and so on—all represent separate sets of cognitive skills. If we omit those areas from the curriculum, we are in effect shortchanging the mind.

Photographs by Constance Wolf

Now, it might not be necessary to nourish these abilities in school if they were developed fully outside of school, but it's obvious that in most cultures—and certainly in ours—there's very little attention to the arts outside of school.

Is it really possible to assess achievement in the arts in a meaningful way?

Even people who are strong advocates of arts in the schools are very much in conflict about assessment. To some extent, they feel that what's most important in the arts is difficult to assess: arts have personal meaning, they deal with emotional content, they're often very subjective. So some people, including people involved in the arts, feel that assessment is incompatible with their purposes. Others, though, feel that we must assess results if we are to justify the expense of offering these experiences in schools. But they often make the opposite error of trying to assess the arts in the same way other kinds of learning are assessed: with multiple-choice tests and so on.

The assessment techniques you're developing are for use with all students, not just those with special talents?

Exactly.

Are they intended as measures of ability or achievement?

In the beginning, we had the mistaken idea that one could assess aptitude apart from intensive involvement with material. We're convinced now that that probably doesn't work anywhere, but it certainly doesn't work in the arts. It's pointless to test people's musical or dramatic aptitude unless they've had a significant amount of experience in artistic thinking. And many kids—even at the high school level—have had virtually no exposure at all. So our approach has been to involve students in very rich kinds of artistic activities. We involve them not only in artistic creation—actually painting, composing, and so on—but also in what we call "projects." These are curriculum modules that involve

fairly long-term kinds of analysis and perceptual discrimination, as well as considerable "reflection" on what they're doing. And after students have had some experience with these kinds of things, we assess them, so to speak, "on the fly" while they're actually engaged in these projects.

As an analogy, let's say that somebody wanted a chess aptitude test. We could give people a chessboard and say, "All right, play with these for 20 minutes, and we'll see how good you are." Or recognizing that they don't know the rules of chess, instead we could see how good they are at counting, calculating, spatial reasoning, and so on. But you would probably find that such related abilities are a poor predictor of actual chess playing, because chess is a complicated activity that also involves "psyching out" what's on your opponent's mind, thinking several steps ahead, that sort of thing. So it's much more sensible to take a hundred people who have never played chess before, teach them the rules, have them play for a while, and then begin to give them chess problems.

That's basically what we're doing: we're assuming that most kids have not had much experience artistically. We immerse them in activities that call for artistic thinking, and after they have some familiarity with an activity, we use various kinds of assessment techniques, including some straightforward ones as well as some that are more unobtrusive.

How can you be sure about the validity of these new techniques?

Well, to begin with, they're not all new. Both Project Zero and ETS have had extensive experience that tells us what sorts of things are *likely* to work and not to work.

But a crucial part of this effort is that, from the very first, we have worked directly with teachers. In workshops we conducted in Pittsburgh, the teachers became familiar with our materials and began to do exercises on their own, and then slowly began to work with students while we looked over their shoulders, trying to make sense

"If we omit [the arts] from the curriculum, we are in effect shortchanging the mind."

of what the students were doing.

The first step, in other words, has been to find out whether the materials we developed were acceptable to teachers themselves, which is often not a trivial matter because some of these ideas are not very transparent. Also, the teachers often make useful suggestions and modifications. Once the teachers think the exercises are usable, they try them with students. Then, if they work, we find that the teachers are usually able to reach general agreement on how to analyze the results.

A good example is music. Because we believe it's important to work with teachers, we started with what music teachers were concerned with: performance. We came up with a set of measures to look at changes in student performance over time: how a clarinet player or an ensemble improves. I am pleased to say that in our first go-around with teachers there was actually fairly high agreement on how to score the results.

Similarly, in the literary area we are developing a complex set of instruments to monitor a variety of different aspects of student writing. We began with poems. We gave the kids a poetic frame with which to work, and then monitored their figurative language, their sense of voice, and so on—there are a lot of things to look at. Again we've been pleased with the initial responses. The teachers have not only caught on to the system but are excited by it.

These measures are intended for use by teachers, then, not by external evaluators?

Our goal is to come up with instruments that make sense to teachers in regular schools and that will provide useful feedback on how students are doing. That's been the goal of the Rockefeller project in general. We're not part of the current critical thinking initiative, but this effort is analogous to it.

Whether there will eventually be a set of National Assessment-type instruments that could be administered without intensive participation by local teachers is a question that hasn't been answered yet. Clearly, that is the sort of thing that ETS might want to do, and I'd be glad to see it happen if it seems feasible.

What are some of the factors to consider in assessing aesthetic growth?

We think one should monitor three kinds of things: production, perception, and reflection.

This idea isn't highly revolutionary, but it's more unusual than one might think. This past spring I spent three months in China. We have a great deal to learn from the Chinese about teaching students to produce great works in the traditional way. But they haven't confronted at all the issue of how people learn to *see* art nor of how they reflect on it.

Now, there's a growing group of American art educators who say our schools spend too much time on producing art and that we ought to teach the arts as we do other disciplines: take a verbal and analytic approach—emphasize historiography, aesthetics. I

From the very beginning, Gardner explains, teachers have contributed their ideas and judgments about assessing student work in the arts to Project Zero.

don't think that's necessarily a bad thing, but there's a great danger that it will slip into the traditional ways of knowing, verbal-analytic and logical-mathematical forms, which are covered pretty well in the rest of the curriculum.

Our approach differs from both the Chinese and the American in two ways. One is that, particularly with the younger kids, production continues to be central. That is, we think artistic learning should grow from kids *doing* things: not just imitating, but actually drawing, dancing, performing, singing on their own. And I mean not just songs they've been taught, but singing their own compositions. That's central to our approach—and it's very different from just learning traditions from the past or just talking about art.

The second aspect of our approach is that, as much as possible (and our exercises strive to do this), production should be linked intrinsically to perception and reflection. Perception means learning to see better, to hear better, to make finer discriminations, to see connections between things. Reflection means to be able to step back from both your production and

your perceptions, and say, "What am I doing? Why am I doing it? What am I learning? What am I trying to achieve? Am I being successful? How can I revise my performance in a desirable way?"

Now, that's quite different from the "discipline-based" approach, which always proceeds in terms of the standard disciplines. Our approach grows out of the child's actual experience with the arts. We don't talk about perception or reflection apart from artistic *activity*. As kids grow older, those aspects can be taught more intensely. I have no objection to teaching art history to 10- or 12-year-olds, but I do object to teaching it apart from actual artistic production.

An example we use describes a student at work on a triptych: portraying images of three faces in a tripartite work. After working on the project for several weeks, she was introduced to the way artists in the Middle Ages put together triptychs. That way the student was much more interested, because she herself had been trying to solve the same problem of producing three distinctive yet complementary forms.

Another example, which I used a lot in China, is theme and variations. You take something like "Happy Birthday" or "Twinkle, Twinkle," which everybody knows, and you make sure kids can sing it or play it on a kazoo. Then you have them do "Twinkle, Twinkle" in different ways: do it sad, do it happy, do it spring, do it winter, do it limping, do it in 3/4 time, and so on. Then you show them that, in fact, Mozart also wrote variations on "Twinkle, Twinkle, Little Star." Again, the children are interested because they've been confronting the same problem as Mozart.

That type of exercise would seem to be generalizable across disciplines.

Many of them are, but not all. Exercises in pitch or in color arrangement don't have direct analogies in other art forms. But at Project Zero we've been working simultaneously or in parallel with a number of different art forms. We try to get maximum applicability but, as you may know, my theory of multiple intelligences holds that no two forms of thinking are exactly comparable.

I'd like to ask about your theory. First, though, will you give one or two more examples of ways to assess growth in the arts?

A good example that begins with perception is the Mona Lisa exercise. We show some slides of fakes of the Mona Lisa along with the original, and we get the kids very interested in which is which. We show a slide and say, "What is this?" . . . "It's the Mona Lisa." . . . "Are you sure?" Some kids say one thing and some another. They talk about the differences they see and the reasons. After that kind of reflection, we get them experimenting on their own, trying to either copy a work like the Mona Lisa or copy things like signatures, so they begin to see what is involved in doing something so that it looks as if it was done by someone else. Now, that task begins with perception, passes through reflection, then eventually goes to production. And we go from a fun puzzle to the serious question of style.

"We think artistic learning should grow from kids doing things: not just imitating, but actually drawing, dancing, performing, singing on their own."

Another form of assessment involves the building of a portfolio. Over a period of time, students accumulate their various efforts, including drafts, notes, false starts, things they like and don't like. Their portfolio becomes a kind of data base that both teacher and student can look at to see what's been done and what's been learned. Some of the measures can be quite explicit: how many entries kids make in their notebooks, how detailed they are, things like that. But others can be more difficult to get exact reliability on; for example, how many different sources of information have been used in trying to improve a work, or when a work has deepened, rather than simply changed.

We think these kinds of data should be enlightening to students, even if the teacher never looks at them. But of course the teacher does look at them too.

I see a lot of implications in this project for teaching and for curriculum design.

And not just in the arts. Almost everybody realizes that the American schools have been disappointing in recent years. But I think most of the reactions to this concern will not be very productive in the long term. Getting higher scores on standardized tests is not the real need, and at best it responds to symptoms rather than to the underlying disease. What we need in America is for students to get more deeply interested in things, more involved in them, more engaged in wanting to know; to have projects they can get excited about and work on over longer periods of time; to be stimulated to find things out on their own. In a way, the arts are a good testing ground for such activities because many members of the educational establishment don't care about them so much, so teachers can afford to take more chances.

A little earlier, you mentioned your theory of multiple intelligences. How does this arts assessment project relate to it?

Well, nobody has to buy my theory to buy the project, and in fact it's only tangential. But it is related in the sense that program officers at the Rockefeller Foundation, our sponsors, felt that many young people are being cheated out of the opportunity to receive a good education—by college admissions criteria and so on—because, while they have many abilities and many achievements, they tend not to do well on standardized tests. There's a lot of agreement about that, even among the testing experts. Having a certain kind of intelligence we might call "test smarts" helps some people scoot through school very well, but everybody knows that it doesn't have nearly so much predictive value for what happens outside, or after, school.

So the Rockefeller Foundation became interested in the possibility that school has focused too much on a certain combination of intelligences—linguistic, logical, mathematical; but that life certainly involves more than that, so school should be concerned with more than that too. They wanted to see whether we could find ways to pick out the kids with skills in some of these other areas, so those kids would have a better chance to get into a good college and to achieve success in life, and would also acquire a better self-concept in the process.

For those who may not know your theory, would you summarize it briefly?

Evidence from a variety of sources, especially new information about development of the nervous system and organization of the brain, indicates that human beings have evolved over a long period of time to think in at least seven ways, which I call "intelligences." I mentioned two of them—mathematical and linguistic—but there's also musical, spatial, bodily-kinesthetic, interpersonal, and intrapersonal intelligence.

Everybody who's normal has the potential to develop each of these intelligences to a large extent, but we don't all have the same profile to begin with, and we certainly don't all end up with the same profile. Most important, strength in one intelligence does not have predictive value for strength in another intelligence. You can be very strong in music and not in spatial, or vice versa. Therefore, psychologists who claim that intelligence is a single entity—educators who think of students as either smart or dumb—are wrong. A person can be smart in one area and dumb in others.

Part of our effort is trying to find how best to define each of the areas and how best to assess aptitude and achievement in them. We're also interested in which forms of intelligence are important in the various arts. For example, linguistic intelligence plays a role in the study of science and history and geography, but it's of central importance in writing fiction or poetry.

As a psychologist, what made you decide to define intelligence this new way?

It was probably less as a psychologist than as a participant in American public school life that I felt intelligence had been appropriated to refer to a very narrow band of abilities. And as long as the word is saved for just those abilities, people have the license to call everybody who doesn't have those abilities "stupid." So I deliberately tried to use the word in a new way to make people realize that there were a lot of tacit assumptions that needed to be confronted.

> **"Getting higher scores on standardized tests is not the real need . . . what we need in America is for students to get more deeply interested in things, more involved in them, more engaged in wanting to know . . ."**

I would have no problem with calling intelligences "talents," as long as people also called language and logic "talents." But they don't; they say that's being smart. The fact that I've annoyed many people by using the word this way is a kind of perverse confirmation that people thought they owned the word and that it had to be used their way.

How is the theory being accepted?

Well, the closer people are to psychometrics, the more they don't like the theory at all—and they probably have good and bad reasons for that. It's a threat to a lot of people who have an intellectual and a financial stake in a certain way of looking at things. I'm pleased by the fact that people who I think are good scientists but who don't have a vested interest in a particular orientation often like the theory. Biologists think it's sensible. And even psychologists—those who aren't wedded to psychometrics—feel it's a useful point of view. Many educators find it appealing. It's not a theory with a capital T; it's a new way of thinking about things, a new way of organizing a lot of information.

A skeptic might say that it is just another way of describing what we've always known: that people differ in their abilities.

I think it's taking two forms of intelligence off their pedestal.

The skeptic might also say that, far from ignoring the other forms of intelligence, schools do a lot to foster them. They certainly pay attention to athletic talent, for example. They do teach music and art. They encourage kids in their social activities, and so forth.

I can't go along with that. Music and art are the first to go when there's a financial crunch. As kids grow older, they get less and less of it. It may be important in kindergarten, but it disappears by eighth grade, except for the kids who are professionally oriented. Probably the most important reason I disagree is that even though there's a lot of focus on the kids who are good performers—who play an instrument well, for example—teachers don't often engage them in musical thinking, in visual thinking. I can only say that these are new ideas to many of the art teachers I work with.

If your theory were more widely accepted, how would that affect school practices?

I think that it is beginning to be accepted. Education is gradually becoming more individual-centered. Surely we've passed the point where we want to teach every kid the same thing the same way. My theory gives educators a way of thinking about individual gifts and how to accommodate teaching to them, but also a way of teaching conventional subject matter in ways more accommodating to the different ways of knowing. A student's profile of intelligences ought to have some effect on the way he or she goes about learning history. Another implication is the realization that, while assessment is important, we need to be much broader in what we assess and much more flexible in how we assess it.□

Howard Gardner is Co-Director, Project Zero, Harvard University, Graduate School of Education, Longfellow Hall, Cambridge, MA 02138. **Ron Brandt** is ASCD's Executive Editor.

Educational Leadership 45 (March 1988): 38-45

RON BRANDT

On Students' Needs and Team Learning: A Conversation with William Glasser

The author of numerous books on counseling and discipline, William Glasser says our failure to use control theory in the classroom and teach it to students is "like asking people to play a game without teaching them the rules." In this interview, he also suggests that if we structure schools to satisfy basic human needs for belonging and for power—for instance, by providing for team learning—students will be less susceptible to destructive influences in their lives and will come to see school as a need-satisfying place. The result will be fewer discipline problems and more learning.

45

Do you think today's young people have more difficulty coping with life than children of earlier generations?

In many ways life is easier for kids today, because there are so many more resources available to them, even if they're poor. What makes it harder, however, is that there are also so many more opportunities to harm themselves with drugs, cars, and sexual activity, well before they're old enough to realize the risks of these pursuits.

Knowing that's the case, what can schools do to help?

Schools must help children understand that, good and bad, most of what they do with their lives is their choice. For example, they've been told that school is good for them, and most believe it when they're small; but when they get a little older a large number, more than half, begin to believe that what goes on in the classroom is not good for them. Rather than to understand that this is a choice, they blame school for the fact that they have stopped working. What they also don't realize is that they are driven by genetic needs that they are not able to satisfy in their classes, and further they don't even know what these needs are.

What are they?

We all have needs built into our genetic structures, and everything we do is our best attempt to satisfy them. For example, we all need to struggle to survive (most children do understand this), but we also have a need for love and belonging. For example, if we ask young children what's the best part of school, invariably—I must have asked 150 of them by now—they'll say, "My friends." We should explain to them that the reason they feel this way is that we all have a built-in need for friendship and caring concern.

Teachers should know this too. Schools, especially primary schools, do a good job of encouraging students to socialize while they work; but most schools, especially secondary schools, would function much better if they made an effort to increase the oppor-

tunities for students to feel that in class they can talk to and work with each other.

While most educators try to make their schools friendly places, they don't pay enough attention to the fact that needs do not turn off in the classroom. In most secondary classrooms, students are taught as if they were supposed to suspend this need, to put it in abeyance: sit still and pay attention to what's being taught and not to each other. But they can't suspend this basic need; they can't even put it in abeyance. Teachers therefore need to find ways in class to give students chances to associate with others in friendly ways and do this as a planned part of this learning.

What are students' other needs?

Another need, perhaps harder to satisfy than friendship, is to gain the continuing sense that "I have some power; I'm somebody; people pay attention to me." When I ask, as I very frequently do, students aged 11 to 15,

> **"When you ask . . . students aged 11 to 15, 'Where in school do you feel important?', they look at you as if to say, 'That's ridiculous! Of course you don't feel important in school.' "**

"Where in school do you feel important?", they look at me as if to say, "That's ridiculous! Who listens to us?" (I'm using the terms "important," "power," and "self-esteem" synonymously.) You can't have self-esteem, you don't feel important, unless you have some sort of power which means at a minimum somebody listens to you.

As I pursue this question, I keep pushing and pushing for some sort of anwer and, eventually, about half of them say they do feel important in school to some extent—but almost *never in classrooms*. It's always in extracurricular activities: athletics, drama, music. In the classroom, only a few of even the top students feel important.

If educators wanted to check this out, could they ask their own students that question?

Educators who've worked with students for years have never heard students answer questions related to their basic needs, and they should ask these questions. And we should keep in mind that teachers also often feel relatively powerless and lonely in school. Teaching traditionally as most do, their needs are hardly more satisfied than their students'.

Indeed.

Certainly. For example, there are three levels of satisfying the need for power. At the first level, the minimum level, we have to feel as if someone whom we respect listens to us. If we, teacher or pupil, don't honestly believe that when we talk someone listens, this need cannot be satisfied. And, in our frustration, we begin to do all kinds of things, many of them antisocial, to get someone to listen. That "effort" is the source of perhaps 95 percent of what we call discipline problems in school.

The next higher level is: somebody listens and says, "You're right." That's even harder to get. Students may get the first, but except for "right" answers, they almost never get the second; and we all need to be told once in a while that what we say counts.

The third level is very hard to get. We can do without it, but it's nice to have. Here, not only does somebody listen to us, but once in a while he or she says, "You know, your way is better than mine. I think we ought to do it your way." That's the pinnacle for satisfying this need and students, especially, rarely have this experience in class.

I believe that frustration of the need for power, even more than the need for belonging, is at the core of today's difficulties, not only in school, but everyplace else in our society where there are serious problems (e.g., in the workplace, in management, in marriages). People who aren't able to say, "I'm at least a little bit important" in some situation will not work hard to preserve or improve that situation.

Many students, however, maintain a good sense of being important that they've gained from home, so they are able to survive the lack of importance in the classroom. But we can't count on a majority of students coming from homes this supportive. In our varied culture, homes provide much less of this than in more homogeneous cultures like Japan, where home support is so strongly a part of the culture that it can support them to work hard in schools that pay even less attention to this need than we do.

You say students' needs for power and belonging are the main problem. What are their other needs?

The others are freedom and fun. They are important needs, too, but I don't think they are at the core of our problems. Students really don't expect to have much freedom in class or in school. They know that you can't have a thousand kids going in different directions; they accept the need for rules and regulations.

The final need is for fun, and it's very important, but if students have a sense of belonging and a sense of personal importance in class, the fun will take care of itself. Even without this, however, few schools are grim; lack of fun is not a major flaw.

How does what you're saying ap-ply to, for example, the teenage pregnancy problem?

The decision to be less than careful about sex and pregnancy is the result of both a lack of belonging and a lack of power. Many teenagers, especially females, feel powerless at home and at school. When a girl discovers that she can use her sexuality, which is one of her most powerful possessions, to get her boyfriend to do what she wants, she feels the satisfying power of increased control. That's the major reason that very young "women" become sexual. Young women who have a good sense of personal importance at home and in school tend not to get involved in premature sexuality.

Another factor is that we revere motherhood so much that most unwed school-age girls who get pregnant are often treated more with respect and love than disdain. Suddenly they're somebody, and this leads others to think, "To be somebody and to get love, maybe I ought to get pregnant too." Unfortunately, pregnancy (not caring for a child) satisfies the

> **"Schools have used the team concept in classrooms less than any other part of society. . . . you sit and work by yourself, keep quiet, don't share, don't relate to one another."**

need for belonging and the need for power but does so in a way that is almost always self-destructive for immature mothers.

There may be no easy answers for educators in this, but at least if they understand—

No, there *are* answers. Not easy, perhaps, but clear: regardless of their homes, girls who find school satisfying and do well will have little inclination to get pregnant. What's more, they'll also pay attention to what the school teaches about avoiding venereal diseases and AIDS. Unfortunately, disinterested students don't listen to what's going on in the classroom, so it does little good to teach them the facts about AIDS, drugs, or pregnancy.

In your book, *Control Theory in the Classroom*,[1] you advise using learning-teams.

Absolutely. If I suggest to educators that they should be running schools that meet students' needs, I have to suggest a practical way to do it. When I learned control theory—and certainly the basis of control theory is these needs we've been talking about—it became apparent to me that the way most of us satisfy these needs is by working in teams with people we respect and care for. A well-functioning family is a team. The extracurricular activities, all of which function superbly in almost all schools and lead students to feel important—the band, the orchestra, athletics, the school newspaper, the drama club—are all need-satisfying team activities.

I'm sure that working teams evolved because we have these needs. For example, in a good team, we satisfy our need for belonging because we care for each other. We satisfy our need for power because we can do so much more than by ourselves. In a team we have lots of chances to contribute our ideas, and people listen to us. And when we work well together, we learn more and it's fun.

Except for tradition, I don't know why schools use so little cooperative learning. It hasn't changed that much since I was in school: students still sit and work alone, and are continually told to keep quiet and keep their eyes on their work.

But it can and should be done differently. Good researchers like David and Roger Johnson, Robert Slavin, and Spencer Kagan have proven the effectiveness of cooperative learning or, as I call it, learning-teams. Here, the teacher, instead of trying to force all the students down a single learning pathway, becomes a facilitator who goes from team to team encouraging, helping, inquiring, and prodding. In this method of instruction, the teacher gets nose to nose with learning, and students are encouraged to branch out creatively and stray from the "common" pathway.

The increased interaction apparently helps students understand and remember.

Especially for those who have difficulty learning. To think things through to an intelligent conclusion, most of us have to bat ideas back and forth. Otherwise it's like going to a movie by yourself and then trying to have a lively discussion with yourself about what you saw. But if you go with a friend, you can probably come up with some really creative ideas. We are by nature interactive creatures who learn by inquiry and disagreement.

Another point is that much of what we do in schools is far too superficial. Teachers have a tendency to teach to the level of the average students, trying to keep them from falling behind, but average is too often superficial. Learning gets interesting only if it gets beneath the surface. When students work together in teams, the teacher can encourage them to go deeply into the assignment, and they almost always can and do.

It sounds easy.

I wish it were. It isn't, because a team lesson is not the same as an individual lesson; it has to be tailored to the team situation. It's like tennis, where doubles is only superficially like singles. In conventional classrooms, students can, and too often do, fill in the blanks or write out questions

"Control theory tells students what their needs are, that they have to make choices to satisfy these needs, and that they have the capacity to evaluate their choices and to make good choices."

at the end of the chapter; and few except the highly motivated students learn from these traditional activities. If, however, you give assignments like this to teams, they don't work at all. And when they don't work, because usually one student answers the question and the others copy, both teachers and the working students get disgusted and say learning-teams are no good.

So that's the tricky part.

Absolutely. It takes a lot of time and effort to work out an effective team assignment, and anything less doesn't work. But if you figure out some good assignments, they can be used year after year. For example, I've written about 18 team-learning assignments to teach students the control theory they need to know if they are to make the choice not to use addicting drugs, and it has taken me well over a year to do

this. It's not easy, but good team assignments are the keys to this educational approach.[2]

You're also saying, then, that control theory offers a practical approach to preventing drug abuse?

Control theory teaches students about their needs and that they have to make choices to satisfy these needs. It also teaches them that they have the ability to evaluate their choices and to make good choices. Anyone can say, "Don't use drugs"; but the point is, if you are unsatisfied as many students are and you don't use drugs, what else can you do to satisfy your needs? Control theory addresses this vital issue directly.

Would you say a little more about making choices?

Well, besides the needs themselves, control theory includes several other important concepts. Although your needs are very general, you can only satisfy them in very specific ways. You can't just go out in the world and eat; you have to find a restaurant or a grocery store. So each of us builds inside our head a kind of hypothetical world—I call it an *"all-you-want world."* Starting at birth and throughout our whole lives we store pictures in it, pictures of what we have found to be need-satisfying for us. In this world we put our mothers, our fathers, our loved ones, our prized possessions, these kinds of pictures.

Once this is understood, then control theory points out specifically where things go wrong in school. In any school you'll see some students working hard and some not working at all. Those who are working hard are getting their needs satisfied, and those who aren't are not. But we also know that those who are working hard have a picture of school inside their heads as a need-satisfying place. Hard-working students will keep it there, even if they run into a couple of bad classes, or a bad year or so, because it's firmly fixed in their minds that "my school is a satisfying place." Most students start with that idea, but in the early years it's not firmly fixed. If they don't actually

> **"Successful programs get kids to put pictures of themselves liking to read or liking history or math into their heads as need-satisfying activities. When they do, the kids expend effort to learn, and the teacher's efforts begin to pay off."**

experience school as satisfying, around 7th or 8th grade, they take this vital picture out of their heads. And when they take this picture out or when they take a subject like math or reading out of their heads, they won't work at it any more. We will only actively pursue what's in our "all-you-want world."

We have many teachers struggling with kids with "learning disabilities," "dyslexia," and so on. Too many are convinced that there's something wrong with these kids' brains; that the wiring is so defective they cannot learn. Many reading programs, however, are successful, but none change the wiring of the students' brains. Successful programs work mostly because they persuade kids to put pictures of themselves liking to read or liking history or math into their "all-we-want worlds," as need-satisfying activities. When they do, the kids expend effort to learn, and the teacher's hard work begins to pay off.

In other words, if students have some sort of difficulty reading, which many kids have, the difficulty is usually severely compounded by the fact that they *stop wanting to read*. All the remedial programs that work make use of involved, caring people who use interesting, relevant materials, materials designed to get kids to say, "Gee, maybe this program is good for me; maybe I'd better try again."

Most of the money spent on testing these children, for specific perceptual or neurological difficulties, is wasted. We are looking for things that don't exist, and, even if they did, we could do nothing to correct them.

I've understood that in fact these kids are different in certain ways.

Not neurologically. The difference is in how they choose to try to satisfy their needs. Psychotic people seem much different from most of us. But if you can figure out how to help them satisfy their needs, they become much like us. Emphasizing behavioral or even possible neurological differences is not the way to help kids learn. That's a bankrupt carryover from the field of medicine, where it's always assumed

that there's something wrong with the structure, perhaps a virus or genetic defect. It's analogous to a computer. If you have a friend who really knows computers, ask him or her, "When a computer fails, how often is it software, and how often is it hardware?" The answer you'll get is, "999 times out of a thousand it's the software."

Well, it's the same with learning disabilities. It's software when the kid says, "I don't think I want to learn." Hardware is the rare instance when a student actually has a wiring defect in the brain. I'm not saying there aren't some kids with brain defects; of course there are. But with most of them the defect is, "I don't really see this work as need-satisfying, and I won't try. But if they force me, I'll say and do all kinds of odd things so they'll give me attention for being 'different' instead of for not trying."

That explanation is consistent with your view of mental illness, which you describe as a choice, right?

Right. There are some mentally ill people, I'll grant that: people with syphilis, tumors, or strokes destroying their brains are mentally ill. But most

> **"Anyone can say, 'Don't use drugs'; but . . . if you don't use drugs, what do you do to satisfy your needs? Control theory addresses this vital issue directly."**

> **"I'm saying that unless we pay attention to what students need, we will continue to have trouble teaching the basics successfully."**

of the people we call mentally ill are choosing behaviors that they believe are most satisfying for them at the time, even though to us they're self-destructive. Alcoholics, for example, choose to destroy themselves with drink. If there were something inherently defective in alcoholics' brains or genetic structures, none of them would recover. But *millions* go to AA and learn to make better choices, and most AAs recover. So, although they may be genetically different, it's obviously not a genetic defect; it's a defective way of satisfying their needs.

And you also say that sometimes people choose to be ill.

Oh, yes. Almost all of our major diseases have a large element of choice in them. Not all—certainly not most cancers. But most heart disease and rheumatoid illnesses are very much related to how people choose to live their lives. Smoking, drinking, poor diets are choices that lead to illness.

Is control theory being used outside of schools?

I teach it in every application of what we would call the helping professions. It's basic to drug and alcohol counseling, and used widely in working with those who have all kinds of psychological problems. I believe it's the best explanation of how all living organisms function both biologically and psychologically.

And you're saying not only that educators should apply control theory, but that we should *teach* it so that it's common knowledge?

Yes. To me, not teaching how we function is like asking people to play a game without teaching them the rules.

Because if kids understand control theory, they'll understand their own motivations better?

Yes. They'll say, rather than, "I feel lousy today," which a lot of us do, "Okay, what need is involved, and how can I satisfy that need? I can sit around and 'depress' or I can do something about it." Little kids, 7- and 8-year-olds, can learn this.

Among some of those having considerable influence on education these days, what you're saying is probably anathema. They say schools must teach fundamental knowledge like geography and history and mathematics, and not get sidetracked into "pop psychology."

I don't want to imply that I'm against basic educational skills. I'm just saying that unless we pay attention to what students need, we will continue to have trouble teaching the basics successfully. Trying to force students to learn has never worked; control theory teaches that we can't force people to do what they don't want to do.

How can educators learn how to use control theory?

The best way is to begin applying it in your own life.

You ask yourself, "All these con-

> "... think back to a time in your life when you really had a hard time ... when you recovered, it wasn't because the world had suddenly become a wonderful place; it was because you made a better choice."

cerns and problems I have. What choices am I making about them?"

That's right. When you sit in the corner "depressing," as I say, that's a choice. And you have the option to make a better choice. If you don't believe me, all you have to do is think back to a time in your life when you really had a hard time, and you'll find that when you "recovered" it wasn't because the world had suddenly become a better place; it was because you made a better choice. You started dealing with it more effectively, instead of saying, "I'm sick; I can't make it."

So control theory is useful both in preventing some problems and in resolving others?

Yes, it can be both. There's no way to live our lives without problems. People don't always do what we want. But as much as we try to control other people, the only person we can control is ourselves.

And yet, as you've said, we all have a need for power. Is there a relationship? If schools make teachers feel more powerful, does it carry over to students?

Let's be clear about what I mean by power. Most people think having power is being the boss, telling others what to do. But few people in our society can be intimidated for very long by someone telling them what to do, especially if the person doesn't pay them. I say we have to understand that management practices built on the old idea of power—that the top person tells the next one and so on down the

> **"... management practices built on the old idea of power—that the top person tells the next one and so on down the line—are totally inadequate, especially in school where students aren't being paid for their work."**

line—are totally inadequate, especially in school, where students aren't being paid for their work.

The way I understand power should be used is that if you're the head of an organization—the principal of a school, or the teacher of a class—there are at least two ways you can use your power that are need-satisfying both for you and for those you're trying to direct. One way is to provide them with material support: the best possible tools, the best possible workplace. The second is to use your power to facilitate what they do. The more powerful you're perceived to be, the more you should listen to what other people say; and in this way your power helps them get some power too. It's really the opposite of the conventional notion of power as exemplified by "Sit down and shut up." The ultimate use of power should be to empower others. That's what our Constitution is all about.□

1. William Glasser, *Control Theory in the Classroom* (New York: Harper & Row, 1986).
2. *Choice*, the Control Theory Approach to Preventing Drug Abuse. A program distributed through the Educator Training Center, Long Beach, CA 90813.

William Glasser is President of the Institute for Reality Therapy, 7301 Medical Center Dr., Suite 202, Canoga Park, CA 91307. **Ron Brandt** is ASCD's Executive Editor.

Educational Leadership 42 (Feb. 1985): 61-66

On Teaching and Supervising: A Conversation with Madeline Hunter

RON BRANDT

M adeline, you have probably had more influence on U.S. teachers in the last ten years than any other person. What accounts for that?

Well, teachers have had a lot of intuitive knowledge, but it's never been based on theory. What I have tried to do is take what research tells us about teaching and translate it into something teachers can use tomorrow morning as they make educational decisions.

Briefly, what do you teach teachers?

That teaching is a constant stream of decisions and that good decisions increase the probability of learning. We now know cause-effect relationships between teaching and learning. Teachers can't control everything, but they can certainly influence it. It's true that you can lead a horse to water but you can't make him drink. You can, however, salt his oats. You can run him hard. You can keep him away from water. So we're looking at every way a teacher can influence a student's motivation to learn, the rate and degree of that student's learning, the retention of what's been learned, and the appropriate transfer of that learning into new situations.

Madeline Hunter

One would think that most teachers would know these things already. Why don't they?

One reason is that they're taught in a way that doesn't transfer. For example, there isn't a teacher in the world who hasn't studied about Pavlov. And yet when a teacher asked me to work with a child who was always making smart remarks, I found that the minute the kid made a remark, the teacher said, "Now what did you mean by that comment?" When I asked the teacher what the boy wanted with his smart remark, she said, "Attention." I asked, "What did you give him?" When she looked surprised, I said, "Have you ever heard of Pavlov?" She said, "What does a slobbering dog have to do with it?" Well, there was no transfer. In his

memory lab, Wundt showed more than 50 years ago that the beginning and end of any sequence are the easiest to learn. And yet teachers use the prime time at the beginning of a class period to take roll, to make assanine announcements, to collect lunch money—because they have to get the job done. We now know how to have them get some learning done along with the job. The knowledge has been around for years, but it was in terms of pigeons and rats, or in terms of the psychological laboratory, so the teacher saw no similarity between it and the classroom.

Well, you've certainly translated it into practice, but why don't others do the same?

I think it's very difficult for researchers in the university to know how their research can be applied in practice. When my husband was trying to produce a plane that would protect the pilot from radiation, he worked with one of the leading radiation theorists at Cal. Tech. My husband would come home pulling his hair out and saying, "That guy is trying to design a Sherman tank for me to put on the nose of an airplane." I said, "Has he ever seen a fighter jet?" My husband said, "I

Ron Brandt is Executive Editor, Association for Supervision and Curriculum Development, Alexandria, Virginia.

don't know. Maybe not." So he took the scientist the next day, put him in a fighter jet, and said, "Now, here's the guy you have to protect—and he has to see where he's going." "Oh," said the fellow.

You can't expect researchers to translate the knowledge they produce because they don't know what the plane looks like—and most of them aren't really interested in that. I'm very fortunate to have been thoroughly steeped in psychology but also in having spent most of my life in the trenches of public schools. So I'm kind of bilingual in theory and practice.

Isn't the research you draw upon quite behavioral in its orientation?

Anybody who says it's behavioral does not understand our model. It's been called behavioral simply because we include attention to reinforcement. If a student is able to generate an elegant hypothesis, we let him know he's valued and he's competent. People look at that, and say, "It's all reinforcement." Well, it's not. For example, we do a lot of work on teaching for transfer, which has nothing to do with reinforcement theory. The one idea we push the most is having students attach meaning to what they're learning, which comes from Merle Wittrock's generative theory of cognition.

There's a lot of interest these days in teaching for thinking. How does that fit in your model?

It fits very well because our model maintains that if students can't take the learning they have and translate it to a new situation, it's worthless. If all you're going to teach are names and dates and facts, you're wasting your time and the students' time. Learning is like money in the bank; it's great to

have it there but it's only useful when you pull it out and use it.

So it's very important to teach for higher-order thinking, but not without building a foundation. I see teachers asking children to compare the governments of Russia and the U.S. when the students don't know anything about either of them.

How do you feel about the ideas of people like Reuven Feuerstein and Robert Sternberg, who believe that the key is to teach the necessary intellectual skills directly?

I agree with them. We factor-analyze what a student needs to do, just as we would factor-analyze what a painter needs to do to paint a house well. That doesn't mean that thinking isn't a lot more complex than painting, but there are similarities: you have to prepare it, you have to sand it, and so on. I'm worried, though, that we may begin teaching these skills in isolation the way we now teach some other skills. We will have a period of thinking skills and then have social studies, with no transfer. In a lot of schools, kids spit and sputter their way through phonic skills and then when they come to a reading task, they don't use the skill.

Whenever you isolate a process and teach the process separately, there's a danger that students will not actually use it. We have to help them make the application. For example, if we teach children about decision making, we need to translate it: "How are we going to decide who's going to be captain? How are we going to decide what kind of cooking to have at the party? How do you decide whether to do your work in your free time or take it home for homework?" Decision making must become a part of the student's real life.

> **"This model should provide the launching pad from which creativity can soar."**

Are there any teaching circumstances for which your model isn't appropriate?

Not at all. I'm always amused when somebody says, "Well, that's fine for drill, but not good for creative learning, or It's all right for large groups, but not for small groups."

I literally teach all over the world. Most recently I was teaching a group of children in China. They happened to speak English; otherwise I couldn't have done it. The Chinese wanted to see me work with a nongraded group, because they couldn't feature children of different ages learning together. I took a group of five- through 14-year olds who had just visited a commune, and I had them categorize what they had seen.

One of the five-year-olds—we would label him a hyperkinetic student—responded to exactly the same techniques that work with children here in the U.S. For example, we categorized first by what humans had made—baby buggies and so on—versus what nature had made, like the rice and the rape seeds. Then we categorized by "Which place would you like to work?" That five-year-old could shift categories like crazy, while one of the "brightest" kids in the school, who could memorize and regurgitate perfectly, found it almost impossible to shift categories. But exactly the same techniques worked with Chinese children as had worked about two weeks before with children in Milan, Italy, and had worked about three weeks before with children in Hong Kong.

There really is an invariance to human learning, as there is invariance to human anatomy and physiology. There are differences, but they're not nearly as great as the similarities.

From your travels to other nations, what can you say about how U.S. education compares with education in other countries?

All countries have fabulous schools and poor schools, just as we have. I do not see all the greatness that is reported in Japan and Russia. I've been in Japanese schools and I've been in Russian schools, and we can learn from them—but if they're so excellent, why are they sending for me? Right now, if I had to pick a country for my own child's education, and I couldn't pick the school, I would choose the U.S.

You're aware, I know, of the findings by John Goodlad and his colleagues[1] that most teachers use a very small number of strategies— mostly talking to their classes or having them do worksheets. If more teachers used your model, would that change?

Very definitely. However, let's not forget that John Goodlad talks a lot to his classes—but he talks very well, so his students learn a lot.

One of our problems is that teachers have been told to have discussion groups but they don't know how. They have been told to have more individual projects. But generalizations like that are not enough; teachers have to learn how to do these things. For example, we have task-analyzed independent learning, identifying step-by-step how you move children from being dependent to becoming more independent. Then we made a series of films starting on day one and moving through the stages until by the middle of the year the students were conducting their own reading groups. But that's a sequence of learning skills, not admonition.

How do teachers learn to use your model?

They go through three stages. First they learn the propositions, such as that the beginning and end of any sequence are the most powerful times for learning. Even though they learned that in ed. psych, they don't understand how it applies to wasting time by taking attendance, collecting lunch money, or cleaning up. Now those things have to be done, but we teach teachers how to use the time productively: "While you're putting away your equipment, be ready to give me a summary statement of what you've learned from this experiment," or "While you're putting your books back in your desk, be ready to say what you think is the single most important facet of Columbus' personality."

When we have taught a proposition like "The beginning and end of a series is your prime time," then we translate it into procedures: how do you do it? First I simulate it while I just talk about it, then we role play an actual teaching episode. By the way, it has to be unfamiliar content. You can't teach people something they already know; that would be violating a basic principle.

Then they have to try it out with students in their own classrooms— with coaching, so somebody helps them see what they're doing well, and where the booby-traps are and how to get out of them. It's a three-stage process of knowledge, procedure, and then conditional decision making.

What do you mean by coaching?

We teach that when you're watching a teacher make what is called a "script tape." It's really a sort of shorthand log of the teacher-pupil interaction. You

"**My purpose is to tell teachers what to *consider* before deciding what to *do* and, as a result, to base their decisions on sound theory rather than on folklore and fantasy.**"

"The model is equally effective in elementary, secondary, and university teaching. In fact, it applies to every human interaction that is conducted for the purpose of learning."

capture what the teacher does just as you would on videotape or audiotape, but you do it in writing. It's a kind of recording that you can play back to the teacher so the teacher knows in temporal order everything that happened in that lesson. That script tape is the basis for your diagnosis of the teaching—just as you'd look at a child's math paper and say, "He knows this and he's ready to learn that." We give the teacher feedback as to what the teacher did really well and why it worked, and we find in many cases that we bring intuitive knowledge to a conscious level.

As I said in your ASCD yearbook,[2] intuition is sterile. Some people thought I meant it was useless, but I meant it could not be reborn in somebody else. A sterile animal—a donkey, for example—may be a very useful animal, but it can't recreate itself. Teachers who happen to create a good learning activity solely by intuition cannot recreate that in a new situation as predictably as they could if they had conscious knowledge, such as that the beginning of a sequence is the most powerful. So we move from intuitive knowledge to articulated and deliberate knowledge. Now, as I said in the article, there's quite enough room for using intuition beyond what we know consciously.

So when we give a teacher coaching and feedback, we identify those things the teacher did well in terms of teacher-student behavior. An example might be, "Madeline, when you went over and stood by the boy who was fooling with the rubber band and he put it away, do you know what caused that? Researchers have found that the closer you are to the authority figure, the more likely you are to behave as expected. So you probably caused the boy to put away his rubber band, and with no loss of dignity."

Then, if there were things the teacher did that caused difficulty, we bring them to the teacher's attention: "You know why the student gave you the wrong answer for that? You had just asked a different question and he was thinking about that. Then you changed the question, but he didn't change with you." The teacher will say, "Oh, is that the reason?"

It sounds like what you're calling coaching is not much different from what some people call supervision.

To me, coaching and supervision are the same. To me, a coach is a person who has the skills to enable another person to perform better. That's very different from practice. Often people recommend that teachers watch each other and give feedback. Now, that's fine if every teacher is very knowledgeable, but coaching takes special knowledge. For example, a football coach will show a player how to throw the ball, how to shift his weight. He might say, "You're not getting enough of your shoulder in that throw; there's too much of your arm and not enough of your shoulder." Then he'll say to that player, "You and Bill go out and practice that." A lot of what people are calling coaching is really practicing: just working together.

Many principals are afraid to coach teachers because they think that to help a teacher they ought to be able to teach better than the teacher. They really don't have to. In fact, it's possible to coach a person in teaching when you don't even know the content. In China, I helped the teachers improve their teaching of Chinese even though I don't know Chinese. I worked with the teachers of German and with our geophysicists at UCLA, and even though I didn't know the content, I could help them teach it better.

Some people contend that a person in a position of authority over a teacher can't really function as a coach. Do you find that true?

No, I think that's a ridiculous notion. I have never found that people resent being evaluated by an authority figure who knows what he or she is doing.

You said earlier that I have influenced teachers. I would like to think I have influenced principals even more, because we know the power of the principal to make a school either more excellent or more mediocre. In fact, I'm encouraging school districts to make principals their first priority.

There seems to be a trend in many school systems to make the principal the primary instructional leader, although in some places there are supervisors outside the school who are considered to have more expertise in instruction than the principal.

Excellence in teaching stands on two feet. One is curriculum, and the other is pedagogy or skills of teaching. You cannot be an expert in every phase of curriculum. We need someone who knows enough about social studies, for instance, to help me know the key concepts that ought to be taught about the Revolutionary War. We need someone who knows what verb form ought to be introduced first, and so on. So we need central office curriculum consultants. But no outside supervisor can be in the school often enough to really help a teacher on a day-to-day coaching basis. The only person who can do that is the principal or the building-level resource teacher. I am all for having resource teachers as an aid to the principal, because the principal does

have other responsibilities—but not in place of the principal. The person who does the evaluation ought to have watched the growth pattern of that teacher throughout the year.

Some people say that principals in large schools simply don't have the time to be supervisors.

I disagree with that. I have been a principal most of my life, including assignments in the ghettos and in the richest and most demanding areas of Los Angeles, and I have never ever had a principalship where I didn't have some time to work with teachers on increasing effectiveness. If you do that, all the other problems go down. Your discipline problems go down, your parent problems go down, your lunch room problems go down, your bus problems go down. The only thing you can't reduce with excellent supervision is the amount of paper coming from the central office. That goes on and on.

Of course, no principal has the time to do all the supervision he or she would like. I would be happy to spend 100 percent of my time in classrooms, but you can't do that when you're running a school. It's a question of both quantity and quality. I know many a principal who says, "I make it a point to walk in and out of every classroom every day." And that principal does nothing but walk in and out of every classroom. I know other principals who may take 15 minutes to visit three classrooms and each of those teachers later gets useful feedback.

If it's not being a threat or lack of time that prevents principals from being good supervisors, what is it?

They don't know how. They certainly didn't learn it in graduate school. Our training programs in teaching and administration are way behind what

we know. It's only recently at UCLA that we've added instructional analysis to our supervision course even though we've been doing it in our lab school for 20 years.

There are some who feel that we're not going to have superior teaching until we change the circumstances under which teachers work: the number of students they have to work with, the countless responsibilities they have. Do you agree that it's almost impossible for a teacher to do an effective job under the circumstances most teachers face?

No, I don't. I think it's possible to do a very effective job under the circumstances, but I don't think it's fair to ask teachers to do it. I've seen teachers do a fantastic job under horrendous circumstances, but it has taken too much toll on them.

I have two children, one in education and one in the film business. They're both fine people, both excellent in their field, they both work hard, and yet one's income—the one in the entertainment business, of course—is far higher than the other. I think it's critically important that we pay teachers a salary more like those of other professionals.

On the other hand, I don't think that just being a teacher should automatically entitle a person to a good salary, any more than just being a doctor or an attorney does. They have to perform well. I have very strong feelings that merit pay is desirable provided you're paying for skill in doing a more difficult job. If there were two teachers, each with 30 of the same kind of children, I would find it unfair to pay them different salaries simply because one was considered to be doing a better job than the other. Excellent surgeons or excellent attorneys make a lot more money, but they work on more difficult cases.

Many educators say that any form of merit pay is impractical because it is so difficult to determine which teachers are best.

But it's very easy to know which students are more difficult to teach. We pay extra for teachers with special credentials to teach the blind—and we don't give them nearly as many students. We're saying the job is more difficult. Surgeons who do heart transplants don't do surgery as often as surgeons who remove appendixes—and they earn more money.

Of course, all parents want a superior teacher for their children whether their child has a special problem or not.

Every child should have a well qualified teacher. I think we have the knowledge to say, "This teacher is a fine teacher; this one leaves something to be desired; this teacher is outstanding." Now it would be nice if all teachers were outstanding, just as it would be nice if all surgeons were outstanding, but if you're to have a sliver taken out of your finger, you won't be nearly as concerned as if you're going to have a cancer removed—because it doesn't take the same kind of skill.

I'm for merit pay. I know we're going to have some terrible errors committed in deciding which teachers should be paid more. On the other hand, I can't think of a more terrible error than to pay a teacher who is doing nothing exactly the same amount of money as a teacher who is teaching his or her heart out.

So much of this is dependent on school principals, as we said. Can you envision a system that would assure standards of professional excellence?

Very much so. For example, in California we now have Senate Law 813, which mandates that every principal must be certified in clinical supervision by 1985. Now, one of the many problems with that law is that it doesn't state what certification means. A group of us have recommended that

to be certified a supervisor would view a videotape of a teacher teaching. After a half hour spent reviewing the script tape he or she had made, the supervisor would confer with the teacher on the lesson. That kind of test would clearly show whether the supervisor was competent to analyze instruction and to confer with the teacher in an enabling rather than in a threatening or disabling way.

Do you think that procedure actually will be used?

We're hoping for it. It's already being used in several school districts.

How do you feel about the idea of a career ladder for teachers, with various levels such as master teacher?

I strongly endorse it. For example, I think a brand new teacher coming into the profession ought to have the coaching and guidance of a master teacher. At UCLA we have seen the difference between putting our student teachers with a master teacher—such as one of our laboratory school teachers—versus putting them with John Doe, who may or may not be expert. In fact we spent a lot of time training our supervising teachers and we turned out student teachers second to none in the world. Now, you can't make a fine teacher in one year, so I strongly urge that beginning teachers have a period of internship—and you don't drop them after that. Even the very finest teachers can still learn. The greatest reinforcer in the world for me is when a teacher comes up and says, "You know, since I've learned this, I'm as excited about teaching as I was at the beginning."

Speaking of growing, you made a career change of your own recently.

I had been trying for ten years to talk myself into leaving the UCLA Lab School, but it is such a fantastic place, it was hard to leave. Before being at the Lab School, the longest I was ever in one assignment was three years, and that only happened once—when I built a training and demonstration school in the inner city of Los Angeles,

and I asked to stay a year and just enjoy it. I had always been a "hopper around." So after 20 years at the Lab School I thought, "you know, Madeline, you can run this school with one hand tied behind you. Practice what you preach." I had a lot of ideas I wanted to try out, I had some writing I wanted to do, and I had been traveling more and more. So I decided that I would just be a professor at UCLA. As a result of that we're making some changes. We're developing a new doctoral program focusing on the analysis of instruction, staff development, and so on.

At this stage in a highly successful and influential career, what about your work is most satisfying to you?

The ability to see that you can make a difference in a student's learning. Just as a doctor has the ability to eliminate a lot of suffering and despair, a teacher can feel fulfilled by seeing students learn and by convincing them that they *can* learn. And I help teachers learn to do that, which is very satisfying to me.

What is most distressing?

The fact that there are only 24 hours in a day. I happen to need a lot of sleep. In my next incarnation I'm going to need only three hours of sleep a night. I just cannot find time for all the things I enjoy doing.

You seem very excited about the future for education.

I think we're in a renaissance. We have the same opportunity we had 25 years ago when Sputnik went up. The only difference is that then we didn't know what we were doing. Now we do—not everything, but a powerful lot!☐

[1]John Goodlad, What Some Schools and Classrooms Teach." *Educational Leadership* 40 (April 1982): 8–19.
[2]Madeline Hunter, "Knowing, Teaching, and Supervising," in *Using What We Know About Teaching* (1984 Yearbook), ed. Philip L. Hosford (Alexandria, Va.: Association for Supervision and Curriculum Development), pp. 169–192.

Educational Leadership 45 (Nov. 1987): 14-19

RON BRANDT

On Cooperation in Schools: A Conversation with David and Roger Johnson

David and Roger Johnson, articulate proponents of cooperative learning and authors of ASCD's popular *Circles of Learning,* believe that developing cooperative structures at all levels will contribute to overall effectiveness in a district.

Roger Johnson

David Johnson

For several years the two of you have promoted cooperative learning among students. Now there seems to be a trend toward more cooperation at the professional level.

David: Yes, we're seeing not only more cooperative learning in classrooms, but collegial support groups of teachers and administrators at the building, and sometimes the district, level. Cooperation needs to start at the classroom level because that determines the organizational climate and atmosphere in the district. If teachers spend five to seven hours a day advocating a competitive, individualistic approach—telling students, "Do your own work. Don't talk to your neighbor, don't share, don't help, don't care about each other; just try to be better," those are the values the teachers are going to have in their relationships with colleagues and their administrators.

On the other hand, if teachers spend five to seven hours a day saying, "Help each other. Share, work together, discuss the material, explain," and make it clear that "you're responsible not only for your own learning but for the learning of your peers"—if they promote cooperation among students—they will look at their colleagues as potential cooperators.

How widespread is cooperative learning at the classroom level?

Roger: In certain areas it's getting very popular: on the East and West coasts—in California especially—and in parts of the Midwest. It's taking hold primarily in suburban upper-middle-class advanced districts, where parents want their children to do well in college.

So parents support it?

Roger: Yes, especially upper-middle-class parents. For example, when I talked to a PTA in a suburban district in the New York area a couple of years ago, a father stood up and said, "I know exactly what you're talking about: it's management training, the same thing we're getting at the First Bank. You mean my kid learns math and gets management training at the same time?" The parents in that district see cooperative learning as a bonus because their children are getting the training in leadership, group decision making, and conflict management they'll need to be successful in later life.

But is there evidence that cooperative learning in fact pays off?

David: Yes. If there's any one educational technique that has firm empirical support, it's cooperative learning. The research in this area is the oldest research tradition in American social psychology. The first study was done in 1897; we've had 90 years of research, hundreds of studies. There is probably more evidence validating the use of cooperative learning than there is for any other aspect of education—more than for lecturing, age grouping, starting reading at age six, departmentalization, or the 50-minute period. And the research applies as much to teachers as it does to students.

There's research on that as well?

David: Yes, in fact most of the work done up to 1970 was on adult cooperation; it was only in the '70s that much research was done in elementary and secondary schools. But from both types of studies it's clear that cooperation increases productivity. At the adult level, cooperation among adult teachers increases teaching effectiveness, while at the classroom level, cooperation increases each individual student's achievement.

"What you want for every child—but especially for those with a lot of ability—is a cheering section urging that student to work to maximal capacity."

There are two possible bases for making those kinds of statements. One is to infer that findings of research done in other settings apply to schools. Madeline Hunter has done that very well with the psychological research on learning. Another way is to apply the research in the new situation and test whether it actually produces the intended effects. Which approach are you citing?

David: Both. We believe the first requirement for a good school practice is a solid theory. The theory for cooperation was developed by Morton Deutsch in the late 1940s. Second, you need research to validate the theory, to determine the conditions under which it's valid, and so on. Third, you have to operationalize it so it can be used in practice. That's basically an engineering issue; if the theory is valid, it's a matter of varying and modifying the system until it works in the classroom and school the way the theory says it should.

There's been a lot of theoretical research establishing that cooperative learning *should* work. I suppose that's the Madeline Hunter approach, and actually it's our approach too. We say, "Here's a conceptual system; now look at the characteristics of your situation, of your group of students, and design a system that works in your classroom with your students." But other researchers—such as Spencer Kagan at Riverside, California; Schlomo Sharan in Israel; David Devries and Robert Slavin at Johns Hopkins—have developed detailed curriculum approaches and have tested and validated them.

One reason I would expect cooperative learning to be effective is its use of positive peer pressure. In conventional school organization, peer pressure seems to restrict students' learning.

Roger: Yes. What you want for every child—but especially for those with a lot of ability—is a cheering section urging that student to work to maximal capacity. You can have high, medium, and low kids in the same group with the low kid cheering the high one on and saying, "Rene, we need you to top out the test and get an absolutely perfect score, so don't watch TV tonight, study!" And you can get the high kid saying to the low kid, "Look, if you get six right we're okay. Last week you only had three, but you've really got to get up to six. I'm behind you all the way." The cooperative system encourages everybody to work to top capacity.

David: And the same is true at the building level with teachers. What you want is teachers cheering each other on so that if a teacher has a particular strength or plans a new unit or comes in with new materials, the other teachers say, "That's terrific."

So there's evidence that cooperative learning is effective—but as we all know, that doesn't necessarily mean that schools will use it. For teachers to use it, research evidence probably is not enough. It has to pay off for them with kids in a way they consider beneficial.

Roger: When teachers use cooperative learning they get a whole variety of outcomes. Achievement goes up—for high, medium, and low students—but they also get higher-level processing, deeper-level understanding, critical thinking, and long-term retention. When students get engaged in discussing material and explaining it to each other, their brains respond differently than if they were only reading and listening.

But another plus is a sense of interdependence. Students learn to care about and get committed to each other's success as well as their own. In a competitive classroom, students really have a stake in other students' failure. The worse other students do, the easier it is to get an A. In an individualistic classroom, students have no stake in other students whatsoever. Each student works independently on his or her own against set criteria. What happens to others is irrelevant. Within a cooperative group students have a vested interest in making sure that other people do well. They start to celebrate when other people learn. Anything they can do to help their groupmates learn the material better, retain it longer, get a better grade on the test, benefits them too. That produces committed relationships in which students really care about each other and provide assistance and help when needed. It promotes more positive peer relationships, better social skills, more social support, and, partly for that reason, higher self-esteem. Students like the class better, they like school better, they're more interested in the subject.

You mentioned social support. Why is that so important?

Roger: In today's schools we're expecting more and more of students and staff. When there's an increase in pressure, there should be an increase in social support at the same time. When students are expected to learn more complex material faster and more thoroughly, they need more social support. When teachers are told to work harder or do a better job, they should have lots of social support.

> "and . . . what you want is teachers cheering each other on so that if a teacher has a particular strength or plans a new unit or comes in with new materials, the other teachers say, 'That's terrific.' "

David: As a psychotherapist I may talk with someone who says, "One of my parents just died, I have a child in the hospital in critical condition, my spouse just left with all the money, and I'm destitute"; but if that person has a set of caring, committed friends that he or she can confide in and talk to, the person may be coping better than an isolated, alienated person who has only—say, lost his job. The point is that the ability to cope is determined not by the amount of stress a person is under, but by the balance between the stress and the support. And much of that support has to come from peers. In the classroom that means other students. In the school it means there must be strong, caring, supportive relationships among teachers. There's no alternative.

In ASCD our emphasis has long been on supervision. We assume that the principal or some other official person is responsible—

David: Yes, but the supervisor's job is not to *be* the support system but to *manage* the support system. A supervisor can't provide all the support and caring that a teacher needs on a day-to-day, minute-by-minute basis. A principal can't be in every teacher's classroom two or three times a day providing help. A colleague can.

I'm sure it's true that a supervisor can't do it all, but now there are moves to create middle-level roles for teachers: mentor teachers and so on. Even leaders of teacher organizations are in favor of having "lead teachers."

David: From the research in social psychology I have to say that such differentiation is a mistake. It's based on a parental model that, to be meaningful, social support and assistance have to come from your superior. Good, constructive, helpful, committed support can come from peers and subordinates as well as from superiors. And in many ways it's better coming from peers than from anyone else.

That may be true, but you also know how important it is in this society to make teaching a more prestigious and rewarding profession, and these programs offer promise of doing that.

David: I can only advise that if a district decides to have master teachers, one of the main criteria for their selection should be the ability to establish collegial relationships with other teachers. I believe that creating hierarchies among teachers can create divisiveness. What most principals want is a cooperative staff that pulls together.

Let's get back to the classroom level. What does it take to make cooperative learning work?

Roger: Five basic elements. The first is what we call "positive interdependence." The students really have to believe they're in it together, sink or swim. They have to care about each other's learning.

Second is a lot of verbal, face-to-face interaction. Students have to explain, argue, elaborate, and tie in the material they learn today with what they had last week.

The third element is individual accountability. It must be clear that every member of the group has to learn, that there's no hitchhiking. No one can sit on the outside and let others do the work; everyone has to be in there pulling his or her own weight.

The fourth element is social skills. Students need to be taught appropriate leadership, communication, trust building, and conflict resolution skills so they can operate effectively. To say it slightly differently, if students have not developed social skills, a lot of the benefits of cooperative learning are lost.

The fifth element is what we call "group processing." Periodically the groups have to assess how well they are working together and how they could do even better.

Getting all that to happen surely isn't easy. We have a history of innovations of one sort or another in schools that can be sustained for a few years by asking teachers to work extra hard. Eventually people wear out and the innovation disappears. Is cooperative learning like that?

Roger: I don't think so. Let me explain why. A workshop or course teaches teachers *about* cooperative learning, but it doesn't teach them *how* to do it. The only way teachers can learn the "how" is in their own classrooms, doing it. That means there must be a support system to provide advice and assistance when the teacher needs it. If a teacher goes to a workshop, goes back to the classroom and has no support, then the first time the approach doesn't work, the teacher will drop it and go back to what he or she was doing before. When that happens, the money and effort invested in the workshop have been wasted.

David: The best support system, obviously, is colleagues. So if you train a team of three, four, or five teachers from the same building, they get established as a collegial support group to sustain one another's efforts; and there's a very good chance that cooperative learning will be there forever.

"**Good, constructive, helpful, committed support can come from peers and subordinates as well as from superiors. And in many ways it's better coming from peers than from anyone else.**"

I can see that an administrator might encourage teachers to attend cooperative learning training, but many administrators would probably be reluctant to do more than that. We generally think of classroom organization as a matter for teachers to decide for themselves without outside interference.

David: Insisting that teachers use cooperative learning certainly wouldn't work and would be inconsistent with the ultimate purpose. Roger and I like a "grassroots up" system; we first give a general awareness presentation on cooperative learning to the whole staff—building or district. Then we begin working with some of the better teachers who get interested and volunteer, training them as a team and building a collegial support group within the building. After that we train new groups in concentric circles: teachers are sent by their colleagues so they can get started doing cooperative learning and join one of the collegial groups.

The principal may want every teacher in the building to be involved in a support group, but we know that to be successful such groups must have a clear purpose, and they must be help-ful to teachers in a day-to-day, nitty-gritty way. So a focus on learning to use cooperative learning is a reason for having support groups that teachers can buy into.

If eventually every teacher in the building is a member of such a group, the principal can then run the building the same way a teacher runs a cooperative classroom. His or her responsibility is to make sure that the support groups have those same five elements. Again they are—first, positive interdependence: the teachers care about each other's productivity and well-being. Second, a lot of face-to-face interaction among the teachers: they talk to each other about professional practice. Third, individual accountability: no freeloading or hitchhiking. Fourth, the teachers have the social skills, the leadership, the group decision making, the conflict management skills they need in order to operate together. And fifth, that periodically the teams review how well they are doing.

You mentioned the need for teachers to have group process skills. That can't be taken for granted.

Roger: No. A critical moment of truth in a collegial support group is when two teachers disagree strongly with each other and argue. Within an organizational climate that's primarily competitive or individualistic, such conflicts turn very destructive: teachers feel angry toward each other, they avoid each other, there's a lot of acrimony and divisiveness among the staff.

When teachers in a cooperative group disagree, they must have the skills to manage the conflict constructively. So the issue becomes: How do you teach teachers the basic collaborative skills they need to be good colleagues? There are two approaches, one direct and the other indirect. We prefer the indirect: by teaching their students how to provide leadership for the learning groups—how to disagree in constructive and helpful ways, how to build and maintain trust within the learning group, how to make group decisions—the teachers learn those social skills themselves and see when and how they should be used with their colleagues.

Our experience has been that if you just walk in on a faculty and say, "We're going to teach you how to resolve conflicts better," many teachers don't see the need for it. They think, "I seldom talk to my colleagues. Why do I need to know how to resolve conflicts?" The same is true at the principal-principal level, by the way. When principals begin running collegial support groups within their buildings, ensuring that teachers have the collaborative skills they need to be good colleagues, they begin to look at other principals differently. And in training teachers how to collaborate effectively the principals develop skills themselves to use with their colleagues. This is important because it's not unusual in many school districts for superintendents to place principals in direct competition with each other. A superintendent may say, "There are five elementary schools, but we have only three special ed. teachers. Every-

body write a proposal; the three best proposals will get the special ed. teachers." In that situation it is in each principal's best interest that other principals do poorly.

If the superintendent wants to build more collegiality among principals, more peer support, he or she does it with the five basic elements: deliberately structure sink-or-swim-together, get a lot of face-to-face interaction among principals in small decision-making groups, have clear individual accountability, make sure the social skills are there, and make sure that the groups think constructively about how well they are operating and how they might do better in the future.

So those five elements apply at every level?

David: Yes. And where a district builds that structure—cooperative learning in classrooms, collegial teacher support groups in buildings, colle-

gial administrative relationships within the district—the whole school district functions better: morale goes way up, absenteeism and divisiveness go down. People are more committed, have more energy for their jobs, there are all sorts of positive outcomes. And it puts student cooperative learning in the appropriate context.□

Reference

Deutsch, M. "Cooperation and Trust: Some Theoretical Notes." In *Nebraska Symposium on Motivation*, edited by M. R. Jones. Lincoln: University of Nebraska Press, 1962, 275–319.

David W. Johnson is Professor of Educational Psychology, and **Roger T. Johnson** is Professor of Curriculum and Instruction; both are Co-Directors of the Cooperative Learning Center, University of Minnesota, 202 Pattee Hall, 150 Pillsbury Dr., S.E., Minneapolis, MN 55455. **Ron Brandt** is ASCD's Executive Editor.

RONALD S. BRANDT   *Educational Leadership* 44 (Feb. 1987): 12-17

On Teachers Coaching Teachers: A Conversation with Bruce Joyce

You and Beverly Showers were among the first to use the term coaching[1] in connection with teachers learning new skills. How did that come about?

We were looking for a term that would capture the relationship that appears to facilitate transfer. We had strong evidence that if we combined study of the rationale of a teaching strategy or curriculum with demonstrations of it, plus lots of practice and lots of feedback, almost any teacher could learn almost any approach to teaching—and that's a very affirmative lesson.

But it turned out there was a second stage of learning—when the teacher would consolidate the strategy and adapt it to his or her own repertoire—and skill alone wasn't enough to facilitate that. What was needed was companionship; especially companionship with peers.

We didn't want to use a term like "supervised practice" because of the hierarchical connotations. And we were heavily influenced by some of the sports folks: trainers like Vic Braden, the tennis coach, who was constantly teaching people how to help each other. Braden had expert coaches, but he would also build a community of people who were studying tennis together.

Have your experiences since that time confirmed the value of coaching for teachers?

The senior author of *Models of Teaching* and several other books on staff development and school improvement, Bruce Joyce is an experienced trainer and advocate of peer coaching for teachers.

Where it's well used, yes. For example, we enjoy a school where the principal has organized her faculty for peer coaching. She takes over teachers' classes quite a bit so they can get together. Actually, though, the teachers don't spend a lot of time observing each other in classrooms. A team of her teachers may deal with, say, cooperative learning, and when they get the cooperative learning group going, other teachers go in for a few minutes, more to see the whole setup than to observe a particular lesson. But the main work is done when the principal gets the group together with a little wine and cheese once a week and they begin with a videotape of one of them. Or they may hold a few kids after school and somebody teaches a "live" lesson in front of the others.

What general circumstances are needed to make coaching successful?

Well, you start with lots of training—and you *continue* the training. There's an understanding that every month or so you'll come together and get more input or share experience. Building in regular times for people to think about whatever they're working on makes a big difference.

And as you might expect, it takes an active instructional leader. The cellular organization of schools makes coaching extremely difficult, and a laissez-faire, friendly, warm, congenial principal doesn't do much good in that regard. He or she has to unblock obstacles, to eliminate the isolation.

What are these active principals like?

Well, most of them are really good detail problem solvers. But even more important, they give a lot of attention to building the necessary shared understanding. That is, they help the group not only to take responsibility for sharing in the problem solving, but also to understand what they're about and why they're about it. If it's done mechanically, teachers simply visit each other and say, "Now we've peer coached." That really doesn't do much.

One of the most wasteful arrangements we saw of this was in a wealthy district that hired substitutes so teachers could be free for coaching but failed to provide training or understanding about what the thing was about. They had a good administrative arrangement for getting people together, but the purpose wasn't there.

Then, of course, it's got to be affirmative. Now, there are principals who are both strong evaluators and strong facilitators, so evaluation isn't necessarily incompatible with coaching. But an evaluation procedure that is at all mechanical or inept will certainly make coaching less effective.

Principals have also got to be part therapists because, due to the isolation, teachers are like tennis players who learned to play on a squash court by themselves. For many of them it's coming out of that box and for the first time getting some sense of whether they're any good or not. Very good teachers are sometimes as anxious as very poor ones—and some who, by our standards, aren't very skilled are comfortable. They'll say, "Oh, I'll teach; it's fine." Both parties manifest the lack of a metric that comes from watching other people play. If you learn to play tennis on public courts with 40 other people around, you form some idea of where you stand.

And you're saying that a good many teachers don't have that information at this point?

They really don't, and without it the prospect of coaching can be very scary. But a trainer can get rid of that fear very quickly. When I'm working with a staff I'll do some demonstrations, and then I'll say, "Now you do it with each other." They'll say, "I'm not ready," and I'll say, "Do it anyway."

It happened with the group I was with today. A couple of days ago, when they were to peer teach the next day, the adrenalin in the air was like that in a plane about to crash. Then the griping began: "You fouled us up, you taught us wrong, you didn't prepare us." By yesterday evening there was elation, and today, when they had finished, we showed a couple of tapes of other teachers working on the same strategies—showed them more or less without comment; just "Watch these

people and reflect on what they're doing." They all paid rapt attention to those tapes, and you could see they were ready for more practice and more feedback. I'd rather do it that way than just pair teachers and say without training, "Now coach."

You'd rather have it public for a while?

Yes, with lots of people right in the training setting, where there can be support from the trainers and we can model the coaching. Actually, by the way, much of the learning from coaching is not from listening to someone who has watched you, but from *your* watching the other person work.

And we tease a lot. Relaxation and getting playful when you teach are tremendously important. I'll say, "Only three people had coronaries last week from coaching. We'll keep statistics; give you a running account." Things like that. "Take your nitro and get into your groups," and all sorts of silly things.

We learned a lot again from Braden, who brings middle-class people who are very competitive to a tennis camp experience. He just makes people laugh and laugh. He brings out a group of tennis rackets and says, "People always ask us what racket to buy. All of these rackets are engineered beyond your capability." What can they say? They just have to acknowledge that that's probably right. They have to get relaxed with their imperfections.

What about after coaching has been introduced and things are moving along?

Well, the first thing is that it won't move along unless everyone starts practicing right away. To learn any new skill, you've got to practice it a lot in the first couple of weeks immediately following training. That's why summer workshops aren't necessarily the best time. We've suggested to teachers that they go out and corral children from wherever, lasso their spouses, or shanghai their neighbors—anybody they can—but they must practice whatever they're trying to learn a bunch of times.

Let's say it's a teaching strategy. Either you're going to get it rolling or you're not. If you can get everybody practicing a thing, if a faculty of 30 people all do it five times in the two weeks following training, you'll be running. If half the people don't do it for a month, their skills are going to erode, and they're going to get more fearful.

Why is it so hard to use a new teaching strategy?

Well, for one thing, you're giving kids cognitive and social tasks you're not accustomed to giving—but that's not the main thing; if you're not used to the model, you don't know how the students are going to respond—and if you don't know how they're going to respond, you don't know what *you're* going to do.

We sometimes use a stimulated recall approach to study the process of teachers learning a new model. We play back a recording of the teacher teaching and ask, "What were you thinking at this point?" The teacher may say, "I was thinking about getting the data to the kids. We were pretty well right on task." Then they ask the kids to categorize the data and you say, "What were you thinking?" The teachers' responses are something like this, "I sure hope they come up with an idea I'm familiar with," or even more common, "I hope they come up with the idea I most want to teach; I hope they don't come up with anything weird," and so forth.

After a while, students work in groups and build categories, and then it's time to share them. Teachers have no trouble making that move; they say, "Now, let's see what you came up with." You stop the videotape and say, "What were you thinking?" and they say, "I was thinking I wished I could go home." At that moment, the first time they do it, they have no idea what the kids are going to come up with. With more experience they find that kids can be reasonably intelligent; they'll come up with most of the things the teacher would have; but even if they don't, the teacher will have developed a repertoire of moves to handle what happens.

It's the thinking parts—what we call the "invisible" skills of teaching—that are the hardest; not what we call the "syntax" of a model, or getting through the major cognitive and social tasks. Particularly tricky are the interactive parts; reacting to what students do or say as the lesson goes on.

That fear of what will happen applies, for example, to cooperative learning, even in its simplest form. About the simplest social task you can give students is to say, "Study this in pairs," but there's as much anxiety about trying that as there is for doing a highly complex strategy like the jurisprudential model, which really places tremendous demands on the teacher: "What am I going to do with these 15 pairs of kids all raising hell?" It's not until they've done it for awhile that they find out, "By George, many productive things are happening."

At this point we ask teachers simply to experiment with having kids study in pairs; not everything—we don't want them writing original personal poetry in pairs—but simple tasks: "Read this and get ready for a discussion" or "Dig up information on this."

> "Because of their isolation, teachers are like tennis players who learned to play on a squash court by themselves. For many of them it's coming out of that box and for the first time getting some sense of whether they're any good or not."

How much time does it take for a teacher to learn a model?

Okay, let's design a little program for a year. Let's take just a single model of medium complexity; the inductive one would be a suitable example. You'd probably want a three-day workshop or the equivalent to get started. It wouldn't have to be three solid days; it could be some other configuration. But then there should be a couple of days a few weeks later to spice it up, see how people are doing, and add a little more. Then another day a few weeks later for polishing and sharing, plus a day of advanced training later. So now you have a picture of the amount of input it takes.

Beyond that, it's going to take teachers maybe 30 trials to get reasonably good at a model, in the sense that they can use it as easily as they use their existing repertoire. To be able to look at a unit or a body of material or section of a text, see how to handle it inductively, and plan it quickly and efficiently, it's going to take them a good 30 trials.

Some might say, "If that's what it takes, forget it. That's an impossible expectation."

Of course. What we're talking about, though, is payoff in student achievement. We're in the same position as saying, "It's a lot of trouble to figure out how to control rocket fuels; let's just stick with the internal combustion engine." "It's going to be a lot of trouble to develop a battery that will operate a car efficiently, so let's just forget it." Anything worthwhile is troublesome and is worth it. But you're absolutely right; putting a system like this in place requires a social change that can ruffle some feathers.

But are you sure a school would improve achievement that much? We know these models make school more interesting, but is there much evidence they do more?

I've been familiar with many of the models in which people are currently trained for quite a number of years, and I can tell you that the research

Ronald S. Brandt

base is much sharper now than it's ever been.

Now, there's a reason for that. If you were to compare the number of research studies of a given complexity done in the last 15 years to all the history of educational research before, I'd guess it would be four or five to one. The vast majority of our research has been done in the 1970s and '80s. Researchers have begun to engineer strategies quietly and systematically that are getting a magnitude of effect far beyond anything anticipated before. Results in the area of mnemonics are the most dramatic. Pressley and Levin[2] are routinely doing studies in which kids learn two, three, and four times as much as they ordinarily would in the same period of time. They're doing it in all sorts of subject areas. Experimenters with advance organizers—a way of organizing lectures—have fumbled along for years with effects of a quarter of a standard deviation. In the last seven or eight years they've reengineered the stuff and are getting effect sizes of up to two standard deviations.[3] In fact, they're actually using advance organizers to increase kids' levels of cognitive functioning.

We think the real payoff comes from combining educational ideas. By teaching inductively you can increase student learning as much as 30 percentile points in a given unit of study.[4] If you use cooperative learning properly, you can get about the same magnitude of effect.[5] If you put them together you won't double it, of course, but we've had some studies where we've increased learning twice as much as control groups doing only one or the other.[6]

I think the notion of effect size is going to have a tremendous impact. Until now, researchers have thought of significant difference, not magnitude. Someone will report, "My research shows this approach works," when it may raise achievement by about a percent. Now, the use of advance organizers is good for a *standard deviation*—and that's one of the simpler models. The memory people are now getting effect sizes *four times* the mean.[7] They are literally producing, in

"We tease a lot. Relaxation and getting playful when you teach are tremendously important. I'll say, 'Only three people had coronaries last week from coaching. We'll keep statistics; give you a running account.' "

short-term training, four times as much as good memorizers working by themselves without the help of mnemonic devices. That kind of finding should greatly affect what educators attend to when they want to make a school more effective.

Authors of literature reviews sometimes give the impression that there is indeed a substantial body of research on teaching, but that it rather narrowly supports direct instruction as the most effective model.

We believe they're wrong. Bev Showers, Carol Bennett, and I are doing a meta-analysis of research on the theory-driven models of instruction, as well as the naturalistic studies of teachers and schools. We're looking at about 3,000 reports of research undergirding just the models of teaching that are in the book, *Models of Teaching*.[8]

Of course, not every approach to teaching that we advocate has the same depth of research base, but most have quite a lot. Cooperative learning is a good example; just having kids work in cooperative groups (if you teach kids how to do it, and do it

intensively) can often get you a standard deviation of gain.[9] That's a lot by standards of the past.

So what are you saying about the "effective teaching" research?

Those studies have definitely shown some things about teaching that make a difference. They have also begun to give us some idea about the nature of the social and instructional climate that aids learning. An affirmative climate is very important. Active instruction is also important. But the naturalistic researchers are hampered because they have to work with the existing teaching that they're able to observe. We, on the other hand, teach teachers different models because we're trying to widen their repertoires.

What proportion of teachers in this country are currently involved in the intensive training and coaching process you've described?

I'd say it's a very small percentage. The average teacher is still getting only about three days of staff development a year—not a lot. We're now establishing relationships with districts that are several years long and that involve 20, 30, 40 days of activity a year. Every time we begin one of these I am struck by teachers' isolation from knowledge of their craft. In the setting where we're working right now, for example, I talked yesterday with a group of teachers who had been working for four days on a very simple version of an inductive model of teaching. They were making plans to use the model in their classrooms, and they said they'd just never seen anything like it. I thought to myself, "How is it possible that they haven't seen inductive lessons?" This is as old as—well, probably the pharaohs had tutors who gave inductive lessons. So, just for fun, I asked the 100-and-some people who were there, "Let's take the five or six models you've seen here and be generous about it; how many of you have seen a variation of *a, b, c, d, e?* The number of hands that went up in any case was a handful of the group. They actually had never seen those models, even though they are regarded as good teachers in a well-organized, strong school system in a major metropolitan area. It seems impossible, but I'm afraid it's an index of how far we have to go.

We generally think that supervisors are responsible for helping teachers learn new skills. Do you reject the possibility of supervisors serving as coaches?

Well, teachers are more numerous, and it's much easier for them to get together with one another. I prefer to talk not about the "supervisor" but the "trainer": someone who has really polished a given approach to teaching, curriculum, computers, or what have you; somebody who really knows the stuff. The question is: what are the roles of that person, of the building administrator, of the supervisor, and so on.

> "If you can get everybody practicing a thing, if a faculty of 30 people all do it five times in the two weeks following training, you'll be running. If half the people don't do it for a month, their skills are going to erode and they're going to get more fearful."

Or we might ask it this way: if you were going to organize a school system for a full-scale training effort, what roles would you want in order to make the most productive use of all concerned?

Oh boy. Well, briefly, peers can follow up each other just fine. Supervisors or principals who don't practice as much as the teachers won't be able to help teachers as much as the teachers, who are practicing the skills daily, can help each other. Unless they intend to go to a very high level of competence, administrators are well advised to be facilitators of the process rather than coaches.

But your question is really about the professionalization of educators, and for that I think there are two essentials. One is that educators have to be hired full-time; there will never be a part-time profession accepted as such by other people or by the members themselves.

Second, and equally important, is to redeploy personnel. I know we've been through all the team teaching, differentiated staffing, and such, with indifferent results, but the fact is we're very awkwardly utilized. First of all, as most teachers are presently assigned, teaching is assumed to be something you can do with almost no preparation (one prep period is not enough time to prepare for five or six classes). To change that, so teachers have more time both to prepare and to analyze what students produce, students will have to spend a lot more time working independently. We can't think just of the teachers; we have to prepare the kids to take more responsibility for their own learning. That's the only way I can see for teachers to have more time to prepare and teach the kinds of lessons that will fuel longer-term learning and to analyze the results of complex assignments.

I really think that the main reason we build schools with classrooms where teachers teach individually all day is to control the students, and I think that's bad in several ways. It means that instruction is always overshadowed by the control thing. You're always with 25 people, needed or not. If we could change these things, build-

> "I've been familiar with many of the models in which people are currently being trained for quite a number of years, and I can tell you that the research base is much sharper now than it's ever been."

ing administrators and supervisors could be real curriculum design people, rather than using so much of their time on clerical and trouble-shooting activities.

If I'm a leader in a typical school or school district, how do I get started in that direction?

First, believe it. Believe that your school can be tremendously better, and that you can invent ways to make it better. Then start inventing.

A lot of educators feel the cards are stacked against them now. The community seems to be saying, "No innovations; just make it like good old school used to be."

Educators have been psyched out somehow; the community is not against better education, by any means. Teachers and principals may think that parents aren't with us, but many parents think we're not with them.

I'm sure you'd agree there's been a conservative trend lately, but do you think we'll be seeing more openness to experimentation again?

I think if *we're* open and *we* have confidence, if we bring people into the game, we'll get a lot more support than we might expect.□

1. B. Joyce and B. Showers, "Teacher Training Research: Working Hypotheses for Program Design and Directions for Further Study" (paper presented at the Annual Meeting of the American Educational Research Association, Los Angeles, 1981); B. Joyce and B. Showers, "The Coaching of Teaching," *Educational Leadership* 40 (October 1982): 4–10.

2. M. Pressley and J. Levin, "The Mnemonic Keyword Method," *Review of Educational Research* 52, 1 (1982): 61–91; M. Pressley, "Children's Use of the Keyword Method to Learn Simple Spanish Vocabulary Words," *Journal of Educational Psychology* 69, 5 (1977a): 465–472; M. Pressley, "Imagery and Children's Learning: Putting the Picture in Developmental Perspective," *Review of Educational Research* 47, 4 (1977b): 585–622; M. Pressley, "Elaboration and Memory Development," *Child Development* 53, 2 (1982): 296–30; M. Pressley and J. Dennis-Rounds, "Transfer of a Mnemonic Keyword Strategy at Two Age Levels," *Journal of Educational Psychology* 72, 4 (1980): 575–582.

3. J. Lawton and S. Wanska, "The Effects of Different Types of Advance Organizers on Classification Learning," *American Educational Research Journal* 16, 3 (1979): 223–239; C. L. Stone, "A Meta Analysis of Advance Organizer Studies," *Journal of Experimental Education* 51, 4 (1983): 194–199.

4. B. Baveja, B. Showers, and B. Joyce, "The Effects of Inductive Teaching on Higher-Order and Lower-Order Student Achievement." Eugene, Ore.: Booksend Laboratories, 1986).

5. D. N. Johnson, G. Marvyana, R. Johnson, D. Nelson, and L. Skon, "Effects of Cooperative, Competitive, and Individualistic Goal Structures on Achievement: A Meta-Analysis," *Psychological Bulletin* 89, 1 (1981): 47–62; R. E. Slavin, "Cooperative Learning," *Review of Educational Research* 50, 2 (1980): 315–342; S. Sharan, "Cooperative Learning in Small Groups: Recent Methods and Effects on Achievement, Attitudes, and Ethnic Relations," *Review of Educational Research* 50, 2 (1980): 241–271.

6. See note 4.

7. See note 2, first citation.

8. Bruce Joyce and Marsha Weil, *Models of Teaching*, 3d ed. (Englewood Cliffs, N.J.: Prentice-Hall, 1986).

9. See note 5.

Bruce Joyce is Co-Director of Booksend Laboratories, 3830 Vine Maple, Eugene, OR 97405. **Ronald S. Brandt** is Executive Editor of ASCD.

Educational Leadership 46 (Sept. 1988): 34-37

RON BRANDT

On Philosophy in the Curriculum: A Conversation with Matthew Lipman

Philosophy is the best answer to the call for teaching critical thinking, says Matthew Lipman, because only through philosophy can we give students the experience they need in reasoning—experience that will prepare them much better than the limited knowledge of the disciplines.

Why do you believe philosophy must become part of the regular school curriculum?

There's a growing awareness that much of what schools teach young people is not particularly appropriate for the world we are moving into, that knowledge grows rapidly out of date, and that the most important thing we can do for children is teach them to think well. If we're serious about wanting to teach students to think, we've got to go about it in a responsible fashion. This means giving students practice in reasoning, through classroom discussion involving concepts that reach across all the disciplines rather than only those that are specialized within each subject. Only through philosophy can this be done effectively.

That's why you created Philosophy for Children?

Yes. Back in the early '70s, when my own children were about 10 or 11 years old, the school they were attending did not give them the instruction in reasoning that I thought they needed. I was teaching logic at the college level at the time, and I felt that I wasn't accomplishing very much with my students because it was too late;

they should have had instruction in reasoning much earlier. So I decided I would do something to help children at the middle school level learn to reason. I realized that the principles of logic would have to be presented in an interesting way, so I decided to write a novel in which the characters would be depicted discovering these principles and reflecting on how they could be applied to their lives.

Which was *Harry Stottlemeier's Discovery?*

Yes. I didn't know how it would work until I tried it with a group of 5th graders in the town where I lived. I got permission from the school to teach it for nine weeks, twice a week, 40 minutes each session. We pretested and post-tested both those children and a control group. And it seemed to work remarkably well: the experimental group gained 27 months in logical reasoning skills over the nine-week period, while the control group remained unchanged.

It was pointed out to me, though, that this trial had serious defects. For example, I had taught the course myself. It would have been a much fairer test if the course had been taught by a teacher I had trained.

Photograph by Will Cofnuk

Still, you showed that it could be done.

Right. I was also curious about whether the effects of the intervention would remain and if they would spread: would the students' improved thinking show up in their work in other school subjects? I was able to ascertain that the effects lasted for two years, but they didn't last for four years. I concluded that unless the results of such an intervention are reinforced, they'll wash out.

That's true of almost every educational approach.

As for the spread, we determined that in virtually every discipline except spelling (which is illogical, anyhow) the Iowa test scores of the students I had taught showed significant improvement. But once again those effects washed out after a few years.

So you saw a need for the program to be more continuous.

Yes. And that meant publishing books and preparing materials for training teachers. I spent the next four years trying to figure out how to do that and the next 14 years doing it.

Since that time, the program has been widely used. Just how widely?

I estimate that it can be found in about 5,000 school districts. Within those districts, it may be in one classroom or many. The materials are taught in other countries as well. They've been translated into about 15 different languages.

You mentioned development of materials for teachers. What have you learned about teacher training? Most elementary teachers haven't studied much philosophy.

We began with a one-semester course. Ann Margaret Sharp and I taught it for two and a half hours a week for 13 weeks. We would teach the teachers, who in turn would teach the same material to their students. When we tested the children, we found no significant improvement in reading or reasoning; and we concluded that the teachers had not been exposed to the material for a sufficiently long period. So the next year we doubled the time of exposure and we did get significant results—and they have been confirmed by other experiments.

So you continue to recommend a full year of inservice—not full time, of course.

No. Two and a half hours a week for a school year—or the equivalent. We now have a variety of teacher-training options.

What goes on in a Philosophy for Children class?

The teacher workshops and the children's classes are very much alike, because whatever the trainer does with the teachers, the teachers will almost certainly do with children. The trainer tries to create a community of inquiry, in which the teachers read the novel and discuss the ideas among themselves with the assistance of the trainer. Then the teachers go to their classrooms and do essentially what the trainer did: they facilitate discussion of the ideas the children find in the novel. From time to time, the trainer goes to the classroom and leads a discussion with the children, trying to show what is meant by a philosophical discussion.

What *is* meant?

It means that students discuss experiences all children have had, such as being embarrassed by not knowing an answer. They may have wanted to talk about these experiences, but not in a

Whatever the trainer does with the teachers, the teachers will almost certainly do with children.

personal way. By discussing what happens to the characters in a novel, they can talk about things in the third person: somebody else is the one involved. They become accustomed to asking each other for reasons and for opinions, to listening carefully to each other, to building on each other's ideas. I've seen 1st grade children, when another student voices an opinion, call out softly, "Reason! Reason!"

In a nonphilosophical conversation, one responds to a question with an answer. But in a philosophical discussion, one often responds to a question by attempting to ascertain the meaning of the question. An example would be asking a child what time it is, and she replies by asking, "What is time?" One reason education is in crisis is that children do not understand what we are trying to teach them, and they lack a procedure that would enable them to reach for that understanding themselves. Philosophy provides such a procedure, by having students probe the questions and reflect upon the assumptions.

Do all teachers need special training to teach philosophy? Don't some teachers already teach that way?

Some teachers need relatively little training; others need quite a bit. It takes a special kind of teacher to teach philosophy: a teacher who inspires trust, so that there's an openness in the classroom; a teacher who is thoughtful and reflective; a teacher who can be critical of students' logical reasoning but who always cites the criteria on the basis of which his or her criticisms are made, so that it's a responsible kind of criticism.

Does the experience of teaching philosophy carry over to the way teachers teach other content?

It often does. And when it does, the results are electrifying. When both teacher and students identify with the methodology and engage in spontaneous and stimulating thinking throughout the school day, you see achievement skyrocket. That's the optimum. But of course some teachers restrict their use of the Socratic approach just to philosophy.

You've collected a great deal of data over the years about the effects of teaching philosophy. Some of it is quite revealing. Without such an intervention, young people's logical thinking seems not to change very much through the years.

Well, it improves a little each year up to about the age of 12, and then it generally plateaus at about three-quarters of full efficiency. Without training in logical reasoning, most elementary and secondary school children get only about three out of four logical problems right. We have to do better than that. You can't do college-level work if you are reasoning at a C level.

That brings up another point. I get the impression that some people think philosophy might be ap-

propriate for especially able students, but not for the others.

Philosophy is very appropriate for the whole range of students. I don't think that ordinary children are incapable of thinking about complex matters. Kids who may be doing badly in school can argue with the manager of a professional baseball team about whether a player should have been suspended or whether somebody should have been sent up to hit. They can cite the batting averages, fielding averages—the kind of criteria that a manager uses to make such decisions. Children do that sort of thing very well when there's sufficient motivation and incentive.

When you see slow learners or disadvantaged students drilling and drilling, when you see the monotony and the drudgery, you begin to think that nobody cares about making school interesting for these students, that nobody cares about having them voice their opinions or enjoy learning. But if you talk with them—ask them about fairness or friendship or why the world is the way it is—you discover that they've been mute and inarticulate all this time only because nobody's ever taken the trouble to consult with them.

In fact, it's often the students identified as gifted who are uncomfortable with philosophy, because it doesn't have ready answers they can recite, and it doesn't have the convergence they're used to. But it does have logic, which they generally enjoy. Unfortunately, with the emphasis on short right answers and factual recall, we fail to prepare children for the ambiguities of life.

Some educators are wary of discussions of controversial issues because they think it's not the business of the school to influence children's ideas in that way, and because they don't want to get in trouble with people in their community.

The students become accustomed to asking each other for reasons and for opinions, to listening carefully to each other, to building on each other's ideas.

And they're right that it's not the business of educators to implant their personal opinions in their students. That would be indoctrination. On the other hand, there's a danger that if nothing is done—if teachers are always neutral about everything—schools are really indoctrinating relativism without acknowledging that that's what they're doing. What must be encouraged is rational inquiry: children should be inquiring into moral issues as a community and coming to experience firsthand the range of community perspectives on these matters. When children belong to a classroom community of inquiry that is thoughtful and considerate, they are likely to become thoughtful and considerate themselves.

But some parents say they don't want their children to be reflective on such matters. They want them to believe what they're told to believe until they're old enough to decide for themselves.

There are some parents who would prefer to reserve some aspects of education for the home. Controversies of this kind are inevitable, and rightly so. These are profoundly serious issues. Go back to the disputes that took place when compulsory education was initi-

ated: "Why do we do this? How can we justify requiring students to go to school?" If we feel that education for reasonableness is needed in order to preserve democracy, and that the alternatives to democracy are unacceptable, then we have a mandate to require that all children be educated for reasonableness. A reflective education should include teaching children to read and write well, to speak and listen well, and to exercise good judgment. Without these skills, students will be ill-prepared to confront the responsibilities of citizenship and the problems of life.

You're saying, then, that philosophy offers an answer to the call for critical thinking in education?

I think it is *the* answer, because it provides all that critical thinking approaches can provide, and a great deal more besides. Instead of teaching isolated, dismembered skills, it concentrates on systematically connecting the skills to one another so that when one thinks about the subject matter of a discipline, one does so in an organized and thorough way. It's of little value to possess individual cognitive skills if one lacks judgment as to when such skills should be applied. The aim of philosophy is to develop thinkers, and that cannot be done by merely teaching skills. Moreover, in Philosophy for Children, our objective is not merely to sharpen students' capacities for dry analysis but to dramatize the life of the mind so that students will develop critical dispositions as they discuss ideas of mutual concern in a community of inquiry. It is through such thinking together that children become reasonable and independent thinkers.□

Matthew Lipman is Professor of Philosophy and Director of the Institute for the Advancement of Philosophy for Children, Montclair State College, Upper Montclair, NJ 07043. **Ron Brandt** is ASCD's Executive Editor.

On Teacher Evaluation: A Conversation with Tom McGreal

Tom McGreal, Chair, Department of Administration, Higher and Continuing Education, University of Illinois, Urbana-Champaign, has consulted with numerous states and school districts on design of staff evaluation programs and is the author of ASCD's *Successful Teacher Evaluation* (1983).

You've often said that the only instrument you need for teacher evaluation is a blank sheet of paper. Do you still believe that?

If we had complete freedom to choose, and well-trained evaluators, yes, but there've been a lot of forces working against this in the last five years. We've been making considerable progress in the use of instructional improvement-oriented goal-setting models. But unfortunately, many of the states—around 30 at this point—have mandated certain forms of teacher evaluation that more often than not require districts to submit plans for state approval that are more accountability oriented. As a result there is renewed attention being given to a rating scale mentality. So even though a lot of us don't like that approach, local districts are asking for help in improving the quality of rating scales.

In what way?

Well, the most significant trend in teacher evaluation in recent years has been the heavy emphasis on the use of the research on teaching as a focus for the criteria.

Rather than a more general "trait" approach?

Yes. We're seeing a tremendous amount of similarity in the criteria that districts and states are coming up with. That's partly because they are sharing criteria, and partly it's a reflection of the limited number of criteria you can generate from the research we now have on effective teaching.

Is there a danger that, because these criteria can only reflect the current state of research, they will be too narrow?

I think that's a clear problem. Like many people who work in this area, I feel fairly positive toward using the research on teaching, but there are many cautions about using it. As everyone surely knows, the criteria that have been developed are much more appropriate for explicit instruction than for other forms of teaching. In a number of the states where I've been working, we've begun to see that instruments using the research on teaching criteria tend to give an advantage to certain teachers. For example, we're seeing a high percentage of special education teachers and mathematics and science teachers showing up very well, perhaps because their training and the content they teach fit more readily, while other teachers—particularly those who try to stress higher-level thinking skills—are put at a disadvantage. So we have to be very careful about use of these criteria, especially if they're tied to incentive plans.

If you have these concerns, there must be some good reasons for going ahead and using the effectiveness criteria anyhow.

There are basic teaching skills that every teacher ought to be able to demonstrate. I think the effective teaching findings have great potential, but they must be used with understanding, and I'm not sure that understanding always exists.

What do people need to understand?

Evaluators—and teachers themselves—need to have some perspective on where the research on teaching comes from, what it says, and what it doesn't say. It's also important to understand the differences between the teacher effects research and the Madeline Hunter material and its derivatives. States, particularly in the South, are mandating that every teacher be trained in the Hunter-derived approaches, such as the Principles of Effective Teaching (PET) program. PET was developed, I think, by Don Roberts and others when Roberts was superintendent at Newport News. He took it to Arkansas when he became

"We can discriminate a competent from an incompetent teacher, and we can usually distinguish extraordinary teaching from the rest, but anything beyond that is virtually impossible with any degree of reliability."

Commissioner of Education there. It's now moving into Texas and South Carolina and a number of other states.

How do you differentiate between the Hunter material and the effective teaching research?

There're obviously some similarities, but they're really two different strands. Local schools and states need to understand that the effects research is a combination of correlational and experimental studies tying individual teacher behaviors to student outcomes. The Hunter material and the programs derived from it are learning theory-based, and are often viewed as directed at the total teaching act. Hunter's is a complete teaching approach as opposed to some of the more visible teacher effects programs such as TESA (Teacher Expectations and Student Achievement) and the Evertson and Emmer (1981) work that focus on certain aspects of teaching. There is little evidence at this point to link the Hunter training to student learning. Now, that's not necessarily a criticism of it, but it is a criticism of states and school districts that promise that it's going to improve student learning. We just don't have much evidence for that. What's more, although Hunter and most responsible Hunter advocates try to keep their training separate from evaluation, there's no question that state department people and local administrators are taking the Hunter terminology and recommendations and turning them directly into rating scales.

You said you have some qualms about the use of rating scales, but you've been helping states and

school systems develop better ones anyhow. What are some ways to make rating scales as good as possible?

I might explain that most of us who specialize in evaluation don't have a lot of faith in most rating scales, but the reality is that they are going to continue to be prevalent despite our reservations, so help should be given to make them as useful as possible. One way districts are trying to make their instruments more objective is by using "behaviorally anchored" ratings: each rating has a brief description of what it means. For example, a satisfactory rating might mean "teacher shows clear evidence of having established goals and objectives." This does add a certain amount of reliability to a rating scale.

The process actually results in a numerical score, then?

Many of the states and local districts expect evaluators to give an overall rating. So their systems are set up with a formula that derives an overall rating from the ratings on individual criteria. For example, in order to get an overall rating of "exceeds district standards," you have to get "exceeds district standards" on at least 9 of 13 criteria and no lower than "almost meets district standards" on each of the other 4. Well, that's tough to do. Among other things, it assumes that all 13 criteria are equally important, which is almost certainly not the case. I recommend not giving an overall rating but, if there must be one, having only two categories: "meets district standards" or "doesn't meet district standards."

If that's not acceptable, I'll try to get them at least to weight the criteria. Some can be viewed as more fundamental than others, and the overall rating should reflect that.

Another thing we need to do is to incorporate what we know about teaching for higher-level learning in evaluation criteria. Right now, other than a few vague references like "uses a variety of questions," such provisions are virtually nonexistent.

As I mentioned earlier, one thing I suggest is to look for ways to weight criteria that are better at discriminating at the lower ends of rating scales versus those that might discriminate better at upper ends. Our ability to

76

evaluate performance is, at best, relatively gross. We can discriminate a competent from an incompetent teacher, and we can usually distinguish extraordinary teaching from the rest, but anything beyond that is virtually impossible with any degree of reliability. So I suggest that criteria like "use of time," "bell-to-bell planning," and "teaching to objectives" be considered fundamental expectations used to discriminate between competent and incompetent or satisfactory and unsatisfactory teaching. Other criteria, such as the teacher's ability to match methods with content and with kids, are much higher-level skills. They should probably be used to discriminate between "satisfactory" and "superior" or between "meets" and "exceeds" district standards, and so on. The purpose is to take some of the pressure off the principals and supervisors who are forced by the system to make discriminating judgments among teachers, and then are provided no guidelines or help in responding to teacher questions like, "What do I need to do to receive a 'superior' rating rather than an 'excellent' rating?" If we were to ask the effects researchers to weight the various criteria, I am sure we would not find

them receptive to this notion. I can understand their reservations since the research was not designed to do this. On the other hand, I think that it's reasonable to suggest that certain teaching variables are more fundamental and should be displayed if a teacher is to receive a minimally acceptable rating, while other behaviors, though desirable, cannot be required to meet minimum expectations. I think we owe local supervisors this if we are to help them cope with the demands that their evaluation systems put on them.

You do believe, then, that an instrument can be helpful in discriminating between the competent and the incompetent?

Yes.

I suppose most members of the general public think that's the main purpose of teacher evaluation.

That's true. And they don't see why it should be difficult, especially when we have rating scales, because we're supposedly getting objective data. But the use of rating scales is actually very subjective.

A fundamental problem is that almost all of our supervisory training

deals with formative data collection: how to write descriptively rather than judgmentally, techniques of clinical supervision, conferencing skills, and so on. So we now have a group of administrators being required to take formatively collected data and make summative judgments from them. Making that transition is very difficult, if not impossible.

A long-standing concern is making the same individual responsible for both, and having teachers never know for sure just what the administrator is up to at any moment.

The evaluation system can be a big help with that. Otherwise the whole system becomes rating-scale driven. It forces supervisors to make one or two observations a year using a wide-angle lens perspective because they have an instrument in front of them which they end up using as an observation guide. The conference inevitably focuses on the judgments the supervisor has already made, and he or she never gets a chance to use the skills he or she has been trained to use.

The system should allow a supervisor to—at least artificially—separate his or her administrative behavior from his or her supervisory behavior. I have found that an individual goal-setting model can help supervisors do this. You have monitoring of performance going on all the time. Teachers aren't evaluated once a year or twice a year; they're evaluated continuously— because they live and work in the same place with their administrators every day. I try to set up a system in which the monitoring of minimum expectations is continuous. Then, less frequently, maybe every other year, the supervisor and teacher sit down and identify one or two fairly specific teaching goals that become the basis for what they will work on together. That puts them in a much better position to use formative techniques. They can focus their observations more clearly; they can use clinical models; they can establish a training, coaching environment.

Using the process you've described, there still comes a time when a teacher may have to be dealt with in a different way.

Right. Poor teaching is still going to show up. In goal setting, the rule tends to be that the less competent or mature the teacher, the more directive the supervisor has to be. The more competent and mature the teacher, the more he or she should be involved in the activities and setting of the goals. Since the majority of teachers in this country are mature and competent, it seems sensible to design the system for them: for the roughly 98 percent who are going to be in that district for a long time.

Do you advocate some kind of special notice for the other 2 percent? Something like, "I am hereby informing you that you are now in a different category. Here's how it will work"?

Yes, we probably have to do that. It keeps the special mechanisms that apply only to the marginal teacher separate from the regular, more formatively oriented system.

But you're also saying that it's difficult to develop and maintain a goal-setting model when you have to comply with mandated systems that require everybody to be treated as though they're on notice all the time.

Yes, state departments need help in somehow walking that line. Now, I don't want to pick on state departments; many times they're required by law to put together rules and regulations for statewide mandates. But it's of particular concern that a lot of these programs—whether they require use of a single system or they force local districts to conform to certain kinds of requirements in order to get approved—take away the flexibility of local districts to build systems that are more conducive to improving instruction.

The other side of the argument, I suppose, is that these laws wouldn't have been necessary if local administrators had been more responsible all along. A little earlier you said that 98 percent of teachers are doing a good job. A lot of people feel that's probably an overstatement; that considerably more than 2 percent need some attention.

> "A fundamental problem is that almost all of our supervisory training deals with formative data collection: . . . So we have a group of administrators being required to take formatively collected data and make summative judgments from them."

In some cases that's correct. The state must insist that school districts that are doing nothing—and believe me, there are some—be brought up to minimum standards. The tendency in recent years, unfortunately, has also been to bring districts that have already seriously addressed the issue back down to the middle.

But to return to your original question, when I say that 98 percent of teachers are doing their jobs, I'm not saying they're all doing the job as well as they could. I'm saying they're doing the job to the point where it would be virtually impossible to have them dismissed; that, because of the political realities and the cost of dismissing teachers, a purely summative evaluation system will probably not affect their behavior very much.

If that's the case, what is a better strategy?

The important thing is relating evaluation to staff development. If teachers feel more involved in setting their own goals, they'll be more committed to improvement.

I thought you said you were concerned about the danger of using the Hunter model in both staff development and evaluation, but now you're saying the two *should* be tied together.

Let me explain. Researchers have helped identify a set of skills that ought to be in every teacher's bag of tools—certain organization and management skills, skills in the use of time, Rosenshine's (1986) teaching functions. We have clearer information about how to improve the quality of seatwork and practice activities. We have a much clearer sense, particularly for junior and senior high school teachers, of what constitutes a climate conducive to learning. We know more about increasing levels of student involvement, opportunities for success, appropriate use of feedback, and so on.

A first stage of appropriate staff development would be to give all teachers and administrators an introduction to this bag of tools. From there you can move to more complex topics, such as learning styles and thinking skills, but we need to have in common this relatively sound base.

Now, these tools are there for teachers to sort through and think about, not always to have to use. One benefit of having a set of fundamentals is that it provides a common language teachers and supervisors can use to talk together. We find that it increases the level of talk about teaching, and that's true of the Hunter material as well.

There are appropriate ways to link this kind of staff development to the evaluation system?

Right. Eventually you change your evaluation system to reflect the staff development program. In many ways the staff development and the evaluation system are subsets of something bigger; maybe it's a five-year commitment to enhance the quality of classroom instruction (I'm purposely using the term "enhance" rather than "improve" because it connotes working with people who are already fairly competent). Still later the evaluation system becomes the means to maintain the staff development. In many states and districts where there's been good staff development over several years, we've seen considerable erosion when the original training is discontinued and staff turnover begins to take its toll. When that happens, particularly if the district is moving toward a goal-setting model, the only mechanism to maintain the staff development is the evaluation system.

You're saying that, even where a district must follow state mandates, it may be appropriate to start with staff development on effective teaching, develop some shared understanding among teachers and supervisors, and then gradually introduce a goal-setting approach when the staff is ready to handle it?

That's exactly what I'm trying to encourage. Even though districts are being required to use rating scales and so on, I'm saying they can still keep alive on an every-other-year basis, or if necessary an every-third-year basis, a more intensive involvement between the supervisor and the teacher.

One interesting development in teacher evaluation is participation by teachers in the evaluation of other teachers. In some cases excellent teachers are taken out of the classrooms for a year or more to spend full-time acting as evaluators.

That sort of thing is going on in a few exemplary places, but it doesn't tend to be transferable to other settings. Those of us who spend a lot of time improving skills of administrators and supervisors are seeing a growing movement toward mentoring and peer coaching. Now I think there's a tremendous need for more interaction among peers, but in the schools I've worked in, the average teacher still does not want to be involved in evaluating other teachers. So while there are extraordinary examples of peer supervision, I think there are many of us who feel that for the near future the real hope of improving instruction is still going to come from improving the interaction between the supervisor and the teacher. I think it is wrong to move toward a model that forces administrators to be responsible only for summative evaluations and asks teachers to make formative evaluations. By providing appropriate staff develop-

ment opportunities and designing evaluation systems that encourage and allow good supervision, we can establish quality supervisor-teacher interaction that can enhance classroom instruction. We have the knowledge and ability to do both.□

References

Emmer, E. T., and C. M. Evertson. "Synthesis of Research in Classroom Management." *Educational Leadership* 38 (January 1981): 342–347.

McGreal, T. *Successful Teacher Evaluation.* Alexandria, Va.: Association for Supervision and Curriculum Development, 1983.

Rosenshine, B. V. "Synthesis of Research on Explicit Teaching." *Educational Leadership* 43 (April 1986): 60–69.

Tom McGreal is Acting Chairperson and Associate Professor, Department of Administration, Higher, and Continuing Education, University of Illinois at Urbana-Champaign, 1310 S. Sixth St., Champaign, IL 61820. **Ron Brandt** is ASCD's Executive Editor.

Educational Leadership 43 (May 1986): 12-18
RONALD S. BRANDT

On Creativity and Thinking Skills:
A Conversation with
David Perkins

A major contributor to Venezuela's Project Intelligence and author of several books on creativity and thinking, including *The Mind's Best Work*, David Perkins is codirector of Harvard's Project Zero. Highly regarded for his broad knowledge of this complex and developing field, Perkins is concerned with cognitive skills and human development, especially in the arts.

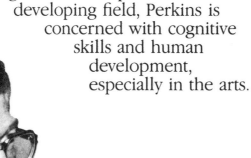

Ronald S. Brandt

To what extent is the current interest in teaching thinking a worldwide movement?

It is certainly apparent in a number of countries. For example, in the early 1980s, the government of Venezuela launched a number of programs to foster the development of thinking skills—not only in school children but in citizens of all ages. Some of the materials for that effort—Project Intelligence—have now been published in English under the title of Odyssey: A Curriculum for Thinking. We evaluated Odyssey in Venezuela with quite positive results on the summative evaluation.[1]

What was your role in the Venezuela project?

I was a member of the curriculum writing team. I wrote the unit on inventive thinking with the collaboration of my colleague, Catalina Laserna. I also did a certain amount of work on teacher training and course evaluation. I made a number of trips to Venezuela, worked with the teachers, observed classes, things of that character.

Your office here at Harvard is called Project Zero. Why?

Well, Project Zero was originally founded by a Harvard philosopher, Nelson Goodman, in 1967. He hoped to better understand the philosophy and psychology of the arts in order to make recommendations for the improvement of arts education. Since then, the project has broadened out considerably. While still working on the arts, now we encompass a number of other interests having to do with cognitive skills and human development.

Anyway, at the time, Nelson's estimate of the state of *general communicable* knowledge about arts education was zero, so that's what he called the project. And we have lived with the name with some agony and some amusement.

Would you say that the state of knowledge is somewhat above zero now?

Yes, I think it is.

What have you learned about creativity that wasn't common knowledge earlier?

One important thing that I have learned from synthesizing the literature relates to testing creativity. Tests of creativity generally call for "ideational fluency"; they ask you to generate lots of ideas and they rate you on the quality and number of those ideas. Unfortunately, performance on that kind of test does not seem to have much to do with real creativity. People of demonstrated creativity, people who are acknowledged by their peers as being among the more creative members of their profession, do not necessarily score high on measures of ideational fluency.

This may seem a minor matter, but it's fairly important, not only because it affects how you measure creativity in students or employees but because it limits the validity of research. I often read in research journals about somebody trying to teach creativity and measuring the results with a test of ideational fluency. Every time I see that, I throw up my hands and say, "Here's a study that could have told us something we might rely on, but because an unreliable instrument was used, we really don't know whether the author has proven something or not."

The best known creativity tests are probably the Torrance Tests of Creative Thinking.[2] Surely Torrance would argue with what you have said, wouldn't he? What would he say?

I imagine he would say the Torrance tests have done fairly well in predicting real-world creativity. Unfortunately, it's not clear whether his tests differentiate more creative from less creative people at the professional level. Nor in general is a test that correlates with creativity necessarily a good measure of improvements due to instruction; one might simply be teaching to the test.

Anyhow, the literature aside, let me tell you something that comes out of my own work. One of my special interests has been the nature of insight. Many of us share a standard romantic picture of insight. An inspiration hits you out of the blue, perhaps because your mind has been thinking unconsciously about the problem for a long time. In one kind of study I've

David Perkins

done, you catch people right after an insight and debrief them. You ask them about their chain of thought: what happened over the past five or ten seconds that led up to the insight. Interestingly enough, you almost always find a chain of thought.

I came to the conclusion that what seems to come suddenly doesn't come as suddenly as it seems. Typically it's provoked by some object accidentally in the environment or some mental wandering you've been doing that sets your mind along a certain track. In five or ten steps you arrive at an insight and are surprised and delighted by it. But you forget about the five or ten steps.

And yet those steps are relatively fast?

Yes, relatively.

In other words, a computer can operate very quickly but lots of things can go on in that short space of time. Is that what you're saying?

I'm saying it isn't some kind of magic. If you look at the steps that might have led from Darwin's reading of Malthus to his insight about natural selection, you find that each step makes sense. Wallace, who discovered the same principle some years after Darwin and also upon reading Malthus, actually spells out his mental steps. Again, each step makes sense. That doesn't mean that each step is a deductive step—we aren't talking about formal logic—but each step is discernibly connected to the previous step, not a leap, not something arriving out of the blue.

Are you suggesting there isn't any unconscious thought?

That needs to be said carefully. I argue that there is no *extended unconscious* thinking.

There's no question that the moment-to-moment life of the mind is largely unconscious. Our digestion goes on, our breathing goes on, and large parts of our higher-level mental functioning are also plainly unconscious. One of the easiest examples is remembering your phone number. If I ask you for your phone number, the answer pops into your head. Now, clearly, your mind has to do something to retrieve that number—to do a good deal, no doubt—but none of that activity shows.

But we're talking about events on a very different scale. For example, suppose you are trying to solve a math problem. You might imagine that you could come up with the answer after having worked unconsciously on it for hours, much as you would work on it consciously. That's what I mean by extended unconscious thinking. And that's what I claim doesn't occur. When it *seems* to happen, short conscious chains of thought that happen quite rapidly really account for the sudden emergence of a solution.

So one of the things your research is showing is that creativity is not some peculiar gift or mysterious process, but something that can be understood in terms of familiar experience.

That's my broadest position in *The Mind's Best Work*,[3] my book on creativity published in 1981.

I suppose there is no single point more important than the one you just highlighted. If you look to the kinds of mental operations that seem to figure in creative thinking, you can virtually always find analogies for these operations in more mundane thinking. You find, for instance, that often a creative insight occurs by recognizing a pattern or by remembering something. Now, not every process of remembering is creative, of course, but the ones that are creative seem to come about by way of the same psychological mechanisms as the ones that are not.

Okay, it's fair to ask, if the mechanisms aren't different, what is different? Why are these moments of remembering creative and those others not so creative? The difference ties in intentionality: in what one asks one's mind to do. If I'm a poet and I am trying to draw from my memory a good word to use, I probably ask myself to remember an interesting word, a word with a twist, not something straight. And my memory obliges. In general, creative people call upon their minds with questions different from those less creative people ask of themselves.

This is very clear, for instance, when one looks into the biographies of scientists who've proven themselves creative. They often quite deliberately seek out a problem that is a little off to the side of the conventional topics or techniques of their colleagues. They're seeking the challenges, the interesting possibilities. The romantic image of creativity is that it bubbles up or blossoms out spontaneously. But biographical data suggest that a lot of creativity comes about because that's what the person is trying to do.

You contend that creativity is not an ability. What is it, then?

I like to say it's a style—a way of deploying one's abilities. We've just talked about one way of deploying those abilities: the creative person asks of his or her abilities that they operate in certain directions. Another very good example is problem finding. Creative people tend to be less solution-minded than noncreative people. They think hard not just about what the answer is to the problem they already have or that somebody gave them, but what the problem should be: how the problem might be formulated, how it might be reformulated. They think about whether the problem is worth addressing or whether they should be addressing some other problem instead—because the other problem gives them more leverage, because it's more provocative, or because it cuts in a more interesting direction. Here again we find in the creative person a different pattern of attention and intention—a distinctive style of deploying one's abilities.

All this relates to personality, in the most conventional sense of psychometric personality measures. Creative people tend to be more individualistic on personality measures. I spoke earlier about ideational fluency measures. Interestingly enough, personality measures detect truly creative individuals with considerably more reliability than do ideational fluency measures.

Then there *are* measures researchers can use to determine whether certain kinds of experiences have contributed to development of creativity?

Yes, we could use personality measures—but the best measure is one's track record. A person's history of creative activities, or uncreative activities, is the best predictor of whether the person will be creative in a certain area in the future. This is documented in the literature. So, ideally, if we want to find out about the impact of, let's say, a creativity course, we ought to track people who took the program and see what they do compared with a control group who didn't take the program. Now, that is difficult to do, and it almost never happens, but it would be the ideal scenario.

As to the content of such programs—the experiences themselves—what have we found out about what schools can do to develop, or at least encourage, creativity?

If you're talking about hard evidence, we've found out surprisingly little. One of the principal reasons for this is the questionable validity of the most popular instruments for measuring creativity. It's been clearly demonstrated that programs of instruction can improve people's performance on these measures, but we don't know whether people who have learned to score higher on such tests behave more creatively in the real world. The courses that improve performance on creativity tests *may* also improve people's real creativity, but in terms of hard evidence, we don't know.

Now, let me talk about somewhat more specialized situations. There is very clear evidence in the literature that mathematical problem-solving skills can be improved. An experiment done by Allan Schoenfeld,[4] for example, got very strong improvements. As part of the Venezuela project, we did some post-testing on inventive thinking abilities on a design task. I should say that the unit on inventive thinking was organized around the notion of "design." We found that on a simple design activity—designing a table for a very small apartment—the treatment group did far better than the control group. I like that kind of task because it has ecological validity. I like Schoenfeld's mathematical problem-solving tasks for the same reason. Both test learners by asking them to do the sorts of tasks you want them to learn to do, rather than tasks that have little ecological validity.

There must be a couple of other cases like these around, although none come to mind immediately. So there are positive signs here and there, most of it in work done since the heyday of measuring ideational fluency. But we would know a lot more at this point were it not for the problem of these ideational fluency instruments.

> **"The romantic image of creativity is that it bubbles up or blossoms out spontaneously. But . . . a lot of creativity comes about because that's what a person is trying to do."**

Your idea of "creativity by design,"[5] then, comes from your study of this field and your feeling that a design approach is probably one of the better ways for schools to encourage creativity in their students.

I came up with that when we were planning a unit on inventive thinking for Odyssey. Design is a powerful concept. In the first place, creativity involves creative products. Whether it's a pun you make on the spur of the moment, or a painting, or the theory of relativity, you can think of that product as a humanly created design—that is, something with a particular structure adapted to its intended purpose.

We can think about both concrete and abstract things as designs. For example, a pencil is designed with a certain structure organized to serve well a certain purpose. But you can also think of the Pythagorean theorem as a design. You can ask about it the same kinds of questions you might ask about a pencil: What purpose is it supposed to serve? Why is it designed this way? Why not some other way?

Thus, there's enormous opportunity in the concept of design to bridge from talking about concrete things like pencils and paper clips to more abstract things like processes: shopping in the supermarket, for instance, or the algorithm for long division, or computer programs. The same holds for constructive as well as analytical activities. You can bridge from designing a highly portable chair to more abstract inventive tasks such as designing a law. Laws are a good example of design because they're so calculatedly worked over to serve certain social purposes. Or to designing a theory. Another richness in the concept of design is that it can bridge across disciplines; one can talk about the design of a poem or the design of an equation. In my *Knowledge as Design*,[6] appearing this spring, I try to detail how instruction can be reframed by the concept of design.

Design certainly goes far beyond the arts.

Far beyond. It's good not only for talking about creative thinking but for critical thinking. An argument, for instance, is a design; it's a kind of truth-testing machine.

We hear more and more about critical thinking these days. How do you relate critical thinking to creative thinking? Do they have similar attributes, or are they quite different? Do you find them in the same individuals, or do some people do one better than the other?

From a philosophical standpoint, the two can't be clearly separated. The creative thinker has to be critically aware, because creative thinking, except in the simplest situations, involves the generation and sifting of possibilities and reworking them. That has to be a critical process.

I've noticed that you stress the objectivity of creative people, and objectivity is certainly one of the qualities of the critical thinker.

Absolutely. And if you're talking about really good critical thinking, you're talking about thinking that is insightful. It's not just nitpicking; it cuts to the heart of the matter—and that, rather plainly, is creative thinking. So, from a philosophical point, one has to acknowledge that the two are hand-in-glove and it can't be any other way.

On the other hand, one can acknowledge that and still talk in terms of balance or emphasis. People produce a lot of products of one sort or another. Some of those products are what you might call *primary* products:

things like paintings, poems, movies, and theories. Some of them are what you might call *critical* products: critical reviews of, or examinations of, the primary products. The better critical products are themselves creative; they represent profound insight into the nature of the primary products. Nevertheless, some people have more of a flair in one direction and some in the other.

The kinds of dispositions and abilities that Robert Ennis talks about as characteristics of critical thinkers might or might not be found, I suppose, in a person who produces the most creative designs. We just don't know, do we?

No, we don't, and there's a good reason why the question is up in the air not only empirically but conceptually. There's critical thinking and critical thinking, you might say. A fair amount of critical thinking has to do with the soundness of propositions and the sorts of grounds one advances for propositions. Now, some areas of creative work are rather propositional, and some aren't.

Let's take psychology, for example. You advance a theory in psychology and try to do experiments to prove it. Part of your competence is to be fairly handy with the sorts of arguments that provide the checks and balances for psychological theorizing. So I don't think it's very likely that in psychology one would find a person of acknowledged great creativity who is just plain bad at the critical side of things, because the evidence wouldn't be any good; the person wouldn't get into the journals and attain renown.

But let's take poetry writing or painting. These are not the sorts of fields in which one as handily tests the soundness of one's position by argumentation or by looking to see whether the evidence is there. So I could easily imagine there being a poet or painter of acknowledged creativity who was not very good at argumentative discourse.

Now, that doesn't mean that this person is not a critical thinker, but rather the critical thinking is very perceptual, very gestalt in character, very much oriented toward statements like—if one wants to put them into verbal terms—"That's too red; it shouldn't be as red as that," "That's too strong," or "That's not strong enough," or "That shouldn't be here, it would work better over here because the result is better balanced"—or "because the result is more interestingly unbalanced"—critical insights like that. Now, such judgments may or may not have some connection with extended, strongly verbal, critical discourse. I don't think I want to say they don't have anything to do with it, but it's just not clear that they do.

And in schools, where we want to develop both creative and critical thinkers, the kinds of experiences we might purposefully provide to do the one would not necessarily be the same as what we do for the other.

Yes. I think it's very important to work on argumentation and, in fact, a lot of my research—apart from the creativity work—concerns ability to handle arguments. But, ideally, I would work not only on argument but also on connoisseurship, where one heightens one's critical perceptions of things. We need to do both, although I admit I know a lot less about how to do the second than the first. We know more about argument and fostering discursive reasoning abilities than

"The courses that improve performance on creativity tests *may* also improve people's real creativity, but in terms of hard evidence, we don't know."

about how to foster the acute eye or the acute ear.

What is the place of exercises like those in Odyssey in developing thinking skills? The exercises educators are used to are ordinarily related to subject matter of some sort. Some of the thinking skills materials—Instrumental Enrichment, SOI, Strategic Reasoning, and Odyssey—do not focus on content; they're intended to develop the mind so that it's prepared to deal with school content later on. Some people say that's not a good idea; we should teach thinking in the context of a subject-centered curriculum.

What we're really talking about here is the problem of transfer: in a program of instruction intended to foster thinking skills, the students do something; the question is what that has to do with the payoffs that may occur in real life and in the teaching of conventional subject matter.

One point is that, if some of these activities don't have much to do with what now happens in the classroom, maybe they should. For instance, one of the units in Odyssey is about decision making. Now, it's pretty clear why one should be a good decision maker, and there are all sorts of situations in real life in which one might benefit from knowing the sort of strategies taught in the decision-making unit. It so happens that conventional school performance may not benefit very much from decision-making skills because students are not expected to engage in making decisions very much as part of their academic programs. But I would say they should be.

The design sequence—the sequence on inventive thinking—is another example. Broadly speaking, life is conducted in terms of products and projects. We design things and engage in projects that yield things. Again, this is the sort of thinking that could well transfer to the classroom if students were doing those sorts of things—but in most classrooms they aren't.

Now let's talk about a different kind of connection. For some of the sorts of exercises you see in Odyssey and in other programs, such as Instrumental Enrichment, this isn't so. The activity is not one you would spend a lot of time on in any everyday context.

For example, there are problems like "What will be the day after the day after tomorrow if the day before yesterday was Wednesday?" Now, that's not the sort of question you go about asking yourself in or out of classrooms. It is the kind of question, however, that pushes you to track very closely what you are doing: to break the problem into parts and approach it systematically.

So what? The research literature shows that there are difficulties in subject matter thinking and in real life or professional level thinking having to do with what you might call cognitive style: being precise, systematic, imaginative, and so on. Some people think that certain sorts of exercises, though lacking transparent connection with conventional subject areas, foster such styles of learning.

This is certainly the case with the work of Reuven Feuerstein.[7] It isn't that Feuerstein assumes that such skills will spontaneously transfer, but merely that they are best learned initially in sharply defined and isolated contexts. Then you shift them over to the application context by bridging activities intended to expedite transfer. Similarly, in at least some of the Odyssey lessons there are activities called "challenges," where the students are asked to take a strategy or process they have learned and plug it into an out-of-school context.

So you're saying that under the right circumstances these exercises could be valuable.

That's what I'm saying, but I'd also have to say that it's not really clear to what extent that's so. With Instrumental Enrichment you have the bridging, so, in a way, the question of spontaneous transfer doesn't arise. But I understand from talking to John Bransford and others that the bridging is often neglected, so by no means do you always get transfer from Feuerstein's materials. Likewise, there may not be enough bridging in some of the Odyssey materials. You give it a try, and hope the teachers are doing the bridging as you asked them to, and see what you get. Maybe in a decade we'll have a lot sharper sense of how much you

"If you're talking about really good critical thinking, you're talking about thinking that is insightful. . . . it cuts to the heart of the matter—and that, rather plainly, is creative thinking."

have to work to ensure transfer. This is one of the fuzzy areas at the moment, although everyone agrees you have to do it.

Some psychologists, particularly Robert Glaser,[8] contend that thinking ability is closely related to the level of one's specialized knowledge. They interpret that to mean that rather than offering separate thinking skills programs, schools should concentrate on teaching science and reading and mathematics in such ways that people learn to think better through those content areas. What comments do you have on that?

Well, that's one way to deal with transfer. By teaching thinking in context, you finesse the transfer problem. First of all, though, to Glaser—and to me—teaching those subjects well does not mean teaching them in the usual way. On the contrary, it means teaching with much more consciousness of the kind of thinking that needs to be done, and with much more engagement of the students in genuine problem solving, genuine inventive tasks, genuine critical appraisal, and so on. So what they, and I, have in mind in fact represents a considerable revision

in teaching style.

Second is the issue of a stand-alone course versus integration of thinking skills with subject matters. Now, that's a very tricky issue for all sorts of reasons. First, it's not an either/or. Given the resources, you might do both—and both may be the best thing to do. Moreover, there's the issue of focused effort with big payoffs versus a broad spectrum approach with modest payoffs. One of the buzz words in the field of teaching thinking is the "power-generality trade-off." What that means is that very general strategies such as Edward de Bono's[9] heuristics, for instance, are unlikely to be extremely powerful in any one application, because an area such as mathematical problem solving or poetry writing has its special lore that is fine-tuned to that application. One reason for teaching a stand-alone course is that you may prefer modest payoffs across a whole range of subject matters. Then again, you may prefer depth rather than breadth, which favors integration.

Yet another issue has to do with the practicalities of the school setting. You can install a stand-alone course pretty easily; all you need is one teacher who's willing to teach it and has the flair and the time for it. There are many such courses around, and some of them seem pretty decent. But is a year's course enough? Integration gives you much more instructional time. But, changing the way a teacher teaches physics or English or history is quite a challenge. Teachers already have their habits of teaching their subjects in a certain way. These habits can be hard to change. You also face the momentum in the text itself and sometimes in the state-prescribed curriculum. You're also not talking any longer about one course that will be taught for two semesters in the first year of high school. Extensive integration with subject matters involves plurals: there are a lot of subject matters and several years of each to worry about. It's not quite clear how you get started on such a grand effort or how you see it through. In summary, there are arguments on both sides—for stand-alone courses and for integration. It's a complex issue that yields no easy resolution.

Recognizing these things, what would you say to a school principal who said, "I'd like to do a better job of teaching thinking skills in this school. How do I get started?"

That is a question I've been asked before, and I keep rethinking my answer. My recipe of the week might go something like this: the first and most important thing is to build up some excitement. Talk it around, have a seminar, circulate some readings.

You need interest on two fronts. You need interest among some teachers—not necessarily all the teachers, not even a majority, but at least a few—and you need commitment at the managerial level: superintendent, principals, curriculum coordinators, at least some of them have to really care. If they don't, an individual teacher may try something, but it will die on the vine or when that teacher leaves. The institutional commitment is most important, because there are always a fair number of teachers who are interested in this sort of thing.

Then the interested teachers and administrators should look at some things that have been done—not a lot, because too much has been tried. It is really self-defeating to wait until one has a sense of everything that has been attempted. Look at a few model cases. I would recommend, in fact, the book *The Teaching of Thinking*, which tries to summarize the state of the art and reviews a number of the existing programs.[10] I would also recommend ASCD's *Developing Minds*.[11]

Most important, don't just read and talk; try some things. Once people start to try things, they really get excited. Of course, that's when things start to go wrong, too, but that's what makes it interesting. There's no reason to expect to magically transform a school system in a short period of time; we all should recognize that and practice patience.

So where do you hope this movement is taking us?

Sometimes I like to put it this way: I hope it's a fruitful fad. It's clearly getting to be a bit of a fad. Now some fads come and go, and some fads settle in. A good example is the ecology fad. A few years ago it was a fad, but now it's part of the culture. You do not see as much protesting and rhetoric, but if you want to do x, y, or z, you had better think about the effects on the environment, because there's a general public consciousness about the problem.

I would like to see that happen with the teaching of thinking. I would like to see enough people concerned, enough school systems to have tried things, enough research to be done, enough policies in government acknowledging and supporting such efforts, that it becomes second nature that we're concerned with students' thinking. Sure, different people may be worrying about it in different ways, but that's okay; if it's part of the atmosphere, good things are likely to happen.

There's another scenario, however, Unless we hit what you might call a critical mass, unless enough people have enough success over the next five years, let's say, for it to be widely recognized that this is a worthwhile thing to do, it's likely to blow over, and we will be back where we were a decade ago. Now, it's not all that easy to foster thinking skills, and if a hundred ways are tried and only five of them really work well, it would be easy for the five to get lost in the noise. Unfortunately, right now most programs are underevaluated.

One difficulty is that the more complex, sophisticated, difficult, and expensive programs are not as widely used because they are hard to do.

That's a problem that should be taken very seriously by the field. In general, then, my hope is for a fruitful fad that matures, settles in, and stays around. I want to help that to happen. I know you and ASCD are working toward that. All of us working in the field need to invest ourselves. We need to *make* it happen.□

1. *Odyssey: A Curriculum for Thinking* (Watertown, Mass.: Mastery Education, 1986); and *Final Report, Project Intelligence: The Development of Procedures to Enhance Thinking Skills* (Cambridge, Mass.: Bolt, Beranek, and Newman, 1983).

2. E. P. Torrance, *The Torrance Tests of Creative Thinking: Norms-Technical Manual* (Bensenville, Ill.: Scholastic Testing Service, 1974).

3. D. N. Perkins, *The Mind's Best Work* (Cambridge, Mass.: Harvard University Press, 1981).

4. A. H. Schoenfeld, "Measures of Problem-Solving Performance and of Problem-Solving Instruction," *Journal for Research in Mathematics Education* 13 (1982): 31–49; and A. H. Schoenfeld and D. J. Herrmann, "Problem Perception and Knowledge Structure in Expert and Novice Mathematical Problem Solvers," *Journal of Experimental Psychology: Learning, Memory, and Cognition* 8 (1982): 484–494.

5. D. N. Perkins, "Creativity by Design," *Educational Leadership* 42 (September 1984): 18–25.

6. D. N. Perkins, *Knowledge as Design* (Hillsdale, N.J.: Lawrence Erlbaum Associates, 1986).

7. R. Feuerstein, *Instrumental Enrichment: An Intervention Program for Cognitive Modifiability* (Baltimore: University Park Press, 1980).

8. R. Glaser, "Education and Thinking: The Role of Knowledge," *American Psychologist* 39 (February 1984): 93-104.

9. E. de Bono, *CoRT Thinking* (Blandford, Dorset, England: Direct Education Services Limited, 1973–75); and E. de Bono, "The Cognitive Research Trust (CoRT) Thinking Program" in *Thinking: The Expanding Frontier*, ed. W. Maxwell (Hillsdale, N.J.: Lawrence Erlbaum Associates, 1983).

10. R. Nickerson, D. N. Perkins, and E. Smith, *The Teaching of Thinking* (Hillsdale, N.J.: Lawrence Erlbaum Associates, 1985).

11. A. L. Costa, ed. *Developing Minds: A Resource Book for Teaching Thinking* (Alexandria, Va.: Association for Supervision and Curriculum Development, 1985).

David Perkins is codirector, Harvard Project Zero, Harvard University, Graduate School of Education, 315 Longfellow Hall, Appian Way, Cambridge, MA 02138.
Ronald S. Brandt is executive editor, Association for Supervision and Curriculum Development, 125 N. West St., Alexandria, VA 22314.

Educational Leadership 46 (Dec. 1988/Jan. 1989): 12-16

RON BRANDT

On Learning Research: A Conversation with Lauren Resnick

You are co-director of a major center for research on cognitive learning. How is research on learning being done these days?

Researchers are beginning to pay more attention to learning as it occurs in real-life settings—settings that include, but are not limited to, schools. There isn't as much study of informal, out-of-school learning as one might wish, but there is some.

Then there's research in the laboratory, which may be just a corner of a classroom where a child comes and works for a time on special problems. But even that kind of research is now likely to be concerned with the learning of complex subject matter. The days of paired associates and nonsense syllables are over.

When I was trained as a teacher, our ed. psych. textbooks listed principles of learning, some of which, I think, were derived from studies with animals.

That's true. There was a long and quite productive period of research in which principles of human learning and the learning of animals were rather closely linked. As long as we were studying forms of learning that were relatively simple, in which ver-

balization was not central, in which the kinds of representational forms that, as far as we know, only humans use, were not so important, it was possible to find strong parallels between human and animal learning. Under those conditions it was more convenient to do the studies with animals. They didn't get bored as easily; they didn't have other things to do with their time.

It has become fashionable in some circles to dismiss that kind of research as "rat psychology."

I wouldn't dismiss it. The arithmetic textbooks of 1950 were quite different

> Just as knowledge is not a collection of separate facts, so learning competence is not a collection of separate skills.

from those of 1900 and much more effective. We have questions now about how much of the math content they were teaching at those earlier times should be at the core of today's mathematics curriculum; but, if you want to teach those computational skills, you can do it well or badly. And we got to know how to do it very well, in large part through the work of psychologists like Edward L. Thorndike, whose work began with cats. These days, of course, we want to do more than teach rote calculation skills. We're reaching for new goals concerned with thinking, reflection, understanding, so those older psychologies cannot answer today's questions.

Does that mean we now have a new kind of research on learning?

Well, it's in progress. We don't have a finished psychology from which to draw clear educational prescriptions. But we have a vibrant research field with definite implications to be explored.

Some inservice trainers claim that we do have a large body of research about how people learn and we simply have to apply it.

If we accept an outdated definition of what it means to know something,

Photograph courtesy University of Pittsburgh

they are correct. That is, if knowledge consists of small bits of information to be accumulated, then we know how it is learned and therefore how to teach it. In that case the pedagogy has to do with how you organize practice, how you structure and sequence the material, and how you manage motivation.

You're saying that, for example, if that's how you view learning, then it's important to know that spaced practice is more effective than massed practice.

Right, but if you view knowledge as something more than an accumulation of little bits, if you want students to understand and be able to use knowledge reflectively, that's different.

Of course, some things should still be taught through drill and practice.

Absolutely. But for some of the new goals that go under the rubric of thinking, we definitely don't know everything we need to know. In fact, the story's even a little worse than that; my hypothesis is that some of what we "know" about learning conflicts with the goal of teaching thinking. There are ways in which the two are incompatible.

For example?

If you believe that mathematics is a collection of specific pieces of knowledge, it is very reasonable to build tests that sample that knowledge. That's what we have in current achievement tests: collections of items, each of which has a right answer. And those tests encourage

As co-director of the Learning Research and Development Center at the University of Pittsburgh, Lauren Resnick is abundantly qualified to interpret the current research on learning. She is recent past president of the American Educational Research Association, author of *Education and Learning to Think*, a 1987 report on teaching thinking published by the National Research Council, and editor of ASCD's 1989 yearbook. In this interview she tells how cognitive research is changing and what it means for practitioners.

teaching that emphasizes bits of knowledge because that's how you improve students' scores. With the kind of teaching those tests promote, children come to believe that mathematics is a collection of questions to which one can find the answer within about a minute, or not at all.

Either you know how to do this particular trick or you don't—

And that is contradictory to the goal of having children come to believe that mathematics is an organized system of thought that they are capable of figuring out.

I use mathematics as an example because a lot of current research deals with mathematics learning, but the same story can be told for literally every subject.

It would seem that this new definition of what it means to "know" would make the researcher's job much more complex.

Well, for one thing, researchers can no longer avoid a certain amount of subject-matter specialization. One of the great luxuries of the old-style research on learning was that you could look for principles that had general validity. Now we believe that we must first immerse ourselves in the study of how people learn particular things in particular environments.

How do researchers go about doing this new kind of research?

Every possible methodology, experimental and observational, has its place. In fact, we ought not to accept a new finding until the phenomenon has been studied by several people using several different methodologies. Our knowledge of learning is a cumulative matter, not a matter of revealed truth coming from any one investigator or any single study.

Can you give an example?

Well, one way to study learning is by watching a single child try to figure out over an extended period of time how certain mathematical structures work. The experimenter would probably also conduct clinical interviews, probing carefully for hints about the

> **With the kind of teaching those tests promote, children come to believe that mathematics is a collection of questions to which one can find the answer within about a minute, or not at all.**

child's understanding. Then he or she might try to build a very detailed analysis of that child's changing knowledge, including what circumstances seemed to produce the changes.

It has also proved helpful to build computer models that "learn" more or less the same material and in much the same way that a child does. These models don't tell us that children are computers; that's not the point. They help us devise strongly specified theories of what children might be thinking.

Some researchers continue to conduct formal experiments, don't they?

Yes. In the experimental tradition the investigator gets a good baseline assessment of what children know, then intervenes in some way, and tracks any changes.

To what extent does the current research on learning focus on what are referred to as "strategies"?

There are mental processes that learners can deliberately recruit to help themselves learn or understand something new, and some researchers and teachers are trying to train people in the use of these "strategies." When I assessed the research literature in this area three years ago, I concluded that strategy training by itself does not get us very far. Just as knowledge is not a collection of separate facts, so learning competence is not a collection of separate skills. Learning competence does indeed involve having certain strategies, but more than anything it seems to involve knowing when to use them and—to put it simply—wanting to bother using them.

I think that attention to strategies will not be effective unless there is also attention to self-monitoring and motivation. Competence is much more holistic than we used to think. The thing that seems to be most general is a perception of oneself as capable of organizing one's attentional resources. I'm inclined to believe that that sense of being in control, rather than any particular set of cognitive strategies, is what turns out to be general.

It may be analogous to our efforts to teach spelling. Many years ago analysts developed numerous rules for how to spell English words. Some children are naturally good spellers, but we've sometimes tried conscientiously to teach the others to follow these rules. The problem is that the kids who are the poor spellers are also the ones who have the most difficulty remembering and applying all those rules.

In addition, the poor spellers have the hardest time noticing when they don't know how to spell a word and therefore need a rule. And that may be the single largest difference between good spellers and bad spellers: good spellers have a kind of built-in monitoring function, so they immediately notice misspelled words.

And you're saying that when we try to teach learning strategies, we can run into the same kind of problem?

Let me put it another way. At the moment we know quite a bit about what discriminates able people from not so able ones. For one thing we know they employ these strategies of various kinds. What we don't know is whether you can directly put the strategies into other people.

And yet the whole business may in the long run be very productive.

Well, some researchers are betting on that and are trying various ways of directly teaching these strategies. Others, however—and I'm among the others—are betting that it's just too easy a way to try to solve this very complicated question. We're betting that the solution includes development of self-monitoring ability, that it includes definition of oneself as someone who's able to do these complex things, and that the specific strategies will have to be embedded in content.

I'm still not sure I understand why the emphasis on content.

This is probably the single most important theoretical issue in the field of learning research, and nobody knows the answers. In fact, nobody even knows exactly how to formulate the questions. We're having trouble figuring out what we mean by strategies and whether self-monitoring and motivation are separate from strategies or part of them. But there's another factor: doing this self-monitoring, and knowing when and how to apply strategies, may turn out to be quite subject matter- and situation-specific.

I mentioned earlier the principles of learning in psychology textbooks. What can you say about the products of this new kind of research? Can the findings be summarized as general principles of learning?

Yes, but they don't translate into instructional practice quite as easily as the earlier findings. What people learn is virtually never a direct replica of what they have read or been told or

even of what they have been drilled on. We know that to understand something is to interpret it and, further, that our interpretation is based partly on what we've been told or have read, but also on what we already know and on general reasoning and logical abilities.

Now, that does not mean that all learning must therefore be through discovery; it definitely does *not* say that. What it does say is that it is not enough just to focus on making an excellent presentation, because you cannot assume that your elegant explanation will be heard and understood in its entirety. In fact, you can be almost 99 percent sure that no child in your classroom will get it the way you said it. Most children will get some portion of what you said but not all of it, a few will get it totally garbled, and a few will go beyond what you said.

Leinhardt (1987) did an interesting study of an expert teacher's teaching regrouping in subtraction. The teacher gave a very clear explanation, she used manipulatives, and so on. She did all the things you could hope for. But when the researcher interviewed the individual children to see what they had learned, she found partial knowledge and misunderstandings, along with a few instances in which children constructed genuinely new explanations. We have to figure out how to teach in ways that don't just "impart"

> ## That's what we have in current achievement tests: collections of items, each of which has a right answer.

knowledge, but instead help students to construct their own interpretations.

And that's true even when the students are motivated, are trying to understand.

Yes, they are constructing knowledge, filling in gaps, and interpreting *in order to* understand. This isn't something that happens only in school. The same thing goes on in conversations: speakers do not say everything that might need to be said, and listeners do not just take in the words of the speaker. No message is 100 percent complete; there are always gaps. Comprehension takes place when the speaker and the listener construct a common space of representation. But it's almost never 100 percent in common. There is usually some difference between the ideas of two people even when they use the same words.

Now this constructivist principle leads us to a new view of errors in learning. When we find an error, we need to see whether there's an underlying idea behind it. Very often there is.

An error is also learning, then, in a way?

Yes. We used to think of errors as just mistakes, something to be gotten rid of, but now we see that errors are frequently the result of a person's trying hard to make sense of something. It follows that teachers may not always want to teach the rules and "tricks of the trade" that get rid of errors, because they might be getting rid of the clues they need in order to follow their students' thinking.

I'm wondering about how what you've said applies to practitioners. As you know, the research on teaching conducted in the '70s and early '80s produced numerous generalizations about the kind of classroom teaching that produces higher test scores. It was relatively easy to summarize and convey to teachers because it was at the level of observable behavior. It described what these teachers did in generic terms: they made their objectives clear, had smooth transitions, gave guided practice, and so on. But the kind

of learning research you are talking about will be less appealing to generalists because it will not be easily generalizable. How does one derive statements applicable to other teachers from descriptions of how excellent teachers teach particular topics in the humanities, for example?

It's very hard. You can produce descriptive statements, but you soon discover that they are not adequate as prescriptions. For example, you might observe that good teachers ask questions that lead students to see analogies. Well, that's fine at the descriptive level; but it isn't much help to the person who says, "Okay, I'll try to do that," because asking such a question in a physics lesson is quite different from asking it in a history lesson. In each case it depends on the teacher's having some idea about what constitutes a good analogy, which in turn means he or she must know the subject matter well. The clear implication is that teachers may be guided by principles of learning, but they will have to rely on their own subject matter knowledge and communication skills in specific cases.

What you have said would seem to have implications for teacher in-service and supervision.

Right. As you know, I believe we must make thinking the main agenda of our schools (Resnick 1987), and that won't happen unless teachers are expected to think. It certainly won't happen if supervisors try to tell them exactly what to do, even if the directives are supposedly derived from research. Research must play a different role; we have to build a new model.

What's the alternative?

Researchers will need to provide a body of research-based theory that will have to be thoroughly understood in the context of the particular subject matter being taught. We will have to get better at communicating what we do know—we don't know enough yet—but practitioners cannot expect from us, if they ever did, simplified prescriptions for what to do next.□

References

Leinhardt, G. (1987). "Development of an Expert Explanation: An Analysis of a Sequence of Subtraction Lessons." *Cognition and Instruction* 4: 225-282.

Resnick, L. B. *Education and Learning to Think.* Washington, D.C.: Academy Press, 1987

Lauren B. Resnick is Professor of Psychology and Director of the Learning Research and Development Center, University of Pittsburgh, 3939 O'Hara St., Pittsburgh, PA 15260. **Ron Brandt** is ASCD's Executive Editor.

Educational Leadership 43 (Nov. 1985): 20-22

RON BRANDT

On Teacher Career Development: A Conversation with Phillip Schlechty

As Professor of Education at the University of North Carolina-Chapel Hill and Special Assistant to the Superintendent of the Charlotte-Mecklenburg schools, Phillip Schlechty helped design that district's exciting and ambitious teacher career development program. In January 1985, he became the Executive Director of the Gheens Professional Development Center in Louisville, Kentucky, where he hopes to develop a model of school-university cooperation while helping to reshape the teaching profession.

What is your new role with the University of Louisville and the Jefferson County Public Schools?

We're establishing an academy that will link the university and the public schools in a very different configuration. In another five to eight years, we hope it will look much like a medical school, with the school site serving as a teaching hospital. People would come into the academy as interns and residents and fellows. There would be systematic training and induction as well as research and development. We're exploring the notion of having a few carefully chosen schools that will become the teacher training centers for the school system.

People will also be coming for continuing education, so university personnel as well as public school personnel will be part of the system. They will operate as equals: some people employed strictly by the academy, others by the academy and the university, others by the school system and the academy.

In short, you're going to have more control over many of the factors that affect career development in our profession.

Yes, and I think we are in a good position to develop this control. We've got a university that's really interested in working in a large urban school system, a board of education committed to improvement of public education, and a business community solidly behind it. There's a superintendent who recognizes that to improve schools we've got to develop people. I think it's an unusual opportunity to bring to fruition a number of ideas that seemed rather radical ten years ago.

In Charlotte-Mecklenburg, was there a great deal of attention paid to working with teachers rather than deciding for them?

Yes, and I intend to follow the same policy here. The very first thing I did was to appoint an advisory committee with heavy representation from teachers' organizations. I spent a vast amount of time talking with teachers and administrators. In fact, I make no decisions without checking with as many teachers and administrators as I can get hold of plus the formal advisory groups: management by wandering around as opposed to management by memo.

At this point, you don't yet have a complete career development plan, right?

We're still working on it. We have identified a building that will be remodeled over the next year and a half to become a full-scale training center. We have developed a means of coordinating the people in-house in charge of staff development, student-teacher placement at the university, student-teacher placement in public schools, and incentives and evaluations. All of these people are operating in connection with the Gheens Center.

To the extent that the career development plan, or whatever it's called, becomes what you personally would like it to be, what characteristics will it have?

What I would like to see is a situation in which people come into the Jefferson County Schools—or into the university, either one—and all their clinical training experiences occur under the guidance and direction of skilled professionals who in one way or another are members of the academy. We will have a management development component, and we will be doing a lot of research; action research will be part of the teacher training curriculum, if you want to call it that. We'll have 15 to 20 school sites where the education of teachers is regarded as important as the education of children.

All this is affected, of course, by teachers' pay and working conditions.

> **"We need a systematic way to assure that the people who pursue lifelong careers in teaching are the kinds of folks we want and that they get the support and encouragement and rewards they deserve."**

It's very difficult. Part of the issue is getting communities to understand what the problems are. Much of it is gaining trust on the part of the teachers. We had a major teacher strike in Jefferson County in 1976, and there are still some scars from that.

But one of the things we see in Jefferson County is that, because of a massive reduction in force over the last ten years—numbers went from something over 7,000 teachers to 5,000—we have an older teacher work force. One of the things we're giving high priority to is developing a systematic induction program for new teachers and new principals because, by the year 2000, most of the people who are presently teaching or running the schools in Jefferson County will no longer be with us. We need to use the talent we've got to develop the talent we're going to get.

How will this influence the roles of people who're now supervisors and principals?

In one of the projects we're trying to get under way, the principal becomes the chief teacher educator. Instead of talking about principals as instructional leaders, we ought to be talking about them as leaders of instructors. One of their primary obligations is the education of those for whom they have administrative responsibility.

Some of the things administrators do now—the things they say keep them from doing what they would like to do—will be diminished, so people who actually like to do those things may find themselves in unimportant roles. People who want to exercise autocratic authority over others, people who want to run massive central staff development, people who enjoy the title "supervisor" because it's got "super" in it, will find themselves a bit threatened. But people who really are committed to human resource development and to the nurturance of professionals will find it exciting.

I believe you have said you agree with Al Shanker that it's pretty hard to get true professional spirit in over two million people. Does that mean that some teachers will be getting higher pay and status than others?

We have to look at this as a 10–15 year project. There are many people who can be good beginning teachers but who do not intend to teach for a career. We need a systematic way to assure that people who do pursue life-long careers in teaching are the kinds of folks we want and that they get the support and encouragement and rewards they deserve.

I want to press a little harder, because I'm not sure I understand your position on differentiation of teacher roles. We're going to have a lot of students out there who have to be taught, which means so many classes to be covered. One way to do it is to extend the responsibility of some teachers and lessen the responsibility of others somewhat. That's the differentiated staffing model, where a team leader has some responsibility for what goes on in other people's classrooms. Now, you've said that's not necessarily part of this model—which suggests that we're back to the one-teacher-per-classroom model.

No, no, no! The Charlotte model, in particular, lends itself to a variety of experiments of that sort. It opens up many possibilities, but it is not tied to any *particular* arrangement. I'm convinced we must try a variety of staffing patterns.

You're not opposed, then, to differentiated staffing plans?

To the contrary. Unless we have different staffing patterns, we simply can't deliver the quality of services the youngsters are entitled to.

Then let's broaden the discussion to talk about the place of educators in our society. You are determined to make teaching more of a profession, and we do see small signs of change. Here and there a state says it's going to have higher salaries, so teachers get a 10 percent or even a 15 percent salary increase. But the next year the legislators seem to think they have taken care of teacher salaries, and it's back to cost of living or less. How in the world do we get real change?

Then there's teacher education. Most people who've spent their lives trying to reform schools of education are exasperated by how absolutely impervious teacher education is. Do you really expect a breakthrough?

When I no longer believe these things can be changed, I'll get out of education. One reason I have great hope is what has happened in the last 15 years in America. A subtle revolution has been taking place in business and industry that has brought us a new breed of leaders who understand that they're really running educational organizations themselves. They have the same kinds of problems that public school people have confronted. The difference is that, because they have had opportunities to explore the issues in different ways and because they have different traditions, they've invented some new responses.

In other words, while there's a great deal of difference between developing youngsters and producing widgets—there's not that much difference between managing public education and managing the production of *knowledge*: for example, managing people who are autonomous professionals at IBM or AT&T or Monsanto. If we can overcome some of our own fears, there's a basis for dialogue between educational leaders and the new breed of business leadership.

So the key, then, is attracting the informed support of these people who are influential in our society?

That's right. And for the first time we have a shared basis and a common urge to support this dialogue.

What might go wrong? What must we guard against?

My greatest concern is that the impetus for reform has come largely from the state level. If we don't watch out the states will destroy excellence by imposing too many minimum standards, which soon become *the* standards. We really need some careful thought about what should be centralized and what decentralized.

You're saying that attempts to change the structure of the teaching profession at the state level may be well intended but questionable?

I think they're a bit premature. We ought to encourage some very strong and sustained local action and then begin to capitalize on that, much as the medical occupation did between 1860 and 1900—because until we've got some firm models that people can believe in, we're really on the cutting edge of ignorance. □

RONALD S. BRANDT   *Educational Leadership* 44 (Nov. 1986): 14-18

On Long-Term Effects of Early Education: A Conversation with Lawrence Schweinhart

You recently reported some new research evidence about the effects of early education.

Yes. We've done a longitudinal study (Schweinhart et al. 1986) comparing three different models of preschool education for disadvantaged three- and four-year-olds. It was a tightly designed experimental study; the three groups of children were very similar to each other on all kinds of demographic characteristics before the study began. And we tried to run each curriculum model as well as we possibly could. The teachers were enthusiastic, they wanted to do the best job possible, and by-and-large, they had the resources to do it. We wanted to find out what the results would be if each of these three programs were done well.

How were the programs different from one another?

First let me mention the similarities. They were all part-day programs—either mornings or afternoons—five days a week. With each program there were home visits that lasted an hour and a half or so every two weeks. In each case the home visits employed the same curriculum philosophy as the classroom components. The teacher-child ratio was about one to eight, which is relatively good but not unrealistic.

Now, the differences: one program was heavily teacher-directed. Basically, we used the model developed by Bereiter and Englemann at the University of Illinois in the '60s that preceded the DISTAR program, now sold by Science Research Associates. Although our version was for preschool rather than school-age kids, we had consulting assistance from representatives of the developers, so we were pretty confident that we were running the program the way they would want it run.

Our other two programs were not so heavily teacher-directed; both focused on child-initiated learning activities. One of the programs was the High/Scope model, in which the teacher and the child engage in collaborative planning. When the child comes in the morning, the teacher says, "Well, what are you going to do today?" After she has encouraged the child to make conscious choices, the teacher's role is largely to facilitate learning. The children go to the various activity areas and the teacher goes around talking to individual children, trying to get them to think about what they're doing and sometimes to elaborate on it in different ways.

The third model was a traditional nursery school in which the teacher tries to respond to the needs of the children as they are expressed. The children choose activities, as in the High/Scope model, but they don't necessarily engage in extensive planning. The important contrast is that the one model is heavily teacher-directed, while in the other two models activities are mostly initiated by individual children.

When we followed the children in these programs to age 15, we found that the young people who had been in the teacher-directed model reported twice as much delinquency as the children who had been in the other two models. We're talking about serious delinquency: those in the teacher-directed model reported five times as many instances of property damage, twice as much personal violence, and twice as much drug abuse. We also found a couple of other things consistent with those findings. For example, the young people who had been through the teacher-directed program reported that their parents didn't think as highly of them (which makes sense since they were engaging in twice as much delinquency). Those students were less likely to engage in sports and other student activities. There was a very clear differentiation between the teacher-directed model and the other two programs.

What about other outcomes?

Well, here's a fascinating thing—and something that raises a serious caution. On short-term measures, such as impact on IQ, all three of these programs were dramatically successful. The average IQ of kids before the programs was 78, while afterward it was 105, 27 points higher!

95

With David Weikart and others, Lawrence Schweinhart has conducted longitudinal research showing that high-quality early education pays off, but their new findings raise questions about the possible side-effects of direct instruction models.

Research Findings Support Child Development Programs

The High/Scope Preschool Curriculum Comparison study (Schweinhart et al. 1986, Weikart et al. 1978) presents empirical evidence in support of the child development approach to early childhood curriculum. This study examined the effects of early childhood programs operating from 1967 to 1970 and using three distinctly different curriculum approaches.

The 68 children from Ypsilanti, Michigan, who participated in the study all lived in low-income families and, according to test results at age three, were at special risk of school failure. They were randomly assigned to three preschool programs, attending them at ages three and four. In each program, classes operated two-and-a-half hours a day, five days a week, with one teacher for every eight children. A teacher visited each child's home for an hour and a half every two weeks, encouraging the mother to engage her child in learning activities that fit the curriculum approach used in that classroom. The teachers were all highly motivated to demonstrate that their curriculum model could be successful, and experts regularly reviewed each program for accurate curriculum implementation. While this study had a small sample of children, it maintained a tight experimental design that generated confidence in its results.

The direct instruction program's classroom activities consisted of carefully prescribed sequences of teacher-child interaction, intended to train children in precisely defined academic skills. For example, a teacher addresses a question to a small group, the children respond with the right answer, and the teacher offers praise. The High/Scope curriculum and the traditional nursery school program represented child-initiated approaches. Teachers in the traditional program encouraged children to engage in free play and activities that matched their needs and interests.

Earlier research had established that, regardless of preschool curriculum received, all study youngsters gained an intellectual head start in school because of their experiences in these well-implemented early childhood programs. The average IQ of study children rose a dramatic 27 points during the first year of program participation, from 78 to 105. Half of this gain eventually disappeared, but at age 10 the average IQ was still 94.

However, in a recent longitudinal study comparing students who participated in the three types of programs, the youths from the two programs featuring child-initiated activities reported that they committed less than half as many acts of juvenile delinquency—including only one-fifth as many instances of property damage and one-half as many of drug abuse. In addition, the teens from the child-initiation programs participated in more sports and extracurricular activities, and their families saw them in a more positive light.

How could early childhood program differences lead to differences in juvenile delinquency? We have not reached definite conclusions, but it's a question worth thinking about. While the direct instruction program was totally teacher-controlled, both the nursery school and High/Scope programs gave children a measure of control over classroom activities, which may have led to greater individual responsibility and initiative. Through home visits every two weeks, the nursery school and High/Scope programs alerted parents to attend to children's needs and interests, while the direct instruction program focused parents' attention on children's performance in academic subjects. In other words, the High/Scope and nursery school programs had explicit social goals for children; the direct instruction program did not.

—by Lawrence Schweinhart

"We're not talking about a panacea for our social problems, but we are saying that here's a workable approach to dealing with these problems—and that's fairly rare."

And that kind of gain was made in what period of time?

After one school year of a part-day program. As usual, by the way, part of the increase wasn't permanent. By age ten, which is the last time we measured it, the average IQ of these kids had fallen, but was still about 15 points higher than it had been originally. So there was some sustained improvement in academic abilities in all three programs.

The point, though, is that if you only look at that—which would be reasonable in terms of the way we evaluate most curriculum models—you would say, "Well, all three of these programs seem to be doing a good job and we recommend them." In fact, we did say that for a number of years. We said as long as you're running a good curriculum model, it doesn't matter what kind it is.

Has this study changed your mind, then?

Yes. We certainly can't make that kind of recommendation now.

But you must have considered the possibility of such a finding, or you wouldn't have run the study in the first place?

Well, originally we may have expected the High/Scope approach to do better, but it didn't turn out that way. So for about ten years, we've not been saying that our curriculum model is the best. In fact, we still don't make that claim on the basis of the data from this study. What we do say now is that *child initiation* seems to be a very important factor: that if you're interested in preventing delinquency, you should give young children opportunities to help design their own learning activities. In other words, you can't do just any kind of a program and expect to get positive results in both cognitive and social areas.

Let me ask a little more about the study. Is it possible that a small number of students accounted for those many acts of misbehavior? How widespread was the delinquency?

The total number of kids in our sample was fairly small—18 per group—but the delinquency was substantial. We were very concerned about the possibility that just one or two kids were responsible, so—for example—we took the one with the highest score and dropped it back to make it the same as the second highest score, and we still found the same thing. We were dealing with a small sample, yes, but it was a real finding for those kids.

A skeptic might say that you probably hoped to find what you found. Is there any danger of experimenter bias? If somebody else had gathered these data, would they have found what you found?

Well, there's a certain schizophrenia in being a researcher who is also interested in program development, because on the one hand you want to see a program work, but on the other you're determined to be very cautious and responsible. In fact, I think the word "conservative" is appropriate, because you want to make sure you don't mess up and make inappropriate claims. There are different degrees of rigor in research; we try to employ the highest standards.

For example, we used completely random assignment. No parent could say, "I want my child in that model." The parent simply agreed to participate in the project, after which the child was assigned to a particular condition on a purely randomized basis.

In this case, you organized and conducted a teacher-directed model—even though you and your colleagues had professional reservations about it—for research purposes. In light of your new findings, would you do that again?

I doubt that the High/Scope Foundation would ever do it again. At the time we did it, we encountered substantial criticism from many early childhood educators. In one case, a teacher said it made her physically sick to see what was going on in that program. Now, I certainly wouldn't go that far; there was no child abuse in any sense. In fact, there are a lot of good things in the program: it emphasizes positive reinforcement, and teachers unquestionably have the highest standards for kids. But the approach apparently has some unintended consequences.

Do you expect the advocates of teacher-directed programs to have second thoughts?

I think they ought to. There'll be resistance to the findings, though. It's a

small study, with only 68 kids in the original group, and we found only about 80 percent of them at age 15. We don't see the study as a basis for public policy, by the way. It doesn't provide answers; it certainly raises questions.

It also suggests that we need more longitudinal studies like yours for other education programs.

It does. They're hard to do, because it's hard to keep samples together. In some cases you have 50 or even 60 percent attrition rates, and under those circumstances it's unclear what you have found. But it's really important.

Let's talk more about that. One of the factors that helps account for the current national interest in early education is the convincing findings of your earlier longitudinal research on the effectiveness of preschool programs.

You're referring to the Perry Preschool Program (Berrueta-Clement et al. 1984), which we evaluated over an even longer period of time. It uses the High/Scope model, so the findings I'll summarize are only for it, and may not apply to all other models.

What we found is that a lot of social problems were prevented. First, the program tended to prevent school failure. It produced higher IQs and therefore reduced the need for special education placement. It ultimately led to a lower high school dropout rate. Then, because it reduced the rate of school failure, the program helped prevent a lot of associated problems. There was a lower delinquency rate, a lower rate of teenage pregnancy among girls. The kids who had been in the program were more likely to be employed, less likely to be on welfare. But let me make clear that these earlier findings were not a comparison of High/Scope with other curriculum models.

They were a comparison of the High/Scope model with . . .

. . .with no program at all. I should say, too, that we didn't find that our program was a cure-all; it didn't *solve* the social problems, although it did help measurably. We're not talking about a panacea for our social problems, but we are saying that here's a workable approach to dealing with these problems—and that's fairly rare.

Your findings provide a rationale for expanding early education, then?

We've done a fairly careful cost-benefit analysis and found that the program pays for itself many times over. That's not just rhetoric; we have data from school systems, from the courts and other sources, that show that our society could actually save money by offering more quality preschool programs.

These findings have proven to be extremely persuasive among policymakers, and they should be. If people want to reduce waste in government, preschool programs are a pretty good bet. We're currently spending more on special education programs than we need to. By that I mean we're treating kids whom we don't need to be treating. We're spending more money on dealing with juvenile delinquency and on high school dropouts than we need to. These problems can be prevented to a degree.

When you say that, you're not talking about just any day care.

No. Because our research has been widely publicized, people sometimes misapply it for their own purposes. We've heard it said that our research shows that Headstart works. It doesn't show that; it shows that it *can* work. It's been said that our research proves day care works, but it doesn't show that either. It shows that day care—specifically *good* day care for *low income* children—*can* work. The findings can't be generalized across the board.

So it's important to say we're not talking here about just any kind of childhood program?

No. There's only one study I know of that's really tried to tackle that issue head-on: the Brookline Early Education Project in the Boston area (Pierson et al. 1984). They found—and I think this is what we would probably find if we did a whole lot more studies—a reduction in academic and social problems among all children who were in a good early childhood program. But the reduction was in different degrees, because the number of problems was different.

Let me simplify to make the point. Let's say that a child at risk will have eight school problems, while another has only two. If both kids go through a good preschool program, in the one case you may prevent six of the problems, so there are two left, while in the other you prevent both school problems. The extent of improvement is not as great, so the return on the investment is not as great. It still may be worth doing, though, because parents and others may consider it valuable for the child to have a little extra edge, socially and academically.

What do you mean by "edge"? Are you talking about learning academic skills earlier?

No. School readiness doesn't mean getting a jump on what you're going to learn in school anyway, and academic edge doesn't mean pushing first-grade expectations down to four-year-olds. The learning of early childhood is different from what needs to be learned in the elementary grades.

School readiness means learning some other things—things that are not self-evidently "academic"; they're not reading, writing, and arithmetic. Young kids don't learn from symbols but from their own concrete, physical environment. They learn from toys, they learn from play, they learn from touching things and moving them around, from their senses, from poking things to see how they react. That's the kind of learning that ought to take place in programs for four-year-olds even if we're tremendously concerned with academic readiness. That's the kind of program that resulted in the reduction in need for special education and in fewer high school dropouts.

You've mentioned that student planning is part of the High/Scope model.

It's one of two critical characteristics that distinguish High/Scope from other child development models. A second is what we call "key experiences": orientation devices that help teachers focus on certain kinds of cognitive and social activities.

An example of that?

Classifying objects: putting things into categories, direct manipulation of objects. Aside from student planning, which is something that's very observable (you can see if it's going on in a classroom or not), the program deals primarily with the orientation of the teacher. High/Scope teachers capitalize on certain kinds of behavior children will naturally engage in and encourage them to take it a little farther.

For example?

If the child is building with blocks, the teacher might encourage him or her to build a little more or to think about what it would be like if this toy car went down that road. It's very simple things like that, as well as cognitive things like, "Have you thought about which car would get there first if one went faster than the other?" Those kinds of questions; lots of teacher-child interaction. It also involves getting kids to work with each other.

You've mentioned a couple of ways the High/Scope program differs from other child development programs. In what ways are they alike?

Basically, a child development program doesn't have desks. It might have tables where kids get together for small-group activities, but not individual desks. It doesn't have a teacher standing in the front of the room. There's probably a rug on the floor in a child development program, because that's where everybody ought to be: down on the floor.

And why is that?

Because little kids aren't very tall, so if teachers want to relate to children on a face-to-face, person-to-person basis, they've got to be down at their level. One of the key elements in all child development programs is that teachers and children talk to each other person-to-person. The biggest danger in programs that don't take this orientation is that the teacher spends too much time talking to the whole group and in some cases almost never talks to children as individuals.

Another hallmark of a good child development program is that toys and other materials are accessible to children without teacher intervention. You will see programs with a different orientation that have similar materials but they're out of reach of the children. Now, that's because the teacher wants to control access—and the reason for that is that the teacher is afraid that the children will misuse the materials. That's understandable, but you've got to create opportunities for them to learn to make choices and to experience the results.

What you've described again and again in this conversation as a "good program" sounds suspiciously like what we used to refer to as "informal" or "open school." A lot of people in our society think that kind of education was thoroughly discredited a few years ago, and they may be surprised to hear you calling it better.

I don't think there was any discrediting. We could talk more broadly about what *seems* to have been discredited, which in fact was *not* discredited: a whole lot of ideas behind the war on poverty fall in that category. They weren't discredited; they just got old. As time went by, the values and expectations of our society shifted. For example, the effective schools and effective teaching movement came to the fore. Now, those movements were basically empirical: they tried to identify the kinds of things going on in schools that were better than other things already going on in schools. So, because well-run open education programs didn't exist in many schools, they never had a chance. In that sense, the effective schools movement is not innovative; it's just trying to make the best of the existing situation.

But we're also talking here about younger children, and their learning needs are different. In any case, if the issue is documentation of what actually works with young children, we have it.□

References

Berrueta-Clement, John R., Lawrence J. Schweinhart, W. Steven Barnett, Ann S. Epstein, and David P. Weikart. *Changed Lives: The Effects of the Perry Preschool Program on Youths Through Age 19.* Monographs of the High/Scope Educational Research Foundation, 8. Ypsilanti, Mich.: High/Scope Press, 1984.

Pierson, Donald E., Deborah Klein Walker, and Terrence Tivnan. "A School-Based Program from Infancy to Kindergarten for Children and Their Parents." *The Personnel and Guidance Journal* (April 1984): 448–455.

Schweinhart, Lawrence J., David P. Weikart, and Mary B. Lerner. "Consequences of Three Preschool Curriculum Models Through Ages 15." *Early Childhood Research Quarterly* 1 (March 1986): 15–45.

Lawrence J. Schweinhart is Director, Voices for Children Project, High/Scope Educational Research Foundation, 600 N. River St., Ypsilanti, MI 48198. **Ronald S. Brandt** is Executive Editor of ASCD.

Educational Leadership 41 (Sept. 1983): 11-13

Harold Shane is currently University Professor of Education, Indiana University, Bloomington.

On Education and the Future: A Conversation with Harold Shane

Harold Shane, author of three books and numerous articles on education and the future, was one of the first curriculum authorities to be recognized as a futurist. When he was ASCD president, in 1974, the annual conference theme was "Creating Curricula for Human Futures" and the keynote speaker was Alvin Toffler, author of *Future Shock*. In this interview with ASCD Executive Editor Ron Brandt, Shane predicts a new renaissance in schooling.

RON BRANDT

Q: Since the early 1970s you've talked with hundreds of leading physical and social scientists around the world. How did these dialogues come about?

Shane: It was largely a benign accident. One evening about ten years ago, I was having dinner with the Commissioner of Education, who asked if I would do a review of some work the U.S. Office of Education was funding at the futures centers at Syracuse and Stanford. I suggested that I might get a broader base by doing 50 or 60 interviews across the country. My report, called *The Educational Significance of the Future*,[1] came out about six months later. One result of the USOE inquiry was that I got involved in a study the NEA was sponsoring for the Bicentennial, called *Curriculum Change Toward the 21st Century*.[2] It was a re-examination of the "Seven Cardinal Principles" made by 50 distinguished Americans to determine if they were still valid after 60 years. Then came the most recent study, which was sponsored by Phi Delta Kappa and funded by the Lilly Endowment.

Q: And that was *Educating for a New Millennium*?[3]

Shane: Yes. It was concerned with what content is essential if we're going to survive and live as decent people. It was based on 132 interviews with physicists, chemists, biologists, anthropologists, economists, and other comparable scientists from all over the world. I wanted to find out what they felt students need to know in their areas of expertise.

Q: Was there much commonality among the views of these scientists?

Shane: They had an amazing tendency to draw on one another's disciplines. Physicists, for example, were very concerned with social trends. Sociologists and anthropologists talked about what they thought was threatening or interesting in the natural sciences. The interdisciplinary tone was very conspicuous, and the scholars agreed as to the nature of the world's problems; they proposed very diverse solutions, however.

Q: Such as?

Shane: Some of the scholars have faith in what is commonly known as "techno-fix" (technological solutions); others— the transformationalists—feel there need to be changes in human behavior. A third group believes we need to restructure and rehabilitate our industrial resources so that the "smokestack" industries—automobile and steel manufacturing—can regain a strong competitive position. Many participants recognized that we also need an infusion of high technology to provide the support system required to make this reindustrialization possible. That's a spectrum of their comments, which I have greatly trivialized by summarizing them so briefly.

Q: From having talked with these scientists, what conclusions did you reach?

Shane: The main concern of the people I've interviewed is whether or not human beings can cope fast enough to deal with the changes and problems that threaten them. John Platt, a biophysicist at Boston University, observed that humans have confronted more changes in the last 40 years than in the previous 600. It reminds me of the old H. G. Wells comment to the effect that we've always relied on a time-lag of a century between perceiving what ought to be done and making an attempt to do it. But now we've got to learn to act rapidly and prudently.

Q: You've been a futurist for some time. How did you decide that educators should pay more attention to the future?

Shane: Back in the early 1960s I was talking with a friend at the Rand Corporation in Santa Monica, and I asked him how it is possible to study things that haven't happened. He said there were a variety of techniques that could be used—the Delphi technique, cross-impact analysis, scenarios, and the like. It occurred to me that perhaps the devastating lag between changing society and changing schools could be reduced if we learned about and applied some of the techniques that were being explored by futurists.

One of the interesting things I discovered was that Rand's long-range forecasts, which were done in the late 50s, had begun to come true by the 60s. These included heart transplants, moon landings, orbiting space ships, and creation of life forms in the laboratory.

Q: Still, many people continue to see futurism as a kind of frivolous activity. Do futurists really know any more about the future than anyone else?

Shane: I have been amazed at the accuracy of some of the prognostications from reliable scholars. For example, Wilbur Cohen, one of the architects of social security, said in 1971 or 72 that social security would go broke by 1980 unless there were massive changes in its funding. That was right on the nose. The energy crunch that peaked during the OPEC embargo was clearly foreseen by most of the futurists I talked to. The ecological problems, the dangers of nuclear warfare, the proliferation of arms, the population explosion—which is disastrous and even more ominous now than it was then—were all predicted.

Q: How well are these problems reflected in the school curriculum?

Shane: I've said for years that there's a chasm to be bridged between acquainting young learners with contemporary trends and the current school curriculum. To the best of my knowledge, there is a whole spectrum of things that ought to be included in English, the sciences, and the social studies. English, for example, needs to emphasize critical listening skills because of the huge amount of auditory and visual input from radio, television, and the computer. We need instruction that can help us interpret the way the media—not manipulate, but—select the news: when, for instance, a reporter tells us what a President has said rather than giving it to us direct. It's not the same as reading a more complete account in the *New York Times* or *Washington Post*. In social studies, science, mathematics, and other fields, we're now moving into an era that is peopled by micro-kids: youngsters growing up in the era of micro-electronics. While it's very important that they have a positive attitude toward the computer and electronic devices, there are also dangers. As Garrett Hardin pointed out, an evolutionary consequence of the computer could be the degeneration of our mental powers as a result of disuse!

Q: Do you believe that some things that are currently taught should be omitted from the curriculum?

Shane: You're asking what we will have to sacrifice? Personally, I don't see a conflict here. It's a matter of enrichment and reshaping what is taught, rather than "chopping block" tactics.

Q: On the other hand, as satirized in *The Saber-Tooth Curriculum*,[4] we have a tendency to teach things we used to need rather than things we will need to know in the future. Mortimer Adler, writing for the Paedeia group,[5] suggests that the way to prepare for the future is to read and discuss great works of the past. Do you agree?

Shane: I think in the sense that our general culture needs to move into a renaissance. We are being encircled, as Marshall McCluhan said, with the "electronic-surround" to the point that to acquire a better understanding of what is occurring we need to have a better general education. A good vocational education, in a sense, is rapidly becoming a good general education and, in a sense, vice versa; general education is acquiring vocational dimensions. For example, there's no place in vocational education for dismantling and reassembling a 1974 Ford or Chevrolet. But there is a very substantial need to help individuals understand not only electronics, but what electronics is doing to our industries and our lifestyles and our educational practices—both in the school and the home.

Q: That suggests an important role for parents.

Shane: Schools must have increasingly close relationships with parents in mediating the way children use equipment in the home. Last weekend, my grandson, who's in the sixth grade, was visiting us and was reading through the Home Box Office list. When I commented that a particular film looked pretty interesting, he said, "Oh, but Grandpa, that's R-rated!" Apparently, there are parents who take some responsibility for TV and other electronic gear in their homes, but there are certainly parents who don't. One of the challenges to education and our society is what to do about this.

Q: In *The Educational Significance of the Future*, you called for certain "fundamental reforms" in the schools. What kind of reforms did you have in mind?

Shane: That particular book, at least in part, was concerned with curriculum organization and structure. The artificial segregation of persons who are not alike is a major problem that has existed in education for many years. What we need is a life-long learning continuum beginning with universal nursery education, and urge that there would be ungraded experiences for children at age four or five who are grouped together until they attained the developmental characteristics of six-year-olds. At age five, six, or seven, and in some cases even eight, children would be grouped with others who had a comparable quality of six-year-old-ness. As Willard Olson pointed out many years ago in his concept of "organismic age," youngsters at a given time are not the same age in any way except chronologically. We need to figure out some way to reduce the ability spread—even though this means increasing the age spread somewhat in a given group.

Q: That's the kind of reform you had in mind?

Shane: Yes. Let me add that our schools have a big problem in doing what the futurists call "retrofitting"—what we used to call "retreading" in times past when teachers needed inservice or graduate study. With the massive changes in production and the new kinds of jobs opening up in the high-tech field, there already are enormous demands on education agencies for the retrofitting, retreading, and re-educating of people; learning experiences which can continue right on through life into our senior years. If our schools do not meet these needs, some other kinds of agencies will—the kind of agencies that already have taken over portions of the instructional monopoly that schools enjoyed in the 50s. One of these, of course, is television.

Q: From current trends and your study of future possibilities, what would you expect to be the condition of public schools in America in the next 10 to 15 years?

Shane: There will be significant and perhaps even a vast increase in flex time and much more learning going on beyond the walls. Many homes will have electronic equipment so that various kinds of distance learning will be possible. In other words, the school under certain circumstances will come to the student. Electronics equipment will make a life-long contribution to education on an increasingly flexible basis.

Q: In *The Educational Significance of the Future*, published just ten years ago, you said, "We have perhaps a dozen years . . . to make basic and educationally relevant policy decisions with regard

to certain crises and problems confronting us."[6] What kind of progress has been made?

Shane: Until recently, I was fairly uneasy about the glacial rate of change in education, sluggish at best, which Goodlad pointed out so eloquently in his Study of Schooling researches. But in the last year or two I have changed my mind somewhat. Back in the 1950s when Sputnik was launched, our society was shaken by the competition implied by Russian technology. A tremendous impetus to education was reflected in funding by the Kennedy and Johnson Administrations. There was an enormously important intellectual and financial transfusion at that time: the "new math" and "new science" era!

We are again on the threshold of a very substantial renaissance in schooling becuase of the coming omnipresent information era. We are benefitted as well as "threatened" by high-tech, as Japan and other nations begin to leave us behind in production races—automobile sales being a good illustration. In view of this threat, I believe a Sputnik-like phenomenon will reoccur. Once again, albeit more slowly, U.S. schools will be more adequately funded.

Q: It seems likely that society will make some adjustment to whatever new forces there are. The question is whether it will be our schools that provide the necessary response. The public schools may not be able to adapt quickly enough.

Shane: There's always that potential danger, and history suggests that we may not. But the situation today is different. Let me put it this way: in addition to the rapid changes that are self-evident—artificial life, fly-bys of the outer planets, gene splicing, the pill—another new element has been added within our generation: people who are moving into positions of responsibility who see their milieu in a different perspective than did educational leaders of the past.

Q: You know a great deal about the future and you are acquainted with the tremendous problems faced by the world and our society. Yet you seem to be somewhat optimistic about the future.

Shane: I am—partly because the rapidity of change and the information society are giving us a spark of the enthusi-

asm analogous to the one that began to glow in the post-Sputnik era. Second, journals like *Educational Leadership* are taking time to speculate and think about the future. There is a growing positive concern—namely, that we have to "make tomorrow work" in school and in society. Furthermore, our young people have "bottomed out" with respect to coping with most of the problems that led to the alienated generation of the 60s and early 70s. Many of them are more thoughtful and task-oriented than they were. I'm not talking about the young returning to mindlessness or bigotry; I'm talking about a general return to thoughtfulness and a departure from the "me generation." This is partly a result of changing parental attitudes, and of growing concerns for the world's future good that are local, national, and international. It may be that the times that are being thrust upon us will, in effect, serve to lubricate our educational efforts to achieve the renaissance that the information society demands.

There's one other thing I really should say. If you're a pessimist, you're likely to just lie down and let the steam roller of the future flatten you. Therefore, I think educators have to be optimists. At his farewell appearance in Washington, D.C., Maurice Chevalier said, "Now zat I am 78 years old, zee reporters zay, 'Monsieur Chevalier, how does eet feel to be 78, eh?' " And Chevalier cocked his straw hat as he used to do and said to his audience, "I zay to zee reporters, 'Eet ees marvelous to be 78—considering zee alternative.' " As curriculum workers, we too have to be optimists or, professionally speaking, face "zee alternative" of decline.☐

[1]Harold G. Shane, *The Educational Significance of the Future* (Bloomington, Ind.: Phi Delta Kappa, Inc., 1973).

[2]Harold G. Shane, *Curriculum Change Toward the 21st Century* (Washington, D.C.: National Education Association, 1977).

[3]Harold G. Shane, *Educating for a New Millennium* (Bloomington, Ind.: Phi Delta Kappa, Inc., 1981).

[4]Harold Benjamin, *The Saber-Tooth Curriculum* (New York: McGraw-Hill Book Company, 1939).

[5]Mortimer J. Adler, *The Paideia Proposal* (New York: Macmillan Publishing Co., Inc., 1982).

[6]P. 92.

Educational Leadership 46 (Nov. 1988): 42-46

RON BRANDT

On Assessment of Teaching: A Conversation with Lee Shulman

Idea man par excellence, Lee Shulman has long set directions for research on teaching. After founding and directing the Institute for Research on Teaching at Michigan State, Shulman, now at Stanford, continues his far-reaching investigations into the interplay of content and pedagogy and into assessments of teaching that faithfully reflect its complexity.

Photograph by Bob Riha

You're working on a process for assessing teachers for national certification. What do you think it will look like when it's finally in place?

I think we'll eventually have a certification process that will unfold over a period of several years, beginning as early as the time a candidate seeks entrance to a teacher education program and continuing into the first few years of teaching. Please understand that I don't speak for the National Board; they are the ones who will shape the policies. But having said that, I foresee a process that will culminate sometime during the first five years of teaching. It will include written tests and performance assessments, but also an emphasis on documenting teaching through building a portfolio.

A lot of people are skeptical about tests.

I'm not prepared to dismiss paper-and-pencil tests as worthless. Written tests, especially objective tests, were invented to solve a very important problem: economically surveying a large range of understandings and ensuring that the same standards were used in a fair and equitable manner for every single person who takes the tests. Tests have their limitations, but you don't want to throw out the baby with the bathwater. Certain aspects of content knowledge and pedagogical knowledge related to content are amenable to paper-and-pencil testing—though not necessarily multiple choice. A format that requires a single best answer does not typically reflect the complexities of teaching.

They've apparently had difficulties with the portfolio idea in Tennessee. Teachers claimed they had to put in so much time building a portfolio that it interfered with their teaching.

We can learn from the problems others have had. We should be able to design checks and balances to ensure that the portfolios represent a legitimate portrayal of the teaching accomplishments of the candidate.

What I have in mind is that after a period of time, during which there is a combination of test taking, documentation in a portfolio, and direct classroom observations of the teacher—with mentoring playing a strong role—when candidates have their portfolios in a certain state, they submit them to the board for review. And only if the portfolio meets stated standards does the teacher go to an assessment center, which I would see as the final stage. The staff of the assessment center will be examining people, in part, over the contents of their portfolios: videotapes, examples of student work, a description of the unit of which the lesson was a part, and so on. In other words, they'll need to make linkages between the assessment center and documentation of performance.

How will this system improve the teaching profession?

Well, first, I think it will make all of us, teacher educators and practicing educators, teachers and administrators, much more reflective about what we're doing. At present, for example, we educators leave almost no record of what we've done. So when it comes time for someone else to learn from our experience, they find it difficult. If beginning teachers are responsible for developing a real portfolio, with test results, performance assessments, and so on, they'll have evidence that will help them look back and think about their performance as a teacher: both what they understand how to do and what they don't. When they apply for a job, teachers will have more than a transcript and a few letters of recommendation. They'll be able to present a portfolio of their work, as an architect can.

Aside from making educators more reflective, the assessment process should improve teacher education. I'm not in favor of assessment only for screening purposes, for selecting people out; the whole idea should be to provide formative feedback to improve the quality of those engaged in learning to be teachers.

It's inevitable that the prospective teacher will see anything of this sort as a set of hurdles to be jumped over.

So you want the hurdles to be valid in themselves; you want them to be meaningful.

What are some other pieces of the total system that need to be in place in order for this process to work?

Well, those of us in teacher education need to radically reconstruct what we do in the preparation of teachers. The worst error we could make as teacher educators is to assume that the problem is one of quality control rather than the quality of the instruction we provide for teachers. Anybody who treats certification as a magic bullet that will somehow select only the best and brightest teachers from an unchanging teacher education process is going to be badly disappointed. We're doing teacher education the same way we've been doing it for 50 years, the process is fundamentally flawed, and we need some utterly new models.

What sort of changes do you have in mind?

I'd like to see much greater use of cases, much like what is done in law and business education. That might reorient the teaching of teachers from the current model, which is either entirely field based, where you have little control over what goes on, or entirely classroom based, where everything is artificial. We have to create a middle ground, where problems of theory and practice can intersect in a realistic way. The genius of the case method, especially in business, is that you use realistic problems, but you can still deal with both the theoretical and the tactical aspects.

A second change is the development of mentoring and induction programs that provide a better transition into teaching, and that will, I hope, erode the boundary between preservice and inservice. I see the mentor as a really new role: a teacher who begins to take on some of the responsibilities of the teacher educator. We have to invent that role; I'm convinced from the case studies of mentors that Judy Shulman has done that this role is for now only a name and not yet a set of well understood functions.

To summarize, my dream for the next decade is for some combination of a reorientation to teacher education in the universities around case methods and the substantive invention of the mentor role to aid the transition into teaching. Assessments alone will not revolutionize teaching.

What about differentiation among teachers: career ladders?

I'm unsure about that. Many of the teachers whom I respect the most and from whom I have learned the most are quite uncomfortable with the hierarchical ladder notion. They want opportunities to differentiate their functions during the course of their careers, but not necessarily in a one-way fashion. We probably need a new metaphor: a ladder may be misleading, because ladders go up, suggesting that something else is down. We need a model more like the one in medicine, where getting better and more respected as a physician does not mean that you've stopped caring for patients. The chief of medicine at a good hospital takes on leadership responsibilities, but continues to be fully involved in practice. And board-certified internists do not necessarily take on different roles from non-board-certified internists. So I have to reserve judgment on differentiation.

The model of certification on which you're working gives a great deal of control over the process to teachers. What are the implications of that for people who now play a larger role in teacher selection, certification, and evaluation?

Well, remember that it's a model for voluntary teacher certification for professional recognition purposes. It's not for licensure, and it's not for the evaluation of performance in a district. The process will be essentially under the control of the practitioner community, with participation from other stake-holding groups. In other words, two-thirds of the members of the board will be teaching professionals,

> **I dream of the day when principals or aspiring principals will first have to be board-certified teachers.**

and the majority will be K-12 teachers—but that still leaves a lot of places on the board for administrators, teacher educators, curriculum specialists, subject matter specialists, political leaders, parents, and so on.

Then I foresee that the very existence of that standards board and that process of certification will exert influence on the processes of licensure and of evaluation, which are of their nature more political and local—not supplanting them, because I think that would be wrong—but providing amplification of the teacher's voice with respect to the standards of practice.

Still, in the long run, it suggests that those in roles typically occupied by ASCD members—principals, curriculum directors—will play a less influential part in such decisions, and teachers will play a larger part.

Perhaps so—but the core of our profession is teaching, and everything else—supervision, administration, teacher education—should build around that core. I dream of the day when principals or aspiring principals will first have to be board-certified teachers: to have demonstrated that they have reached a certain level as instructors before they can claim to be instructional leaders. I feel the same way about those who supervise instruction. The results should be not a "we and they"

kind of business, but a "we," in which we all share the same core and build differentiation of roles out of that.

If someone were a board-certified teacher and also a principal, would she still be considered a teacher?

Absolutely. Let's remember here the etymology of the word *principal*. Principal did not begin as a noun, but as an adjective, "principal teacher."

There are some educators who wouldn't mind having teachers as individuals play a larger role in decision making. They do worry, though, about teacher unions playing such a role, not because they dislike unions but because they feel that's just another way of limiting individual teacher prerogatives.

That's something that's got to be dealt with. I think the members of the two major teachers' unions who are represented on the national board—but are far from controlling the board, which is the nightmare that some folks seem to have—will have to think through the incompatibility between traditional images of adversarial collective bargaining on the one hand, and notions of a unified profession that includes administrators and supervisors, on the other. They can't play it both ways. We're going to have to come to terms with that one, but I'm not smart enough to figure out how. I'll leave that to others.

Some people object to the idea of performance assessment for teachers because zeroing in on a particular model of good teaching necessarily limits the options and implies that we have now decided what good teaching is and that we will shut out other alternatives. Does that concern you?

One would have to be terribly naive not to worry about that, but it isn't the creation of a national board that suddenly introduces this danger; we're living with it already. A good many current teacher tests and teacher evaluation instruments are limited to the teacher effectiveness model of teaching. I actually see the new assessment approaches we're talking about as part of the solution, because they are much more open-ended: the whole idea in these assessments is that teachers produce their own responses to a situation.

But we have to recognize that at some point somebody somewhere has to say, "Here's where we draw the line." That's not been popular in education, and some decisions that will be made may be unpopular. But I don't see any way of doing a responsible job of educating teachers, evaluating them, or selecting them without making some such tough choices.

I can see that some current state models may be mistaken, but the difference is between a variety of state models, which makes it possible to see by comparison over a period of time that a particular plan may be a bad idea, and a single system that might dominate all of education.

Yes, we've had that problem in medicine. When I got into medical education for the first time back in the late '60s, the worst problem we had was the National Board of Medical Examiners, because it was locked into what we felt was a conservative view of medical preparation. For about 10 years, it was a real impediment to changes in medical education. That board has come around, though. It is now becoming much more innovative. If this national board thing works and really does the job we dream it can do, in 20 years we could conceivably have that problem.

One of the themes you've emphasized in recent years is the importance of content knowledge. For many people that's a new way to look at the research on teaching. How would you characterize the state of the art?

We know by now a great deal about classroom organization and management, and much of that work is being applied quite successfully. Some of the research doesn't get classified as classroom organization, but it really is, like the work on cooperative small groups by Slavin and others. But it too is rather generic.

We're just beginning to get a second generation of classroom research that is domain-specific, for example in mathematics, where teaching is typi-

One of the most important things we find that teachers do is to draw analogies.

cally built around problem sets you give as homework, and you therefore have to review homework as problem sets, so you can see whether the students are making specific errors. The management and organization of the mathematics classroom has a certain character that follows from that characteristic of the discipline. Gaea Leinhardt at Pittsburgh has done some fine work on this. A math teacher has to be able, as economically as possible, to check to see if the students understand the homework they've done, to get a quick impression of both what problems they have and who's having the problems, and to do it fast enough to get on with the lesson for the day. It turns out that if you break that down, as Leinhardt has done, that's a very difficult thing to do. Leinhardt has documented that novice teachers have a terrible time doing it.

That's an important kind of second generation research. But notice that it applies in only a limited way to the teaching of history or literature, which doesn't involve use of problem sets. What does it mean to make a mistake with respect to the Declaration of Independence or *Madame Bovary*, if by mistake you don't mean simply an error of fact but that the student didn't get a strategy right or an interpretation right? What I see happening now is a move from the first generation of research on teaching, which helped us understand generic teaching skills, to

second generation work looking at content-specific management.

But there's also a third generation of work beginning to be done, which is trying to understand what kind of representations and transformations of content understanding are needed to teach complex ideas well.

Your attention to content pedagogy makes me think of the statement by Lynne Cheney of the National Endowment for the Humanities, who concluded that educators value process more than content. I rankled at that, and many educators did too; but she apparently got that impression from listening to testimony from expert teachers.

I met with Cheney when she came to Stanford and she gave us that diagnosis at the time. I argued with her that the education community has overemphasized generic processes; but her solution, which is simply to forget process because it's irrelevant, is incredibly naive. As we're finding in our research, deeper and deeper content knowledge does not in and of itself produce better teaching. It is taking that content knowledge and transforming it for teaching purposes that makes for good teaching. Cheney missed that point entirely. She has decided the cure for education is the amputation of pedagogy, and that's insane.

But again, what triggered the thought is that the content has become so subordinated when we think about what we do that even great teachers aren't aware of the role of their own content knowledge. They understand *Huckleberry Finn* well enough that they can read it in different ways, like a literary critic. They select the interpretation that best fits with these students in these circumstances, and then blend some cooperative methods with some discussion methods with some lecture methods to put together an instructional unit. When you ask them what they did, they usually don't talk about their content knowledge; it's second nature, and they don't realize how subtle and deep it is. In my chapter for the *Handbook of Research on Teaching*, I called it "the missing paradigm," in the sense that paradigms are semiconscious ways we organize our thinking about a whole domain. Content has been the missing paradigm; we never talked about it.

Cheney would not only amputate pedagogy; she would amputate most of the people who are concerned with it. What you're saying is a challenge to people who purport to be experts in curriculum and supervision.

That's right. But it applies to my own group as well. Those of us who teach psychology and philosophy of education, and sociology of education, have to make the content of what is being taught central to what we teach. This isn't something I'm prescribing for curriculum and instruction courses alone. When I teach a course in the psychology of education, half of the reader I put together for my students should consist of excerpts from actual texts the students will use in their teaching. When we teach an idea from cognitive psychology, we'll use as the vehicle a chapter from a biology or history textbook. We'll ask, "How do these notions of misconceptions and preconceptions, or of higher and lower order thinking, relate to the teaching of this particular set of ideas regarding natural selection or to this Shakespeare sonnet?" We've got to bring it all in.

That has overwhelming implications for researchers. If more and more research is reported in terms of particular content, how can it ever be pulled together to make a picture of teaching in general?

I think we've got to start working from the bottom up. We will continue to find general principles of teaching, but I'm going to trust them only when I know that they have first been discovered with regard to particular content areas and then slowly generalized from topics to curriculum areas to teaching more generally. I no longer trust the approach of ignoring the content and looking only for the generic. We're going to need a long time in which, as physicians do, we do case studies of the actual teaching and

The drawing of analogies, the generation of metaphors, rests on what other things you know.

learning of particular topics. My guess is that we'll find we can generalize the findings within a domain very rapidly after that.

It suggests, though, that educationists will have to be well educated people themselves, with a huge range of knowledge. It means we should be familiar with content that many of us, in fact, are not.

It makes clear why a really good liberal education is an absolute prerequisite for both teachers and teacher educators. When you realize how tightly bound up the content and process are, you begin to appreciate how profoundly difficult teaching is, and how much we draw on our understanding of the things we teach. One of the most important things we find that teachers do is to draw analogies, because one of the ways you make something clear to a student is by comparing it to something else they already know. The drawing of analogies, the generation of metaphors, rests on what other things you know. A liberal education, then, is not simply a nice thing to have because it gives you stature and proves you're smart; the contents of a liberal education are absolutely basic to teaching particular things to particular kids.

When there's more awareness of this content relationship you refer to, when everyone begins to recognize the complexity of what we need to think about, the audience for research on teaching may be a bit less interested. Generalist administrators who in recent years have been confident because they've had a clean, relatively simple model will now be told they can expect to read research on how to teach *Huck Finn*. They may not find that very appealing.

That's right. I guess one of my goals in life is to bring more profound discomfort to those administrators and supervisors. I don't want them to believe any longer that they can walk into a class in which *Huckleberry Finn* is being taught and, without any understanding of that novel, of the teaching of literature, of the teacher's goals for the teaching of literature to this group at this time, do a responsible job of teacher evaluation.

And yet the generalist administrator can't know the content of every course that well, yet is obligated to supervise and evaluate every teacher as well as possible.

I recognize some of the dilemmas with respect to union contracts, teacher evaluation, and so on. And these dilemmas are being addressed in Toledo, for example, Rochester, and Redwood City, California. We'll come to see that the evaluation and supervision of a teacher is not the exclusive province of the administrator. Administrators can evaluate some things, of course, but they have to recognize the limitations of generic evaluations and the need for additional data reflecting content-specific pedagogy relevant to a particular setting. The task is not to disqualify the general administrator—heaven forbid!—but to take the notion of instructional leadership much more seriously.□

Lee S. Shulman is Professor of Education, Stanford University, 507 CERAS, Stanford, CA 94305. **Ron Brandt** is ASCD's Executive Editor.

Educational Leadership 45 (Feb. 1988): 30-36

RON BRANDT

On Changing Secondary Schools: A Conversation with Ted Sizer

Former Dean of the Graduate School of Education at Harvard University and Headmaster of Phillips Academy at Andover, Massachusetts, Ted Sizer is the author of *Horace's Compromise*, the report of a five-year study of adolescent education. Now Chair of the Coalition of Essential Schools, Sizer insists that high schools can do better by doing less, by concentrating on what is essential to students' intellectual growth.

You're doing your best to change American high schools. Why?

Because they're not serving either kids or teachers as well as they might. The evidence from solid research over the last 10 years—research conducted from different points of view—demonstrates a pattern of problems which we must address.

How would you summarize these problems?

We try to do too much. And the way we organize youngsters' and teachers' time doesn't make sense in light of how kids learn and how we might teach them. The result is that a majority of kids don't perform as well as they ought to, and a significantly large number of teachers are frustrated because they feel a sense of responsibility to those youngsters.

You've often expressed concern about "docile" students. What do you mean by that, and what causes it?

I mean youngsters who are not in the habit of taking a problem and solving it on their own. This is not surprising, as there are few incentives in high schools for kids actually to engage their minds deeply.

You saw this yourself in your recent study of high schools?

Right.

What did you find that was so convincing?

The similarity of the problems in a wide range of schools: small ones, big ones, public ones, private ones. When you see a disturbing pattern repeated over and over again, its importance increases. I also learned of the deep frustration of many of the very best people I listened to. And there was a clear readiness among them to move—to ask the big questions and to make fundamental changes.

Let's talk about the project you're involved in, an effort to work in partnership with some schools to make these changes.

The project is a group of about 50 schools, a varied group in 19 states and 1 Canadian province. All have agreed to a simple set of ideas about schooling; and all of us believe that every community, every school, is necessarily different from any other. That is, we don't have a model to plug in; we have a set of ideas. Each school is shaping those ideas into a program in a way respectful of its local situation.

Does that mean you think that in the long run schools ought to be different from one another?

Absolutely.

But surely there would be some things one would expect to be similar.

General principles, yes, but the way they play out should be different. What's right in Ansley, Nebraska, may not be right for Portland, Maine, and vice versa.

Is it possible to generalize about the sorts of things schools in the project are trying to do?

Yes, there are patterns. They arise from the ideas that we share. Those ideas are old chestnuts; read them and you'll say, "Good grief. What's so new

about that?" And nothing is—that's one of their joys. On the other hand, taking them seriously forces some issues that previously were simply papered over.

A key view among us in the Coalition of Essential Schools is that the most important purpose of schooling—without exception, for all students—is intellectual development. Everybody says, "Sure. How do you express that in programs?" What you see in these Coalition schools are programs focused much more on helping youngsters to use their minds well. It's particularly impressive to see that priority pushed with kids who are turned off, who have done badly in school, who are likely to drop out.

How do the schools do that?

One way is to get the ratios way down: the number of kids for which each teacher feels a sense of responsibility. One of the common ideas of the Coalition is that no high school teacher will ever be responsible for more than 80 students (some of my friends in schools that enroll quite demoralized kids say even 80 is too many). But bringing those ratios down within roughly the existing per-pupil expenditure means drastically simplifying a school's program.

Does that mean schools are actually dropping parts of their curriculums at this point?

Absolutely. For example, a school serving a high proportion of demoral-

Photograph by John Foraste/photographer Brown University

ized kids may have a very simple program taught entirely by teams: a humanities team and a science team. It has a three-period day, the first period being a tutorial or an advisory period in which every adult in the building (except one person who answers the phones to say that everybody's busy) meets with a group of 13 or 14 kids—and that is a ratio that's possible within an existing budget. In the tutorial the teachers gather the kids, go over homework, arrange for students to have breakfast if they haven't had any, try to soften the clatter that a lot of these kids bring in at the beginning of a school day. Then there's a two-and-a-half-hour block of time for English, art, and history. After lunch there's a math-science block. You find in some of the schools all of the kids working within—let's say—mathematics and science, or a common general theme such as "vision and light" or in the humanities, "revolution." You're immediately struck by the apparent lack of course electives. But the teachers in these schools will say that, because the program is very simple, the faculty can concentrate on personalizing their teaching. They can create sensible personal "electives," electives that emerge from what each youngster is like and what he or she really needs.

So the big computerized master schedule is much less a factor?

Some of these schools could be scheduled over a coffee break. Now, having said that, let me point out that the real issues of timing and grouping simply have been moved to another level. You have your 3 teachers and 90 kids in a Humanities group—how do you group those 90 kids? And how do you regroup them every fortnight? Now *that*'s a complicated scheduling problem. These schools skip the "scheduling problem" by pushing it way down so that the decisions are made by the adults who know the particular kids best.

It would seem that parents and community members would be very influential in determining whether these programs succeed.

Oh, yes. In communities where the schools compete—that is, private

> ## "One of the common ideas of the Coalition is that no high school teacher will ever be responsible for more than 80 students."

schools or competitive schools in the public sector—it's a marketing problem for the principal and faculty: they get the kids whose parents want them to come. In other situations—a one-high school town, let's say, that everybody attends—it's a combination of two things. One is persuading the parents that simplification and focus, placing a greater demand on the youngsters, serves traditional interests even better then the status quo. Second is that their youngsters are going to have more options in the future with this kind of approach.

Some of the big high schools which aren't schools of choice have elected to create, at least initially, the Essential School program as a school-within-a-school option for parents and kids to choose. All the schools that have taken this approach have started with either 7th or 9th grade and will move gradually to full-scale operation. In several of the schools, when the Essential School-within-a school gets to its full size, it will have more than half the student body.

If one believes in choice and there's only the one local school, maybe alternatives should be available within that one school.

Yes, unless the community is convinced that the status quo is not working, and that is the case in one of the Coalition's rural schools. Clearly the kids were not going anywhere, and the

community as a whole—represented by the school board and by a very vigorous parents group—felt that the risk of trying something new was far less than the risk of standing still.

Is it difficult for a faculty of a large comprehensive school where they've tried to do a little of everything to begin to take seriously the idea that "less is more"?

It certainly is. The very expanse of curriculum provided turf, and people's jobs depend on turf. When you say you're going to redefine turf, that threatens people's jobs. Some teachers go to the wall and say, "I will teach only chemistry; and if I can't do that, I won't do anything." Others will rise to the challenge and say, "Okay, I'll just dust off my college work in physics."

But, inevitably, in a school determined to make these kinds of changes, some teachers will probably lose their jobs. And that is actually happening?

Yes.

Let's talk a little more about these schools' strategy for change. High schools are generally regarded as bastions of tradition. I think I remember from the RAND studies of the 1970s that not a single high school project was regarded as successful. What makes you such an optimist about the possibility of reforming high schools?

As a historian I would characterize high schools less as bastions of conservatism than as mirrors of society. American society does not really value adolescents very much. I still shake from reading the fifth chapter in David Cohen's *The Shopping Mall High School*—a devastating critique not so much of schools but of the American people, who seem willing to live with the hypocrisy of an elaborate graduation ceremony with diplomas that some of the recipients can't even read.

So why my optimism? I sense in the current mood of the country a sustained interest in substantial change. Enough people in politics and education apparently realize that the situation is so serious, both in the schools and in the fact that the United States is in a competitive race for its very life, that the old complacency won't work anymore.

So as a historian who sees a close relationship between schools and society, you can account for the fact of considerable stability in the high school for much of this century, but you also know from history that when circumstances reach a certain point, things happen. And this may be the time.

Right. An analogy isn't perfect, but it's worth mentioning: the great push toward a common Americanizing curriculum that followed turn-of-the-century immigration. People in the Northeast and Midwest saw a crisis because of so many ''foreigners,'' and big city school systems grew very rapidly in response to the political perception of a real emergency. We may be in a similar situation now.

Your analogy makes me rethink my statement about stability because the high school really did adapt dramatically.

The biggest change was its growth, which can be explained in two ways. One was recognition by the public that adolescents should have access to schools on a full-time basis. That is, the country didn't want—indeed, didn't need—adolescent labor. The second factor was that the country was wealthy enough to pay for it. The explosive growth of high schools in the first two decades of this century and again right after the Second World War, not surprisingly, corresponded with excess revenue in the tax coffers that followed economic booms.

That raises another basic issue. We have had a major split between the Mortimer Adlers, who have insisted through the years that all students should have an intellectual education, and most practicing educators, who are convinced by their own experience that that is simply unrealistic. I've often heard educators say—I've said it myself—''Let them try. We work with these kids, and we know there are certain kinds of adapta-

tions that must be made.'' Are the Essential Schools rethinking that whole issue?

The Essential Schools take a Jeffersonian view that, aside from a small percentage of students with profound special needs, every youngster has a mind; and democracy depends on the wise use of that mind. If people be-

lieve that some members of society cannot learn to use their minds well, then they'd better move to Sparta. Our whole system of government depends on the wisdom of the individual citizen. Maybe such a sentiment is naive, but it happens to be democracy.

Well, it's a wonderful statement; but if I had been teaching in a

---

The Coalition of Essential Schools

Adelphi Academy
Clinton Vickers, Headmaster
8515 Ridge Blvd.
Brooklyn, NY 11209

Alternative Community School
Dave Lehman, Principal
111 Chestnut St.
Ithaca, NY 14850

Andover High School
Mr. Richardson, Acting Principal
Andover, MA 01810

Bishop Carroll High School
Bernard Bajnok, Principal
4624 Richard Rd., SW
Calgary, Alberta T3E 6L1
Canada

Brighton High School
Thomas Jones, Principal
1150 Winton Rd. South
Rochester, NY 14618

Brimmer and May School
Anne Reenstierna, Headmistress
69 Middlesex Rd.
Chestnut Hill, MA 02167

Bronxville High School
Judy Codding, Principal
Pondfield Rd.
Bronxville, NY 10708

Bryn Mawr School
Barbara Chase, Headmistress
109 W. Melrose
Baltimore, MD 21210

Catholic Central High School
Sr. Joan Flynn, Vice Principal
1200 1200 E. High St.
Springfield, OH 45505

Central Park East School
Deborah Meier, Director
1573 Madison Ave.
New York, NY 10029

Elizabethtown Area High School
Dustin Peters, Principal
600 E. High St.
Elizabethtown, PA 17022

Episcopal School of Arlington
Rev. V. Stanley Maneikis, Headmaster
805 Sharpshire Dr.
Grand Prairie, TX 75050-6322

Gordon School
Darcy Hall, Headmistress
Maxfield Ave.
East Providence, RI 02914

Heathwood Hall
J. Robert Shirley, Headmaster
3000 S. Beltline Blvd.
Columbia, SC 29201

Hope High School
Paul Gounaris, Principal
324 Hope St.
Providence, RI 02906

Hixson High School
Tom McCullough, Principal
5705 Middle Valley Pike
Chattanooga, TN 37343

Irondequoit High School
Eugene Horrigan, Principal
260 Cooper Rd.
Rochester, NY 14617

Ballard High School
Alexandra Allen, Principal
6000 Brownsboro Rd.
Louisville, KY 40222

Doss High School
Gordon Milby, Principal
7601 St. Andrews Church Rd.
Louisville, KY 40214

Pleasure Ridge Park High School
Charles Miller, Principal
5901 Greenwood Rd.
Pleasure Ridge Park, KY 40258

Seneca High School
John Whiting, Principal
3510 Goldsmith La.
Louisville, KY 40220

Mayme S. Waggener High School
Donna Ludwig, Principal
330 S. Hubbards La.
St. Matthews, KY 40207

Park Heights Street Academy
Deneauvo Robinson, Headmaster
3901 Park Heights Ave.
Baltimore, MD 21215

Paschal High School
Radford Gregg, Principal
3001 Forest Park Blvd.
Fort Worth, TX 76110

The Judson Montessori School
Gay Jones Judson, Director
705 Trafalgar
San Antonio, TX 78216

Finn Hill Junior High School
Robert Strode, Principal
8040 NE 132nd St.
Kirkland, WA 98034

Juanita High School
Kathy Siddoway, Principal
10601 NE 132nd St.
Kirkland, WA 98033

Lincoln High School
Douglas Molzahn, Principal
1433 S. 8th St.
Manitowoc, WI 54220

Mass. Advanced Studies Program
Chuck Burdick, Director
Milton Academy
170 Centre St.
Milton, MA 02186

Meridian Junior High School
J. Clifton Ernst, Principal
23480–120th Ave., SE
Kent, WA 98031

Metro High School
Mary Wilcynski, Principal
1212 74th St., SE
Cedar Rapids, IA 52401

Mid-Peninsula High School
Philip Bliss, Chairman
870 North Carolina Ave.
Palo Alto, CA 94303

Miss Porter's School
Rachel Belash, Headmistress
60 Main St.
Farmington, CT 06032

Nova High School
Larry Insel, Principal
3600 SW College Ave.
Fort Lauderdale, FL 33314

Nova Middle School
Suzanne Alvord, Principal
3602 SW College Ave.
Fort Lauderdale, FL 33314

The Park School of Buffalo
Thomas Fulton, Headmaster
4625 Harlem Rd.
Snyder, NY 14226

Parkway South High School
Craig Larson, Principal
801 Hanna Rd.
Manchester, MO 63021

Portland High School
Barbara Anderson, Principal
284 Cumberland Ave.
Portland, ME 04101

The Putney School
Barbara Barnes, Director
Elm Lea Farm
Putney, VT 05346

St. Andrew's-Sewanee
Rev. William S. Wade, Headmaster
St. Andrews, TN 37372

St. Xavier Academy
Joyce Blum, School Liaison
225 MacArthur Blvd.
Coventry, RI 02816

School One
Bill O'Hearn, Principal
75 John St.
Providence, RI 02906

Schools Without Walls
Dan Dramcich, Program Administrator
400 Andrews St.
Rochester, NY 14604

Springdale High School
Harry Wilson, Principal
Springdale, AK 72764

The Stowe School
David Gibson, Headmaster
Mountain Rd.
Stowe, VT 05672

University Heights Alternative School
Nancy Mohr, Principal
University Ave. and W. 181st St.
New York, NY 10453

University School of Nova University
Joseph Randazzo, Headmaster
7500 SW 36th St.
Fort Lauderdale, FL 33314

Walbrook High School
Sam Billups, Principal
2000 Edgewood St.
Baltimore, MD 21216

Walden III
Charles Kent, Principal
1012 Center St.
Racine, WI 53403

Westbury High School
Bill Morgan, Principal
5575 Gasmer Rd.
Houston, TX 77035

Whitfield School
Mary Burke, Headmistress
175 S. Mason Rd.
St. Louis, MO 63141

high school for the last 15 to 20 years, and I had been used to tracking students and providing quite a different curriculum for the low track, it would be hard to convince me that somehow I'd been wrong all along.

But "you" *have* been wrong. Jeannie Oakes' book, *Keeping Track*, makes that very clear.

And schools in the Coalition intend to change that?

Absolutely. We're giving it a noble try. We're assuming that everybody's going to make the grade. Essential Schools group students according to what they need to learn, and they regroup frequently; they don't hammer any youngster permanently into the structure of the school, saying, "This kid is in the General track, and that one is in the Honors track, forevermore." Behind all of this is the assumption not only that every youngster can use his or her mind well, but that if we give up on that goal, we give up on democracy.

A series of books by Allan Bloom, E. D. Hirsch, Jr., Lynne Cheney, Diane Ravitch, and Chester Finn have charged that schools are neglecting the teaching of cultural knowledge, especially history and literature, and that they've been emphasizing process and skills too much instead. Is that a concern of schools in the Coalition?

Yes it is, though I think most of us agree with part of the critique but not all of it. The idea that schools put too much emphasis on process and not enough on content doesn't square with my experience or that of others who spend a lot of time in schools. What strikes me about all too many high school classrooms is the churning out of disembodied data which the kids are supposed to spit back. It's facts, facts, facts at their absolute grotesque worst. If Hirsch, Cheney, et al. think we're teaching skills, well—sorry, friends; it's worse than you think.

They may have reached that conclusion by looking at textbooks.

"American society does not really value adolescents very much."

That's like making a judgment about the telephone system by looking at the phone book. To be blunt about it, analysis of schools on such a limited basis is poor scholarship.

You've been in a lot of high school classrooms, and you haven't seen too much "process"?

Right. And John Goodlad's people spent years visiting schools and found much the same pattern. But I don't mean to be contentious about cultural literacy. I think Hirsch and the others are making a very important point. Take an example from social studies. For a young American there is no part of the school curriculum that is more important than that addressing the United States Constitution; and for a 16-year-old to really understand the Constitution, time is needed. Or take another pivotal document, the Declaration of Independence. Mortimer Adler argues that you can spend three hours on just part of the first sentence. The Bill of Rights needs very careful work—lots of examples, case studies, Socratic dialogue, role-playing, and so on. Otherwise the kids will not get to the bottom of those fundamental ideas that drive this country, not understand them enough to use them. I think that's what Lynne Cheney and Diane Ravitch are talking about.

Now, I use that example of the

Constitution because it's so easy to defend. Not many people would say, "Oh no, it's more important that students know about X." Choices get more difficult when you get out on the margin and begin to argue, for example, whether the current waves of immigration from Asia are as "important" in "history" as the waves of immigration from southwestern and eastern Europe since the 1890s. Our view is to join these issues: "Let's make some very hard decisions about what is most essential and teach this thoroughly."

So you disagree with some of what Hirsch says, but you think he is calling attention to an important issue?

Oh, yes. And to be fair about it, I am less criticizing what Hirsch says than what some enthusiasts think he says. Professor Hirsch is under no illusion about how complicated these things are.

A related question. In his book Hirsch also takes a couple of swipes at schools' efforts to teach critical thinking, because he says that distracts them from teaching knowledge.

In good schools that issue is a straw man. The way to get serious critical thinking is to get kids' minds focused on substantial matters. Give them the text of the *Brown vs. Board of Education* decision, give some background for that decision, and then go into the kind of Socratic dialogue that Mortimer Adler so admires. I don't know how you teach truly critical thinking without consequential subject matter—just as I don't know how you teach consequential subject matter without resourceful thinking.

Would it be accurate to say that these issues seldom arise in typical faculty meetings, but that in the Essential Schools they are being argued?

That's right. That word *essential* in the name of our project has a double meaning. On one hand it is essential that we restructure overloaded and ineffective schools. And our project also involves figuring out what is essential in the way of education. The toughest part is "the politics of subtraction." That is, if you're going to teach the United States Constitution adequately, you're not going to be able to give much attention to the first administration of Grover Cleveland. You have to decide what is fundamental. Facing such choices is consistent with the current mood.

Where, in your opinion, does vocational education fit in the secondary curriculum?

In one respect I don't think it fits at all. In the current economy, jobs change so fast that any type of job-specific training is a very short-range proposition. So to say that schools should prepare students for specific entry-level jobs may be a nice objective but, if you can't do everything in high school, a low priority.

Put another way, in a rapidly changing job market the most important vocational training is general education, which is exactly what the Committee on Economic Development and other business groups have been saying over and over for five or six years. So, in many of our schools that serve kids who mostly don't aspire to higher education, wise principals are now saying to students, "Look. This program we're putting together may not seem to speak to your immediate job prospects; but in fact it is the most important vocational education you can get, because it's teaching you how to teach yourself in a constantly changing situation."

I must also say that some of the vocational education courses I've seen are superbly taught, because they force the kids to do the work. In shop after shop, I've seen teachers who are in the habit of pushing the problem out to the kids, engaging them. Happily, some of those teachers are prepared to use their talents teaching general education. One whom I admired most—a teacher of electricity—I wrote about in my book. He was just magnificent, and under no illusion that he was teaching for entry-level jobs: he was teaching basic educational skills. It's that kind of imaginative

Bronxville High: An "Essential" School in Process

Sherry P. King

When the 9th graders in our interdisciplinary elective no longer saw their teachers as teachers of discrete subjects, we knew we were on the way to success. On a given assignment they might seek help from the English teacher as readily as from the social studies teacher—or from the art teacher, for that matter.

Key principles of the Coalition of Essential Schools, of which we are a partner school, are driving forces in our evolving program: personalization, the student-as-worker, exhibition, and the concept of "less is more." Three teachers—Joanne Duffy in social studies, Mary Schenck in English, and Linda Passman in art—are assigned to one course; art is as much a part of the content as English and social studies. We attempt to integrate the disciplines, attending to the basic skills and knowledge each requires as well as to connections among the three.

We piloted the interdisciplinary program in 1986–87 with one heterogeneous class that we scheduled for double periods several times during our eight-day cycle. The content was the same as the regular curriculum—The Ancient World through 1715—but the third teacher and the possibility for different blocks of time allowed us to alter our focus. Perhaps the best way to capture the essence of our program is to describe one of the units.

We began with study of the ancient world. Students were reading The Odyssey, a 9th grade required text, and studying Greek culture, with a focus on the norms of society, including notions of hospitality and the value of arts and entertainment. At the same time, students were learning about folios, scrolls, and illustrated manuscripts. Moving deeper into the unit, the teachers struggled to find a creative way for students to exhibit their understanding of the period.

The teachers decided to have students create an additional chapter of The Odyssey—not a unique assignment, but other dimensions of the project enhanced it. They had a storyteller come to class as Odysseus and tell his adventures. While the students were working on their own stories, the storyteller, knowledgeable about both the assignment and The Odyssey, responded to their drafts by challenging students to try their characters in new situations. He offered provocative responses from his point of view as Odysseus. The final assignment, or exhibition, was to prepare a folio, a scroll, or an illustrated manuscript with their stories. We invited the visiting bard back to join us for a classic banquet, with oral presentations of the stories as its entertainment.

Our approach has produced problems along with successes. Our most prominent hurdle is time—time to plan, time to cover the content, time to be with students. We also struggle with the knowledge that not all students are in this program. Thus we are torn between our desire to encourage divergent thinking, our need for the time required to help students make connections, and our commitment to cover The Ancient World through 1715. We struggle, too, with grading policies: how can we promote collaborative learning and still evaluate individuals fairly; how can we ask students to take risks and then have to evaluate them?

Despite these possibly unanswerable problems, we would find it hard to teach any other way. We have seen students learn to read, think, and generalize in ways that go far beyond their peers of similar abilities. We have seen students willing, even eager, to investigate subjects independently and in depth. Our students have maintained high individual standards but have developed a sense of caring for each other as they help one another learn.

We have grown along with our students, becoming facilitators of learning more than disseminators of information. Our daily conversation and collaboration have broken the isolation of teaching. We are piloting a similar class in 10th grade, and expanding our 9th grade program. In our enthusiasm to increase connections among disciplines, we must remember not simply to add content, but to heed our own belief that "less is more."

—Sherry P. King is Assistant to the Principal, Bronxville High School, Bronxville, NY 10708.

teaching, which I've seen often in voc-tech programs, that some science and social studies departments could well copy.

There's something I'm curious about. If these public schools are successful in their efforts, they will look more like what private schools have looked like all along. Your professional experiences have been mostly in non-public schools. Are you simply trying to shape public schools to look more like private schools?

No, no. I've been very aware, particularly during the years when I was able to wander around and visit, that there's a stereotype of public school and a stereotype of private school. Everything I admired in the large private school in which I worked in the '70s I've seen working in public schools.

Let me put it another way. There are, for instance, some big Catholic high schools which, if you didn't notice the crucifixes on the wall, you couldn't identify as public or religious schools. And I can show you some public schools which—due to, for example, the social class segregation of the community—have an ambience which is stereotypically attached to a high-tuition private country day school. Public and private schools aren't all that different. Indeed, one of the embarrassments of American education is how similar all our schools—private and public—are, given our rhetoric about local control and the need for professional freedom.

Can you say more about exactly how the schools are undertaking the changes you are talking about? I can hear a high school principal saying, "Sounds good, but I don't see how they do it. This is a complex institution, and people are very busy just getting by. How do I get teachers to read about these ideas; how do I get them to even consider the possibility?"

There are as many approaches as there are schools in the Coalition, but

let me describe a kind of prototype. In every school where something is under way, there is a core of people, usually including the principal, who feel that (a) the school is a good school, and (b) it can be a hell of a lot better. Those folks start talking; and, if the talk gets beyond immediate things such as merely "Let's add a period to the school day," an ambitious plan evolves.

It's at that point that the Coalition tends to get involved. Where principals and teachers know about the Coalition, and find that their own thinking is running along similar lines, they get in touch. At that point there's more talk, parents are brought into it, the superintendent and key school board members add their backing, and a plan is worked out. In some cases the plan has been subject to a faculty wide vote. Where there is a strong union and a quite specific contract, amendments to that contract have even been voted by an entire citywide membership.

So the process starts with a group of people who have pride in their school and a conviction that they can do better. It continues quite slowly, evolving into a plan which then has to get—if it is a plan of any consequence—wide support. Then, in a big high school, it usually starts with a school-within-a-school; or it starts with a series of well-planned and carefully staged changes in the overall school.

So the general pattern is to start small and grow.

Yes. And it takes time.

Do you see indications that these schools are in fact bringing more people in? Are they making headway on changing the whole school rather than remaining a small, relatively separate unit?

Yes. One example, where the whole school is involved, is in a city with five high schools where there's open enrollment: most students go to their neighborhood school, but they can go to another school if they have a particular reason. And at the end of its second year the Essential High School is outdrawing the competing schools.

Students from all over town want to go to that school. It has exactly the same per pupil expenditures, but it is set up in a simplified way; and it's getting a reputation among the youngsters of the community: you're not a cipher there; you're not anonymous. There's not nearly as much listless listening to teachers as in a regular school; there's a lot more "doing," which means that the kids are held accountable, and they like it. Oh, they complain to me when I visit about having to work harder than kids at the other schools, but attendance rates are way up, discipline rates are down, and the dropout rate is infinitesimal.

Now, when you do that for two years, superintendents, the school board, and parents begin to pay attention—and the program accelerates. Oh, it could blow up tomorrow; I'm under no illusion that there's a panacea here. However, even in some troubled communities you find real progress.

Can you identify some things these schools are learning that would be useful to other high school principals and administrators across the country who'd like to improve their schools?

One thing they've learned is that planning requires a major investment of time: the time needed to think through these matters carefully must not be underestimated. Another truism: everything important in a school affects everything else that's important. For example, if you want to rearrange your program to make the kids more active, to let them derive answers rather than simply memorize them, that obviously affects not only the speed with which you move over the subject matter, but also the blocks of time necessary for the kids to engage in it. The teachers and principals will tell you this can't be done piecemeal. That means that planning must be comprehensive indeed.□

Ted Sizer is Professor and Chair, Department of Education, Brown University, Box 1938, Providence, RI 02912. **Ron Brandt** is ASCD's Executive Editor.

Educational Leadership 46 (Oct. 1988): 22-29

RON BRANDT

On Research and School Organization: A Conversation with Bob Slavin

At the Johns Hopkins Center for Research on Elementary and Middle Schools, Bob Slavin directs the elementary school program and monitors research findings on a broad scale. Here he explains Success for All, an early intervention that organizes resources to ensure that students arrive at 3rd grade with adequate skills, and calls for practitioners to make stringent demands upon researchers for experimental trials of instructional techniques.

Over the last year or so you've looked at a lot of research on various ways to organize schools. Why?

I am broadly interested in what makes a difference in achievement, particularly in the elementary grades. When I run up against an issue, I do a thorough review of the literature so that I am confident about what the research actually says. Before I write it up for others, I first have to convince myself.

How do you do it? Do you personally search out the original research reports, analyze them, give more weight to some studies than others, and so on? Is this "meta-analysis"?

I have my own method, which I call "best evidence synthesis." It owes a good deal to meta-analysis but pays more attention to the quality of the studies—to substantive issues rather than only statistical issues—in deciding what to include and what not to include.

One topic you looked at this way was ability grouping (see Slavin 1988). What are some others?

Mastery learning, class size, cooperative learning. Those are the ones on which I have done complete, formal best evidence syntheses.

When you put all your findings together, what sort of model of school organization do they suggest?

To make schools markedly more effective, they really have to be quite different from the way they are now, particularly in serving students who have the greatest difficulty. It takes a three-part strategy to meet the needs of kids in difficulty. First and most important is much more emphasis on prevention: on picking up on problems very early and making sure that kids don't get into the special education or the remedial cycle. Second, we must change instructional methods to use systematic programs that have clear evidence of effectiveness. Only after we implement effective preventive programs and classroom change programs should we be looking at the

Photograph Courtesy the Johns Hopkins University

third issue, which is remediation. As one example of this kind of approach, we are currently doing research on a program that uses one-to-one tutoring, a completely restructured reading curriculum, family support services, and other components to try to make sure that kids in an inner-city school don't arrive at 3rd grade without adequate skills.

So you have in fact devised a comprehensive model?

Yes, it is called "Success for All."

And it reflects what you have learned from looking at the research on grouping, class size, tutoring, and so on?

Exactly. It doesn't just load it all in, of course. The various components have to work together in a coherent and meaningful way—but you want to be on firm ground as you make each choice.

What are some characteristics of the model that reflect the research on school organization?

One is the use of tutoring, which really came out of looking at class size research. A lot of people ask whether there isn't a critical point at which class size begins to make a difference, and the answer is yes, but—that critical class size is one student. You don't really see a lot of difference even when classes are very, very small; but one-to-

one tutoring is vastly more effective than even one-to-five teaching.

That finally led us to try to get away from the Chapter I approach of pulling out small groups, a mild treatment that may go on throughout the student's entire elementary career. Instead we decided to invest our resources in one-to-one tutoring that would get kids up to grade level rapidly and then try to maintain them within the regular classroom.

Another aspect of the program is a form of the Joplin Plan: grouping students across grade lines according to reading levels. First, 2nd and 3rd graders who are all performing at the 2-1 level may be in a class together. We do this because, as I said in my review (see Slavin 1988), the kind of grouping that has the greatest research support is cross-grade grouping.

We also have evidence from other sources about the uselessness of the workbook activities that students usually do in reading classes. Then we have the time-on-task literature and some of the direct instruction literature, which suggest that it is beneficial to increase the amount of time that students work actively with the teacher.

We also provide extended day and preschool programs because of the strong evidence for effectiveness of preschool and extended kindergarten for disadvantaged kids. In these programs we use the Peabody Language Development Kits, which also have strong research support.

How long will it be before you know whether this model is effective?

We now have data for one entire school year—we also assessed the students every eight weeks to check on their progress, to regroup, and to decide who needed tutoring—and we have seen remarkable progress. Our promise is that a kid who starts with us in preschool will get to 3rd grade with adequate skills; that no child will fail unless he or she is severely retarded. It may be three years before we know whether we can fulfill that promise, but we know that mean scores have increased this year.

We decided to invest our resources in one-to-one tutoring that would get kids up to grade level rapidly.

Is the program quite a bit more expensive?

Oh yes. We are proposing a shift of Chapter I monies to earlier grades so there will not be so much remediation to do in the upper grades. We already know that we can reduce special education referrals, so we may be able to demonstrate cost-effectiveness even before the students get to the middle school level.

Let me turn to another topic. One of the more controversial conclusions you reached in your reviews of the research literature is that mastery learning is not nearly as effective as claimed (see Slavin 1987). How did you decide that?

It is actually very simple. I did a number of things in my review, but if this were all I did, it would have been enough: I required that the studies had to have taken place over at least four weeks. The studies that produced the big effects—the ones that Bloom talks about and that are cited in a lot of other mastery learning syntheses—were conducted in three days, one week, two weeks, three weeks. Requiring that the treatment had to be in place for at least four weeks brings down the mastery learning studies to a very small number, and I think that even four weeks is really too short.

Another attribute I looked for was use of a control group. I think a control group is essential, because a lot of people evaluated mastery learning programs during the period 1979-1985, which was also a time when people were discovering all kinds of other ways to increase their test scores: curriculum alignment, retaining students in grade, things like that. When scores were reported for control groups within the same district, then everybody was operating under the same ground rules—how the tests were given and so on. But in studies with control groups the difference between the control groups and the mastery learning groups was practically nonexistent.

But for many educators it seems pointless to argue with mastery learning. Surely we should try to

Our promise is that a kid who starts with us in preschool will get to 3rd grade with adequate skills.

be clear about the outcomes we want, to assess student learning periodically, and not to go to the next level of difficulty until students have the prerequisites. It seems self-evident.

There are lots of principles in education that are correct but that don't result in educational gain. The concept of mastery learning *is* almost axiomatically true, but the issue is what it means in actual practice. I am talking here only about group-based mastery learning: if you have a 10-day lesson, you teach for eight days and then give a test. The kids who need correctives get corrective instruction, while the other kids get enrichment activities. What may be going on is that two days of corrective instruction are not enough for kids who have serious problems, but two days are too much wasted time for kids who don't have a problem. In other words, Bloom's Learning for Mastery model may actually be too limited a response to student differences in learning rates.

So it's not that it's too sophisticated; it may not be sophisticated enough. If you are going to do something different from traditional instruction, why not do something better?

Precisely. I think it does not go far enough to ensure students' success. We use mastery learning principles in our Success for All model, but we use them more directly. The purpose of the tutor is not to teach something different, but to ensure that each child has learned what the classroom teacher has taught. If a teacher teaches long "a" in the morning, the main task of the tutor is to be sure the students get long "a," so that tomorrow they are ready for the next lesson. That's clearly a mastery learning concept, but we do it daily and with a one-to-one tutor to make sure that the kids actually get it.

But as you say, it's in accord with the principles of mastery learning. I doubt that Benjamin Bloom and other advocates would quarrel with your design.

Yes, but another problem with some mastery programs is that they chop knowledge into little pieces, and that's unnecessary. What is critical about mastery learning or any other program is how it's done. Another good example is individualized instruction. Nobody would quarrel with giving kids instruction suited to their needs; but in the '60s and early '70s, when educators made individualized materials and had the kids work on them all by themselves, the effect on achievement was disastrous. The concept was correct, but the way in which it was operationalized was foolish, because while you were accomplishing one goal—adapting instruction to individual needs—you were interfering with other goals, such as providing students with explanations by quali-

Bloom's Learning for Mastery model may actually be too limited a response to student differences in learning rates.

Response to Slavin: Mastery Learning Works

James Block

This year marks the 20th birthday of mastery learning. In schooling, concepts that last even a few years are powerful and rare. As such, it is not surprising that mastery should draw periodic potshots. Slavin's is but the most recent.

I am disturbed by Slavin's interpretation of the cumulative mastery learning research record. Mastery advocates (e.g., Guskey and Gates 1986, Guskey and Pigott 1988), as well as more neutral parties (Stallings and Stipek 1986, Walberg 1985), have repeatedly reported exactly what Slavin proposes—"experimental-control comparisons over realistic periods of time with suitable measures of effectiveness." The most recent review, in fact, involves some 83 quasi-longitudinal studies ranging from years to over a decade (see Block et al. 1988). These studies have concluded, almost without exception, that mastery works. The basic strategies move the student who achieves at the 50th percentile to somewhere between the 65th and the 88th percentiles; this movement occurs in ordinary elementary and secondary school subjects; and the change registers on well-known standardized tests (Block et al. 1988). Enhanced mastery learning approaches do even better (Spady and Jones 1985).

I am also saddened by the dampening effects that this interpretation may have on communication between mastery learning and "Success for All" practitioners. There is a striking resemblance between Slavin's agenda for improving schooling and mastery learning's (see Block et al. 1988, pp. 49-57). Slavin's interest in the development of component approaches to instruction parallels mastery's promotion of the development of functional ones. His interest in the prevention of student learning difficulties jibes with mastery's, too. His interest in advancing "cooperative" learning overlaps with mastery's interest in developing "self-determined" learners. Lastly, his interest in tutoring clearly correlates with mastery's interest in the development of talent.

So I hope Slavin will not dismiss these comments out-of-hand. They are meant to caution him, his followers, and fair-minded observers not to throw out the proverbial mastery learning baby with the bathwater. That baby is now a young adult. They are also meant to suggest to Slavin and his followers that collaboration rather than confrontation is now in order. There are good reasons for the vitality and longevity of the mastery concept. While Slavin waits three years for data on his ideas, we are willing to share our 20 years of experience now.

Block, J., H. Efthim, and R. Burns. *Building Effective Mastery Learning Schools*. New York: Longman, 1988.

Guskey, T., and S. Gates. "Synthesis of Research on the Effects of Mastery Learning in Elementary and Secondary School Classrooms." *Educational Leadership* 43, 8 (1986): 73-80.

Guskey, T., and T. Pigott. "Research on Group-Based Mastery Learning Programs: A Meta-Analysis." *Journal of Educational Research* 81, 4 (1988): 198-216.

Spady, W., and B. F. Jones. "Enhanced Mastery Learning and Quality of Instruction." In *Improving Student Achievement through Mastery Learning Programs*, edited by D. U. Levine. San Francisco, Calif.: Jossey-Bass, 1985.

Stallings, J., and D. Stipek. "Research on Early Childhood and Elementary School Teaching Programs." In *Handbook of Research on Teaching*, 3rd ed., edited by M. C. Wittrock. New York: Macmillan, 1986.

Walberg, H. "Examining the Theory, Practice, and Outcomes of Mastery Learning." In *Improving Student Achievement Through Mastery Learning Programs*, edited by D. U. Levine. San Francisco, Calif.: Jossey-Bass, 1985.

James Block is Professor of Education, University of California, Santa Barbara, CA 93106.

fied teachers and motivating students to learn.

Some of the things that you say don't work have been advertised as based on research. How would you describe the state of educational research these days?

It's not at the stage I wish it were, but in the last 15 years educational research has come into its own. We have a lot of promising developments: for example, the process-product studies of effective teaching. I am encouraged by the emphasis on what's really going on in classrooms.

We use mastery learning principles in our Success for All model, but we use them more directly.

Let's clarify the term *process-product*. What does it refer to?

Studies in which a large group of teachers are carefully observed and the teachers whose students made the greatest gains are compared with those whose student gains were much smaller. A lot of the teacher behaviors people are talking about now in terms of classroom management, components of the lesson, and so on are direct outgrowths of that approach.

What are the advantages of that kind of research?

One is that you don't go in with preconceived notions that you try to impose on teachers. You are focusing on practices you know are realistic, because they already exist in classrooms. That is also a limitation, of course; you won't discover anything very surprising, because the only practices you will see will be those in fairly widespread use.

There are two major strands of research that contribute directly to practice. One is *correlational* research—of which the process-product research is a good example—where researchers identify the best of current practice. The other is *experimental*, where researchers try to increase the range of variation by introducing new methods

that a teacher might never stumble on otherwise. My own belief is that until you've done experimental research, you shouldn't be talking to teachers at all. I feel that a lot of the correlational and descriptive research is valuable in *suggesting* what kinds of things we should look at, but that it should never be used as a guide to practice.

Why do you say that?

I think that in order to tell teachers, "Do this and your students will learn better," you must have compared the results of that kind of advice using control and experimental groups. For example, if you studied basketball players and found that the taller ones did better, you might then say, "Well, we've learned that taller basketball players do better, so let's start stretching our shorter players." The correlational finding is correct; it is a useful thing to know. But it doesn't mean that a stretched player is the same as one who is naturally tall.

Similarly, with teachers we often find things from correlational research that are truly characteristic of the best teachers—but that doesn't mean that

Response to Slavin: Who Defines Best?

Thomas R. Guskey

Robert Slavin is a respected educational reseacher who has made a number of valuable contributions. Yet his recent work involving what he labels "best-evidence" syntheses and his application of this technique have evoked strong criticism from many within the research community. "Best-evidence" synthesis procedures were proposed by Slavin (1986) as a way to focus more attention on the quality of the studies being synthesized. But what has become apparent is that "best," in this particular sense, is a relative term (Joyce 1987) and that the best-evidence syntheses Slavin conducts include *only* those studies that he, and he alone, considers best (Gamoran 1987, Hiebert 1987). The results of these best-evidence syntheses, therefore, are often potentially biased, highly subjective, and likely to be misleading (Guskey 1987).

A case in point is Slavin's best-evidence synthesis of the research on mastery learning (Slavin 1987). In this review Slavin threw out all studies of less than four weeks' duration, even though previous reviews of mastery learning research that have specifically investigated the influence of study duration have consistently shown it has no effect on study results (Block and Burns 1976, Guskey and Gates 1985). He also threw out all studies which compared the results teachers attained before-to-after their implementation of mastery learning and studies involving multiple teachers, each teaching different subjects. For a significant portion of the review, he threw out all studies in which teachers used class time to help students with their corrective work and included only those studies in which correctives were done outside of class as independent work. In addition, he rejected all studies that did not use results of standardized, norm-referenced achievement tests as a principal outcome, even though mastery learning has always been based on the premise that student learning should be evaluated in terms of criterion-referenced standards. In the end, he had only seven studies, looked at their results, and concluded that mastery learning doesn't work. But if you narrowly restrict the way in which an innovation is implemented, alter a basic component of that innovation, and then evaluate its effectiveness in terms of an outcome poorly aligned with its intended goals, why would you expect positive results? What is most unfortunate, however, is that while many people now know this was Slavin's conclusion, very few understand the rather idiosyncratic process by which that conclusion was reached.

There are, at the same time, several unusual ironies in all this. Some years ago Benjamin Bloom (1984a, b) and his graduate students (Anania 1981, Burke 1983) conducted a series of studies emphasizing the especially powerful effects of tutoring. The model that Slavin now describes emphasizes the use of tutoring. Also, Slavin those are the best things to teach to other teachers. The process-product people admit, at least in private, that a lot of the individual teacher behaviors that they have found to be characteristic of effective teachers are really just indicators of hard-working, intelligent, insightful, very active teachers. Now, how do you get other teachers to exhibit these behaviors? That's a very different question.

It seems reasonable to try to teach those same behaviors to other teachers.

But in actual fact many of the programs derived directly from the process-product research have failed. One clear example is the Madeline Hunter programs. Everything Madeline Hunter talks about is very well established, either in laboratory research or correlational research or both; but when assembled into an experimental program, will it work in actual practice? We now have enough evidence to say that it doesn't.

What makes you say that? A lot of people think it works very well.

I don't think they would if they looked at the research. The study that Jane Stallings did in Napa, California (Stallings and Krasavage 1986); a study in West Orange, New Jersey (Donovan et al. 1987); a study involving the entire state of South Carolina (Mandeville 1988)—all three found essentially no difference between control classes and those using Hunter's methods.

Aren't there other explanations for the results in each of those instances?

Even with the problems that people cite, if there had been big effects, researchers would have found something, but in South Carolina, for example, where 15,000 teachers were trained in the Hunter method, researchers found nothing at all.

You're saying that in rushing to devise programs based on correlational research, educators may have jumped the gun a bit.

I'd be delighted if people were rushing out to design programs based on that research and then were carefully evaluating them. But I think it's

---

now criticizes mastery learning because some programs "chop knowledge into little pieces, and that's unnecessary." Yet his program would insist students master such discrete skills as "long 'a'." A final irony: in 1981, in *All Our Children Learning*, Bloom outlined his ideas on a comprehensive model of schooling, which considered the characteristics of teachers, students, and their interaction; the curriculum and instructional materials; peer groups; and the home environment. Slavin's comprehensive model, which includes "one-to-one tutoring, a completely restructured curriculum, family support services, and other components" is labeled "Success for All." Researchers hope, as descriptions of this model are developed, they will include appropriate citations.

Anania, J. "The Effects of Quality of Instruction on the Cognitive and Affective Learning of Students." Doctoral diss., University of Chicago, 1981.

Block, J. H., and R. B. Burns. "Mastery Learning." In *Review of Research in Education, Vol. 4*, edited by L. S. Shulman. Itasca, Ill.: Peacock, 1976.

Bloom, B. S. *All Our Children Learning*. New York: McGraw-Hill, 1981.

Bloom, B. S. "The Search for Methods of Group Instruction As Effective As One-to-One Tutoring." *Educational Leadership* 41, 8 (1984a): 4-18.

Bloom, B. S. "The 2-Sigma Problem: The Search for Methods of Group Instruction As Effective As One-to-One Tutoring." *Educational Researcher* 13, 6 (1984b): 4-16.

Burke, A. J. "Students' Potential for Learning Contrasted Under Tutorial and Group Approaches to Instruction." Doctoral diss., University of Chicago, 1983.

Gamoran, A. "Organization, Instruction, and the Effects of Ability Grouping: Comment on Slavin's 'Best-Evidence Synthesis.'" *Review of Educational Research* 57 (1987): 341-345.

Guskey, T. R. "Rethinking Mastery Learning Reconsidered." *Review of Educational Research* 57 (1987): 225-229.

Guskey, T. R., and S. L. Gates. "A Synthesis of Research on Group-Based Mastery Learning Programs." Paper presented at the annual meeting of the American Educational Research Association, Chicago, April 1985.

Hiebert, E. H. "The Context of Instruction and Student Learning: An Examination of Slavin's Assumptions." *Review of Educational Research* 57 (1987): 337-340.

Joyce, B. "A Rigorous Yet Delicate Touch: A Response to Slavin's Proposal for 'Best-Evidence' Reviews." *Educational Researcher* 16, 4 (1987): 12-14.

Slavin, R. E. "Best-Evidence Synthesis: An Alternative to Meta-Analysis and Traditional Reviews." *Educational Researcher* 15, 9 (1986): 5-11.

Slavin, R. E. "Mastery Learning Reconsidered." *Review of Educational Research* 57 (1987): 175-213.

Thomas R. Guskey is Professor, Department of Educational Policy Studies and Evaluation, College of Education, University of Kentucky, Lexington, KY 40506.

Research is never going to inform practice as it should until practitioners demand top quality experimental evidence before they adopt programs and practices on a large scale.

Response to Slavin: Toward a Greater Variety

Benjamin S. Bloom

When used correctly, mastery learning does improve student learning. However, no single method of improving learning will work well for all teachers, all school subjects, and all students.

We must have a greater variety of methods and programs to ensure good learning for most of the students in our schools. I am delighted that Robert Slavin recognizes this.

In a recent paper, I described needed improvements in mastery learning, initial prerequisites in a new course or subject, the support of the home environment, developing automaticity in reading, and teaching the higher mental processes (Bloom 1988).

Perhaps at some time in the distant future, even Robert Slavin will declare a truce in his opposition to mastery learning.

Bloom, B. S. "Helping All Children Learn Well in Elementary School—and Beyond." *Principal* 67, 4 (March 1988): 12-17.

Benjamin S. Bloom is Charles H. Swift Distinguished Service Professor, Department of Education, University of Chicago, 5835 Kimbark Ave., Chicago, IL 60637.

---

not appropriate to design such programs on the basis that "correlational research supports this, so it has to work in the classroom, and that's my proof."

What does that mean for the future of educational research?

In my view, research is never going to inform practice as it should until practitioners demand top quality experimental evidence before they adopt programs and practices on a large scale. They will also have to conduct, or allow to be conducted, good experimental studies of new methods within their own districts when they try them on a small scale. Until we have practitioners who say, "I'm not going to use that until I've

Until you've done experimental research, you shouldn't be talking to teachers at all.

seen good experimental evidence for it," we're going to continue on the educational pendulum with the "miracle of the month" and will not make much serious progress.

One response to what you're saying is that much of what we're doing right now doesn't have any validity so we have to keep trying what appears to be better even if we don't have the data.

You have to use your best judgment, yes. But we must demand better data for making important education decisions.

The other problem, of course, is that researchers argue among themselves about what, in fact, is true. One of the best-accepted tenets in recent years has been that mastery learning has powerful effects—and now you tell us it isn't so.

It would certainly be helpful if we had widely agreed upon standards for evaluation and more third-party agencies that were conducting evaluations. It would help us get away from some

Response to Slavin: What's the Best Evidence?

Herbert J. Walberg

Robert Slavin does me great honor by criticizing me along with Benjamin Bloom, who ranks with Gary Becker, James Coleman, Piaget, Carl Rogers, Skinner, and Margaret Wang among this century's great educational theorists. Credit for mastery learning research and synthesis, however, should hardly be accorded to me, since my part has been to calculate and compile estimates of the learning effects of many successful and popular educational interventions, including mastery learning (Walberg 1984).

The best recent estimate of mastery effects is large and close to Bloom's estimate and the one I cite (Kulik and Kulik 1986). To conclude that more time yields more learning or that short-term mastery studies show bigger effects than longer ones requires comprehensive evidence—dozens of studies of mastery—not Slavin's hand-picked "best evidence." The same may be said for other interventions for which we now have substantial evidence: some 8,000 studies and 112 reviews of them in my latest collection.

Slavin makes an expansive and unfilled promise; he claims "remarkable progress" with "Success for All" despite his apparently incomplete, uncontrolled, and unpublished single study. Yet he calls for "third-party" evaluation. Interested readers will find such evaluation of Slavin's work on mastery learning, cooperative learning, ability grouping, and class size in the highly critical commentaries on his theories, methods, and conclusions by about a dozen researchers that have followed his recent articles in the *Educational Researcher* and *Review of Educational Research*.

Kulik, J., and C. L. Kulik. "Mastery Testing and Student Learning." *Journal of Educational Technology Systems* 15 (1986): 325-345.
Walberg, H. J. "Improving the Productivity of America's Schools." *Educational Leadership* 41 (May 1984): 19-27.

Herbert J. Walberg is an Educational Psychologist and Research Professor of Education, University of Illinois at Chicago, 522 N. Euclid Ave., Oak Park, IL 60302.

Response to Slavin: Improving Teacher Decisions

Madeline Hunter

I heartily commend Robert Slavin for his endeavors to take a research-based analytic look at what can make a difference in education. I also appreciate the time he has spent becoming familiar with our teacher decision-making model since he wrote "The Hunterization of American Schools," where he characterized it as "rigid and mechanistic." Now he correctly states that the model is based on research that is "well established either in laboratory research or correlational research or both," before he claims the evidence shows it "won't work in actual practice." Let's examine that evidence.

● The Napa Project, given its flaws, presented hard data that test scores escalated when teachers were applying what they had learned. What the project really validated was that newly learned professional skills do not maintain themselves without encouragement and refinement from coaching. In addition, the teaching "skills" were used only for reading and math; therefore the teachers did not perceive them as generic elements in every teaching decision regardless of content or teaching mode. I criticized the project for the omission of the transfer theory that is central to the model.

● Manatt reports positive results with the SIM Project. An associate and I were active in establishing the integrity of content and the certification of its transfer from information to knowledge to judgment to wisdom, for both teachers and administrators. Without judgment and wisdom there is a danger of teachers' becoming robots.

● Although I have been involved in some workshops in West Orange, New Jersey, I cannot attest to the integrity of use of the model. I have serious questions about the general rigidity and "assembly line procedure" of some of the New Jersey Academy's work.

● In terms of the South Carolina study, the researchers state, "The unfortunate truth is that higher-level coaching skills are crucial to teacher improvement." Those skills were missing in many of the coaches. This condition also prevailed in the third year of the Napa Project. The amazing result in both projects was that teachers' attitudes were very positive.

I have cautioned educators in South Carolina against both the mass production of courses and the use of trainers with little or no certification of competence or content integrity. There I also cautioned the state superintendent against rigidity, lack of decision-making skills, and the adoption of a checklist. This fall I will be working with trainers in South Carolina and Arkansas to build correction into the "assembly line" aspects that unfortunately have developed.

Slavin ignores the original validation of the model (Project Linkage) conducted by an independent investigator, Rodney Skagar, which substantiated impressive gains by students in an inner-city Los Angeles school where the integrity of the model was certified. Also, how does he explain the 20-year escalation of acceptance all over the world? Surely educators are not that gullible—they must be seeing results.

There is no aerodynamic research available to support, and there is much to refute, a bumblebee's flying. But the bee flies! If practitioners really said, "I'm not going to use that until I've seen good experimental evidence for it," our classrooms would be immobilized. What research does Slavin believe is supporting current practice?

The Hunter model is an effort to change teaching decisions, many of which are based on tradition, folklore, and fantasy, to theory-based judgments and wisdom. Only by so changing can we move classroom teaching into behaviors that more closely approximate the success of tutoring, something we'll never be able to finance and which, with expert teaching, will seldom be needed.

Madeline Hunter is Professor of Education, University of California–Los Angeles, Department of Education, Moore Hall, 405 Hilgard Ave., Los Angeles, CA 90024-1521.

craziness had no bearing on what they do on a day-to-day basis. Because we don't have well recognized standards for what constitutes an adequate evaluation, Walberg took the approach of taking the studies that had "mastery learning" in the title, putting them all together, and reporting a number for them.

Your advice to practitioners then is to look more carefully at the data.

Yes. Before you accept the next program that comes down the pike, demand experimental-control comparisons in real schools over realistic periods of time with suitable measures of effectiveness.

You're saying the evidence is out there?

Yes. And there'll be a lot more—if people start demanding it.□

References

Donovan, J. F., D. A. Sousa, and H. J. Walberg. "The Impact of Staff Development on Implementation and Student Achievement." *Journal of Educational Research* 80 (1987): 348-351.

Mandeville, G. K. "An Evaluation of PET Using Extant Achievement Data." Paper presented at the annual convention of the American Educational Research Association, New Orleans, April 1988.

Slavin, R. E. "Mastery Learning Reconsidered." *Review of Educational Research* 57 (1987): 175-213.

Slavin, R. E. "Synthesis of Research on Grouping in Elementary and Secondary Schools." *Educational Leadership* 46 (September 1988): 67-77.

Stallings, J., and E. M. Krasavage. "Program Implementation and Student Achievement in a Four-Year Madeline Hunter Follow-Through Project." *Elementary School Journal* 87 (1986): 117-138.

Walberg, H. J. "Improving the Productivity of America's Schools." *Educational Leadership* 41 (May 1984):19–27.

Robert E. Slavin is Director, Elementary School Program, Center for Research on Elementary and Middle Schools, The Johns Hopkins University, 3505 N. Charles St., Baltimore, MD 21218. **Ron Brandt** is ASCD's Executive Editor.

of the arguments among researchers about what constitutes adequate evidence. If, for example, you told practitioners clearly that much of the evidence on mastery learning that Herb Walberg (1984) summarized in his synthesis was taken from studies of one week's duration, in which the corrective instruction, which the control group did not receive, was given in addition to regular class time, they would know immediately that such

Educational Leadership 45 (Oct. 1987): 35-39

On Teaching Thinking Skills: A Conversation with B. Othanel Smith

Teaching should not be reduced to models. Instead, teachers need to understand the logic of their subject matter and should master a set of pedagogical skills to use as necessary.

In 1925, when B. O. Smith received his Bachelor of Science degree in Education from the University of Florida, he was a pioneer in a new field. Now a major architect of teacher education and evaluation, he draws upon his years of service at the Universities of Florida, Illinois, and South Florida to share his reflections on the most promising route to improvement of the teaching profession.

You've worked for years on a topic of current interest to educators: thinking skills. How did that come about?

Some of us who were working with public schools in the Chicago area in the 1950s thought that if we could teach teachers the logic of their subject matter, their students would understand the subjects better. We tried this for two years, but our efforts were largely unsuccessful, primarily because we approached the problem from the standpoint of informing teachers about logic rather than how to handle subject matter in a logical way.

Why the emphasis on logic?

My primary interest from the beginning has been in the logic of teaching. My doctoral study was on the logic of measurement. Dewey's logical studies attracted me in the '20s, and I discovered Piaget in the early '30s. In fact, in 1937–38 I prepared a book-length manuscript, never published, on the teaching of thinking. Well, I came back to that work in 1956 and did a study of classroom discourse to find out what teachers actually taught about the logical structure of knowledge.

What did you find?

That teachers use all the logical operations, if you treat them in a very general sense, that you find in the logic books. But teachers are unaware of using them because these operations are partly built into the language and partly into the structure of the content. For example, definitions are an important part of instruction—teachers simply cannot teach without defining terms—yet defining is often poorly done because teachers aren't acquainted with the nature of definitions.

What do they need to know?

Well, there are different kinds of definitions: classificatory definitions, operational definitions, stipulative definitions, and so on. Here's one difference. If you want to define "rain," you're in difficulty if you try to use any other than a stipulative definition. For example, if a corporation insures a ball game against rain, they can say, "If it rains a specified amount, it will be counted as rainy; but if it doesn't, it is not a rain and we won't pay." It's like defining a bald-headed man: how many hairs can a man have and still be

described as bald? Some definitions are open-ended like that, while others are not.

So teachers need to understand the basis for a definition before they can teach it to students?

To develop and teach clear concepts, teachers need to understand the nature of definitions. A definition, of course, is a verbal counterpart of a concept. When you have a clear verbal definition, and you understand the referent of that definition, then you know the concept.

That's just one aspect of the logic of teaching. Explanation is also a part of logic. Teachers are constantly involved in explaining, but there are different kinds of explaining. There's explaining in the narrative sense: to explain how Lincoln was assassinated, we use a narrative approach; we describe sequences of events. If you're trying to explain why an object floats, you use an approach that entails relations among variables.

Are you saying teachers need to understand this kind of complexity in order to do their jobs?

It depends. If we want students to understand the content in depth, yes. All of us have gone through school, and even though we may not have such understanding, we usually do fairly well, but the deeper we go in any field the more we come to understand what I have been talking about. The question is whether we want a larger portion of the population to get a fuller glimpse of the sort of understanding that the more highly educated get now.

Isn't that what some of the curriculum developers of the '60s were trying to do? Develop a better understanding of the essence of the various disciplines?

I think so, but they didn't get very far because they got hung up on models. Any time you try to reduce teaching to a model you're in trouble, because models give us formulas, and formulas squeeze the life out of teach-

ing. The highly effective teacher will design his or her own way of teaching.

I was brought up on models. When I was an undergraduate student, it was "the project method." Then there was the Morrisonian "unit method"; before either it was Herbart's model. Every teaching procedure that becomes formalized becomes deadening. We should teach teachers the skills of teaching—skills of working with children and skills of handling content—and then let the teacher put these skills together.

Is what you're saying related to the kind of teaching models that Bruce Joyce and Marsha Weil have written about?

Yes, although they have assembled a number of effective skills, and that is an important contribution.

But otherwise you reject that approach?

Yes. I reject reduction of teaching to any sort of formula.

Is what you're saying related to the work you did in the '50s and '60s that you mentioned earlier?

In a sense, yes. I found no consistent patterns in the performance of teachers in the best schools or even in the performance of the most highly successful teachers.

I believe you once thought of yourself as a humanist but don't like that terminology anymore. Is that correct?

I don't think I ever made a point of calling myself a humanist, although I have talked about humanistic behavior in the classroom. Anyway, what sort of humanism are we talking about? There is scientific humanism, classical humanism, and there's social humanism. So it's not clear what sort of humanism we're talking about.

What about humanistic education?

I prefer to reduce humanism to pedagogical skills.

What's an example of that?

Say that you're involved in working with a child and another child comes up and asks you a question. You could say somewhat harshly to that child, "Go sit down; I'll get to you later." Or you could say to the child you're working with, "Why don't you go ahead with that part now," and then, speaking kindly to the other child, give some momentary help and say, "We'll do more on that later." That's what I would call a humanistic way of dealing with that situation.

Well, the one certainly sounds preferable to the other. But in what sense is that a skill?

I mean by skill a performance that you can modify according to circumstances. For example, talking to another person can be a skill. As I talk with another person, I can respond to what I'm saying in the same way as the other person responds. In fact, if I find myself saying something that may not be appropriate, I can rectify it immediately.

You may even interrupt yourself?

Yes. That's what I would call a skill: a physical performance. It's an act that I can respond to and modify.

That's a fairly behavioral way of looking at it, isn't it?

Yes, but it's cognitive as well. Whenever I start to say something, I can think about whether it's appropriate or not—that's a cognitive operation—and may change my direction. If an act is not under the control of a cognitive operation, it is sheer habit.

I want to ask you more about good teaching, but since we're talking about skills, let me ask you about the idea of teaching thinking skills. Is it defensible to refer to thinking as a set of skills that can be taught?

Yes, thinking can be a set of skills. It can come in many sets. It's a cognitive performance that has a physical manifestation in the way we handle information. A skillful thinker deals with data or information in ways not possible for the unskilled.

I am asking because I assume that skills can be improved with practice and coaching.

> "Any time you try to reduce teaching to a model you're in trouble, because models give us formulas, and formulas squeeze the life out of teaching."

Yes. We improve thinking by practice. It is appropriate to talk about teaching thinking skills; that is, ways of collecting and organizing data in order to classify, explain, predict, test, and so on. As one performs these skills, he or she can become more flexible and thereby more effective as a thinker.

What do you mean by "flexible"?

Experimental work, some as far back as the '30s, shows good results when teachers convey to students, "Look, don't just approach it one way; if that doesn't work try another, and if that doesn't work try something else." If students do that, the possibility of their coming up with more fruitful answers is increased. Of course, there are many ways of increasing students' flexibility.

Is being flexible really a skill?

Well, if a child gets to the point where he or she routinely says, "I'm doing this, but I'll try to do that—and if that doesn't work, I'll try to do something else," I'd look on that as a skill. Some would call it a disposition, and I wouldn't quarrel about that. Pedagogically it probably makes no difference.

What are some other teacher behaviors we should be encouraging if we want students to be better thinkers?

Let me discuss the question in this way. As a teacher, I may say, "Here are some problems I want you to solve." Now, what do I mean? I really mean that I am giving them problems that I have illustrated how to do. There are rules—procedural rules—for working

them. There are givens in the problem, and there are definite answers. That's what we mean, at least in school, by "problems." Psychologists now regard that sort of problem as "well-structured." We need to teach children to work such problems, but a lot of problems are unstructured: we don't know what the givens are, and we don't know whether there's a definite answer or not.

A good many of the situations we encounter in real life are like that.

They require an unstructured approach. They're comparable to what Dewey called "perplexing situations." These problems require skills different from those needed to solve well-structured problems.

Structured problems are more content specific. You can find illustrations of how to proceed with some of them in mathematics books. When it comes to unstructured problems, we are somewhat less certain about what to do. We can teach about experimentation: how to control variables, about correlation, about proportionality. These entail fundamental skills of thinking and should be mastered by teachers as well as by students. In addition, there are simple devices, like scatter diagrams, that can help show relationships among variables.

You seem to be saying, though, that we must depend on teachers to get this kind of information to students—that this is a matter of building teacher knowledge and skill, and not just of designing better curriculum materials.

That is correct. Student learning materials alone will not suffice. In ill-structured problems such materials can be a hindrance. The teacher must perform the skills of handling the content at high levels of thinking, at the intellectual level expected of the student. That sort of teacher performance is more important than anything else in the process of teaching students to think more skillfully.

> ## "The effective teacher is one for whom the valid skills of teaching and student management are second nature."

But you do want to provide more complete knowledge to teachers about what these mental processes are, don't you?

Not exactly. Teachers do not work with mental processes, but with knowledge and materials. We can name these processes, at least some of them, such as perceiving and judging, but we know very little about them. Our access to them is through materials and teacher performance. It cannot be overemphasized that the teaching of thinking does not take place by working directly with mental processes. It is the way teachers work with the content of instruction that affects the way students learn to think effectively.

In recent years you've been a strong advocate of use of the teaching effectiveness research. Is that the reason?

Yes. The prospective teacher has a very brief time to prepare for a tremendously complex task—more complex than any other profession. I want that teacher to get the skills and knowledge that we know constitute effective teaching, at all levels of thinking, and to the point that he or she can use them in the classroom as automatically as possible. To the extent they are automatic, he or she can give attention to other things. The effective teacher is one for whom the valid skills of teaching and student management are second nature.

Some say the kinds of behaviors that have been identified by the teaching effectiveness research are too narrow; that they only take us so far and no further; that, in fact, some of the things we want as teaching for thinking are contrary to behaviors that have been found to be associated with higher test scores.

Part of what you say is a truism: we never have complete knowledge; we're always wanting more, and rightly so. But the idea that effective skills of teaching are in conflict with teaching people to think has yet to be demonstrated. No, I don't see any incompatibility.

Schooling is short, and the amount of dependable knowledge we have about teaching is very limited. Anything that diverts that knowledge—that replaces valid pedagogical principles, concepts, and skills that teachers desperately need to handle knowledge successfully at any intellectual level—comes at a high cost.□

Reference

Joyce, Bruce, and Marsha Weil. *Models of Teaching*, 3d ed. Englewood Cliffs, N.J.: Prentice-Hall, 1986.

B. Othanel Smith is Professor of Education Emeritus, living at 854 Island Way, Clearwater, FL 33515. **Ron Brandt** is ASCD's Executive Editor.

Educational Leadership 43 (Oct. 1985): 50-53

NELSON QUINBY

On Testing and Teaching Intelligence: A Conversation with Robert Sternberg

Most IQ tests measure only a part of real-world intelligence, says Robert Sternberg, author of the new book, *Beyond IQ.* In this interview, he explains his triarchic theory, which incorporates individual experience and practical or social intelligence along with the mental mechanisms measured on most tests—and he contends that the main purpose of testing intelligence should be to diagnose individual strengths and weaknesses in order to train for improvement.

As an expert on intelligence, do you think schools should be using intelligence tests?

If the scores are used constructively, they can serve a valuable purpose. The main use should be to diagnose students' strengths and weaknesses and then capitalize on their strengths and remediate the weaknesses. But testing without training—without implications for instruction—is vacuous.

What kind of training? How do we bridge the gap between what an intelligence test measures and what is done from day to day in classrooms?

It depends on the test. With a conventional group intelligence test that gives one overall score, it's very hard to do. But we have to get away from thinking in terms of a single level of intelligence and think more in terms of a profile of strengths and weaknesses.

What tests are available that give such a profile?

Quite honestly, there is no test that I'm totally happy with yet. An individual test like the WISC—Wechsler Intelligence Scale for Children—gives some diagnostic information; the Differential Aptitude Test, which is fairly widely used at the secondary level, and the Cognitive Abilities Test give some differential information.

In the test I'm developing, which is based on my triarchic theory of intelligence, there is a section on applying thinking skills to everyday life. For example, we give the children an advertisement and ask what conclusions can legitimately be drawn from it. So they have to apply thinking skills to a situation they're confronted with frequently in their everyday lives. That's an example of what we call the *contextual* part of the test—and of the training program that's associated with it.

Another example of an important thinking skill is something we call *route planning*. Suppose you have an algebra problem. What are you going to do to solve it? In both the test and in the thinking skills training program, the students have to apply this planning skill to doing a series of errands. They are asked to decide what's the best possible sequence for doing the errands so as to maximize what they can get done.

The point I'm trying to make here is that a more nearly complete test or program will assess or train thinking skills in a broad everyday context.

You refer to thinking skills, but we were talking about intelligence. What is the relationship between the two?

Intelligence includes thinking skills, but there is more to intelligence than that—learning, for example, and certain kinds of perceptual skills. I think it is important to test for and train thinking skills but to do it in a broad rather than a narrow way.

What's an example of a broad way?

Some thinking skills programs are essentially disguised IQ tests. They have analogies, matrices, series completion; things that have very little to do with what goes on in school or in a child's life. A better thinking skills program will teach not only such abstract matters but will also help the child *use* thinking skills—*transfer* the thinking skills to everyday kinds of situations.

Wouldn't it be better to infuse thinking skills throughout the curriculum rather than having a special program?

I think that is a false dichotomy that unfortunately a lot of people in the thinking skills business have helped to propagate. The answer has to be both, because when it's only one way or the other, there are problems.

You need a separate program, especially initially, because if the thinking skills instruction is supposed to be infused, it tends to get lost. On the other hand, if you only have a separate program, there is often very little transfer. So I feel the best thing to do is have a separate program—one that emphasizes transfer of thinking skills for use in school and in everyday life—but also for teachers in other classrooms to understand what is being taught, and to be able to infuse at least some of the thinking skills into their programs.

In a way, it's like reading and writing skills.

Yes, that's a good analogy. When I was in school, teachers would often grade our compositions with two grades—one for soundness and originality of the content and another for how well the paper was written. For years I got better grades on the first than the second, and I never quite understood why, until in college my wife pointed out that my sentences didn't follow one from another. I realized that she was right, and I began trying to change my writing—but with direct instruction, I might have been able to correct it earlier. That's why I believe that direct teaching of thinking skills can be very helpful.

How does a teacher or an administrator decide what thinking skills

"...a more complete test or program will assess or train thinking skills in a broad everyday context."

are the most important to teach? As I review the literature, I'll see that someone's program has 112 thinking skills. Another will have four major categories with several subcategories, and so on.

The situation is not quite as bleak as it might appear, because although there are different taxonomies, they very often map into each other. Joan Baron, at the Connecticut State Department of Education, and I are editing a book on critical thinking based on a Connecticut state conference. The task fell to me of integrating various essays. I discovered the surprising extent to which people are saying the same things in different words.

The framework I use for both testing and training is to divide the set of mental processes involved in thinking into three kinds. One kind is what you might call *executive processes*: planning what you're going to do, monitoring while you're doing it, evaluating when it's done. For example, to do an algebra problem, you need to decide what formulas are relevant. Then, as you go through the problem, you need to keep track of where you are and where you need to go. When you're done, you evaluate whether your answer makes sense. I call these processes *metacomponents*.

The second set of components are *performance* processes: actually doing what the executive processes tell you to do. For the algebra problem, it would be plugging in the numbers and using the formulas.

The third kind of mental processes are what I call *knowledge-acquisition* components or learning components. It's learning how to do the problem solving in the first place.

So far you've been talking about three subdivisions of *one* aspect of intelligence, right?

Yes, the processes or components of thinking. A second aspect of intelligence is dealing with novelty: what's new. One of the problems in many tests—as well as training programs—is what I see as too much emphasis on

critical thinking: seeing what's wrong with things; being analytical. It's interesting that by the time students get here to Yale or other colleges, they may be quite good as critics: they can write a paper on what's wrong with a point of view. But they can't go beyond the information given; they can't come up with their own ideas.

You can look at this as *synthetic* or creative thinking. Can they see new problems in an old way? Or old problems in a new way? It's something that I think is grossly underemphasized both in teaching and training because, in later life, the creative skills are probably even more important than the analytic skills. It doesn't matter what field you get into; for example, in your field of school administration, there is some correlation between effectiveness and IQ, or even between effectiveness and critical thinking skills, but probably not much. It's more important to be a creative administrator: someone who can take a school and make it what it needs to be, who has new ideas for how the school can function. The same is true for scientists, writers, mathematicians, and so on. It's the synthetic thinkers who really make a difference. So that's the second aspect of intelligence that is important for tests to measure and programs to train for.

The third aspect I would stress is the real world, or *contextual* aspect. If you look at the large majority of intelligence or thinking skills tests, you see items that bear very little relation to the outside world. That would be okay if it turned out that performance on that kind of test was highly predictive of what happens to the child later on in life or even in school. But it turns out that the predictive power of such tests is quite limited. That's because, as many studies in psychology have shown, one gets very little transfer from such abstract matters to the real world. In a study of college teachers and business executives, we found that IQ is really a poor predictor of performance in those fields.

This third aspect of intelligence, which is scarcely measured by existing tests, depends in part on what I call

tacit or informal knowledge. It's what the student needs to know to succeed in the classroom and elsewhere that is almost never explicitly taught. You can look at it as a kind of *social* or *practical intelligence*. In our studies we have found that students who pick up this tacit knowledge—by a kind of osmotic process—tend to be the ones who are highly successful in school and later in life. For example, to be a successful teacher or principal, there are lots of things one needs to pick up from practical experience that are never taught in schools of education. I think it's important for a complete test of intelligence to measure this ability to acquire tacit knowledge.

Does your broader definition of intelligence help explain the controversy over bias in testing?

At our current state of knowledge, between-group comparisons are extremely hard to make, and the literature is deceptive on that. There have been lots of fancy statistical analyses showing that there isn't that much bias—*if* you accept the researchers' assumptions. But there are several reasons why the tests are not completely fair: first, even if children from different environments *were* using the same mental factors, structures, processes, or whatever, an important aspect of intelligence, as I mentioned, is coping with novelty, and a given test item may be much more novel for some people than others. For example, on an abstract matrix problem, even if a kid from, say, the ghetto, uses the same mental strategies as a kid from an upper middle-class background, that kind of problem may be very unfamiliar to him or her, while the kid from the middle-class background may not even need the directions; she may be able to solve it without reading the stuff.

A second point is that all parents raise their kids to be intelligent. But one of the things we have found in our research, and in research by anthropologists and others, is that parents in different subcultures can have different notions of what it means to be

"Bodies of knowledge . . . often become outdated. Thinking skills never become outdated."

intelligent. One study found, for example, that black parents often emphasize nonverbal communication skills very heavily in training young children, whereas white parents emphasize verbal communication skills.

That same study compared upper-, middle-, and lower-class white environments. In this particular group, it was found that parents from the lower social class background saw intelligence as being able to remember very well, so they trained their children in rote kinds of strategies. The middle- to upper-class parents, on the other hand, emphasized reasoning skills. When the kids went to school, those who were brought up to emphasize reasoning and problem solving were at an advantage. The point is that there can be all kinds of strengths and abilities in kids who don't do well on conventional tests and who don't look good in conventional classrooms.

What needs to happen for schools to do a better job of teaching students to think?

Several things. I think ASCD is doing a fine job already. ASCD is the one major education organization in the U.S. that has made this a major goal. So educators can learn a lot about the subject by reading journals like *Educational Leadership*. A second way is for ASCD and other organizations to sponsor conferences and workshops for teachers and supervisors. A lot of this has to start at the administrative level. If the superintendents and the principals and the curriculum coordinators don't understand it and back it, nothing is going to happen.

And there has to be continuing support. In a fairly large proportion of the districts where I have given talks, very little has happened by way of follow-up. The teachers get excited, they go back to the classrooms and are ready to go, but then it dies. There should be some kind of action committee, a small group of people who make plans to carry things forward.

Boards of education will put up money for program development—for sending people to con-

ferences—but they want to see results in one year. Is that realistic?

We have gotten significant results in as little as five weeks—but that was with fairly intensive training. But you're probably referring to the larger problem of evaluation.

There are lots of people who are eager to get thinking skills programs implemented but not to have them evaluated. Sometimes people are afraid that the results won't be favorable; that's what happens when program developers have more of a stake in their program than in educating children. But administrators and teachers also resist evaluation. Now, I see testing and instruction as inextricably related: if you have a program you should have a test, and if you have tests you should have programs. We have had all this intelligence testing for years with nothing done about it, and the attitude that nothing could be done about it. That's wrong.

One reason for nothing being done has been the ETS mentality—or whatever you want to call it—that intelligence is a fixed entity that can't be improved. With that notion, I really question what good the tests are going to be.

I have the opposite point of view. In the triarchic approach there's a test, and there's a training program, and the whole purpose of the training program is to make the post-test scores higher. The idea is not just to train for the tests; I am not recommending a Stanley Kaplan approach. If you simply train students in how to do the type of items that appear on a particular test, you're not really improving intelligence; in fact, some of the things you can do to raise conventional intelligence test scores might actually make students stupider. Your purpose is to *really* teach intelligence or thinking skills and then if you have a good test, the improvement in thinking will show up in higher test scores.

So, to summarize, your investigation of the nature of intelligence

has convinced you that intelligence includes three kinds of mental processes that you call components. It also includes two other things: the ability to cope creatively with new situations, and practical skills—tacit knowledge—that enable people to succeed in everyday life. You believe not only that schools should be in a position to measure all three of these types of abilities but that they should take responsiblity for developing them further. Isn't that a pretty tall order for schools to take on?

The education of children always has been and will continue to be a tall order. The question is where we want to place our priorities. If one takes the view that the major purpose of schooling is to help students become good problem solvers and to recognize what problems are worth solving; to become good decision makers and to know when decisions need to be made in the first place—if we want students to improve and make the most of the abilities they have, then we really don't have any other alternative.

Bodies of knowledge are important, of course, but they often become outdated. Thinking skills never become outdated. To the contrary, they enable us to acquire knowledge and to reason with it, regardless of the time or place or the kinds of knowledge to which they're applied. So, in my opinion, teaching thinking skills is not only a tall order but the first order of business for a school.☐

Reference

Sternberg, Robert J. *Beyond Intelligence: A Triarchic Theory of Human Intelligence.* New York: Cambridge University Press, 1985.
Robert J. Sternberg is Associate Professor, Department of Psychology, Yale University, Box 11A, Yale Station, New Haven, Connecticut 06520. **Nelson Quinby** is Director of Secondary Education, Joel Barlow High School, 100 Black Rock Turnpike, West Redding, Connecticut 06896.

Educational Leadership 40 (May 1983): 24-29

JERI RIDINGS NOWAKOWSKI

Q How did you become involved in the famous Eight Year Study?

Tyler: Let me begin by describing the public mood at the time of the Great Depression in the fall of 1929, shortly after I arrived at the Ohio State University. People were worried about their material losses and blamed much of it on the banks, the government, and the schools. The newspapers were reporting how bad the schools were, and a big conference was held in 1933 on "The Crisis in Education: Will the Schools Survive?"

Jeri Ridings Nowakowski is a post-doctoral fellow at Northwestern University, Evanston, Illinois.

On Educational Evaluation: A Conversation with Ralph Tyler

Ralph W. Tyler's leadership in education and evaluation spans half a century. In this interview, the "father of educational evaluation," now 82, explains his role in some of the more significant developments in American education, including the Eight Year Study, the General Education Development Test, National Assessment, the regional laboratory program, and the Center for Advanced Study in the Behavioral Sciences.

Since these accusations included no evidence of school decline, I wrote to the superintendents in Ohio asking them whether they had any of the tests from 25 or more years before. We found a number of communities where old tests were available, and we gave them again. We found, as was discovered in Indiana a few years ago,[1] that students did the same or better than those of the past. The public acceptance of the notion that in some way things are deteriorating seems to be due not to a presentation of facts but to the feeling of people that things are bad because they are not as well off as they expected to be.

Q: Do you feel that's true in 1983 as well?

Tyler: Yes, I do. When you look at National Assessment results, for example, you find there are more children able to read now than there were ten years ago. But the public doesn't pay as much attention to the National Assessment results as it does to the College Board report that the SAT scores were declining slightly: 30 points, which is only 2.4 points in raw score.

Q: You've brought up National Assessment, a project you began working on in the early sixties. Was National Assessment your brainchild?

Tyler: Well, I was asked to design the plans and was chairman of the exploratory committee to develop an effective operation that could be taken over by the Education Commission of the States.

Q: Has it turned out to be all that you'd hoped?

Tyler: Oh, nothing is ever all that one hopes for. But certainly it has begun to provide helpful data about the problems and progress of education in the United States.

Q: We were discussing your work at Ohio State.

Tyler: I had gone there because the Ohio legislature was concerned that half of the students who were enrolling in the freshman year never came back for the sophomore year, so they appropriated funds to be used to improve teaching and learning. I was to work half the time with faculties at the university and the other half with schools in the state. I began helping faculty members in departments that had required courses, such as botany and zoology. I would point out that the typical so-called achievement tests simply tested what students remembered about things that appeared in their textbooks. I would say, "Surely that isn't what you're after . . . you are not just teaching them to memorize." This led us to talk about the instructors' objectives—that is, what they really hoped their students would learn. Because the term "test" was usually interpreted as a collection of memory items, I suggested use of the term "evaluation" to refer to investigating what students were actually learning. As we developed evaluation instruments and began to use them, we obtained information about what students were

learning and not learning; how quickly they forgot information; and how long they remembered basic principles. This was going on during my first five years at Ohio State.

Without going deeply into the background of the Eight Year Study, one could say that it developed from a realization that the depression had brought into the schools many young people who did not plan to go to college; in fact, they didn't really want to go to high school, but they went because there was no place else to go. Youth unemployment was nearly 100 percent.

By 1929 we had reached a point where about 25 percent of an age group went to high school. In my day it had been only 10 percent, but as the depression went on, 50 percent of an age group were in high school. It doubled the enrollments. Many of these young people didn't find the curriculum for college entrance meaningful to them. And the other common program, the Smith-Hughes Vocational Education Program, was highly selective. It enrolled only those who were definitely planning a particular occupation like garage mechanics, homemaking, or agriculture.

High school principals realized that the schools should have a different program for these new students who were now in the high schools because they couldn't find work. But the course requirements of high schools then were pretty largely determined by, on the one hand, college entrance requirements and, on the other hand, the requirements of state education departments.

The Progressive Education Association, which was interested in innovations, took the responsibility of getting together a conference of school and college people, including the state departments, to determine what could be done. Out of that conference emerged the idea that a small number of schools (ultimately 30 schools and school systems) should be encouraged to develop programs designed to serve the high school students of that period. These 30 schools were to be given eight years in which to develop and try out new educational programs. During that time they would be freed from meeting the specific requirements of the state and of college entrance subjects in order to provide freedom for experimentation.

But there was a stipulation in the arrangement agreed to by the colleges and state departments: there would be an evaluation. First, records were to be available about the performance of students that would furnish information to help colleges make wise selections. Second, there would be an appraisal of what students were learning year after year in the high school so that the school would get continuing information as to whether they were learning something important. Third, there would be a follow up after graduation. The first year of the Eight Year Study (1933–34) the directing committee expected to use the General Culture Test developed by the Cooperative Test Service for the Pennsylvania Study of School and College relations. But this was just a test of information students recalled about the things presented in widely used textbooks in the various so-called basic subjects. The schools rebelled; that wasn't what they were trying to teach, so it would not be a fair measure of their efforts. They threatened to drop out of the study. This produced a crisis in the summer of 1934 at the time of the annual meeting of the participants.

At this point, a member of the directing committee, Boyd Bode, a well-known philosopher of education who had his office across the hall from me in The Ohio State University said, "We've got a young man in evaluation at Ohio State who bases evaluation on what the schools are trying to do. He works closely with them and doesn't simply take a test off the shelf. Why don't you see if he will take responsibility for directing the

evaluation?" I was interviewed and agreed to accept a half-time appointment as director of evaluation for the project.

Q: Would you say that Tylerian evaluation, as we understand it, was born during the Eight Year Study?

Tyler: Well, it depends on what people want to call Tylerian evaluation.

Q: I have heard you discuss the evaluation process when you train evaluators, and it sounds a good deal richer than the six or seven steps often used to describe objectives-based evaluation.

Tyler: Oh, surely you can't use just objectives as the basis for comprehensive evaluation, but it is very important to find out whether teachers are accomplishing their purposes. When people think of "Tylerian" as a single process it's like saying Dewey only mentioned child interests; there is no way of summarizing very simply any human being's notions about something complex. But for convenience we are likely to give a procedure a name, rather than describing it more fully.

Q: As you worked with teachers to produce objectives, you must have had an impact on curriculum.

Tyler: I think so, especially in areas where there had not been much clarity in curriculum descriptions. For example, the teachers of literature would usually repeat some trite phrase like "the students should learn to appreciate literature." I said, "Well, that sounds sensible. What do you mean by that? What have you observed that you are trying to help young people learn that you call 'appreciation'? Is it that they can tell you who wrote a book? Is it that they can make critical judgments of a literary work in terms of some criteria, such as unity or illusion of reality?" We discussed such things until we began to agree that ultimately with literature we were concerned with comprehension, interpretation, and appreciation. They meant by appreciation that readers respond emotionally and thus their lives are richer. All that came out of discussions, and from continuous reminders: "Don't look at some taxonomy to define your objectives. You're a teacher working with students. What have you found students learning that you think is important?"

> **"To learn something you can't use means that in the end it will be forgotten. One must consider the learners: what they have already learned, what their needs are, and what their interests are. . . ."**

Q: So, it's a matter of articulating some things that teachers know how to do, have been doing, but probably need to refine. You approach educational problems with a great deal of common sense.

Tyler: The only problem with common sense is that it's so uncommon.

Q: One could say that while there might not have been a formal step for assessing the worthwhileness of objectives, that was in fact always going on in the "Tylerian" evaluation process.

Tyler: Yes, of course. The schools were helped not only by the evaluation staff but by a curriculum staff working under Professor Alberty. In 1938, the schools were saying they were getting more help from the evaluation staff than from the curriculum staff. Alberty explained this by saying: "Tyler has a rationale for evaluation and there isn't any rationale for curriculum." So when we were having lunch, I said to Hilda Taba, my right-hand associate, "Why, that's silly, of course there's a rationale for curriculum." I sketched out on a napkin what is now often called "the curriculum rationale." It indicates that in deciding what the school should help students learn, one must look at the society in which they are going to use what they learn and find out the demands and opportunities of that society. To learn something you can't use means that in the end it will be forgotten. One must consider the learners: what they have already learned, what their needs are, and what their interests are, and build on them; one must also consider the potential value to students of each subject. After lunch I said to the curriculum people, "Here's a rationale you might want to follow," and from that outline a rationale began to be developed.

Q: It seems that in the early days of educational evaluation you really couldn't talk about evaluation without talking about curriculum; that they were completely intertwined.

Tyler: Well, if you are talking about evaluation of education, of course.

Q: But as evaluation has prospered, the two have grown apart. Educational evaluation has taken on a life of its own and is really not attending to curriculum.

Tyler: That happens in all professional fields; medical research has often forgotten the patient, who has become clinical material, and forgotten the role of the physician as a health counselor. It was as if in some way, once the physician knew what was going on in the human body, automatically the patient would get well; but we know that only the patient can get himself well—just as only the children can learn; you can't learn for them. So there is all this evaluation business up here without considering what it is the learner is doing.

The same problem exists with social work; social workers sometimes think of clients as having no minds of their own. But when, for instance, people discover that money can be had for aid to dependent children, some are tempted to say, "That's a way to make my living. I'll just have more children and get more money." You've got to consider the social situation and what it means to the so-called clients. They're not inert objects out there to be worked on. You can do that if you're working on plants, but you can't do that with human beings.

Q: Yet the federal money that moved evaluation forward brought us . . .

Tyler: Has it moved us forward?

Q: Well, it brought us large funded programs and with them program evaluation, which has grown and become more methodologically diverse. I guess the question is whether program evaluation has co-opted curriculum evaluation in the public school system.

Tyler: I think there will be much less money from the federal government for that kind of evaluation and that may help people stop chasing dollars and try to consider what is really involved in effective evaluation, and who the clients are. One of the problems is that they see the clients as being the federal government: the Department of Education, NIE, or the Congress, instead of the teachers and other people who operate schools, and the parents and children. When you have those clients, you have to have different considerations.

Q: In 1938 you moved from Ohio State back to the University of Chicago, where you had earned your doctorate. At Chicago you became chairman of the department and later dean of the Division of Social Science.

Tyler: I went there to do two things. One was to head the Board of Examinations responsible under the Chicago plan for determining students' completion of their educational programs. The other was to take Mr. Judd's place, who was retiring, and so to be head of Education.

Q: Egon Guba said to me that while people know you as a researcher, a theoretician, and a statesman, you were also a wonderful administrator and a very good dean. Did you enjoy administration?

Tyler: Yes, if you define administration as Lord Acton did: "the art of the possible." I like to help people find ways of using their talents most effectively, and that's usually by giving them an opportunity for a time to do what they think is important. Then, from that experience, try to clarify what they can do best in that context.

I think that Guba was especially influenced by his own major Professor, Jacob Getzels. I found Getzels teaching social psychology in the Department of

Human Relations at Harvard and brought him to Chicago. He said he was a social psychologist and asked, "What do you want me to do?" I said, "I don't want you to teach anything until you feel you've got something to teach. I'd like to have you go around to schools and see what is going on in education that could be understood by utilizing social psychology." He told me later that he didn't really believe me, so when the quarter started he said, "What am I to teach?" I said, "Whatever you feel is important to people in education." "Well, I don't know." "Until you find that, just go on observing schools and talking to school staff." So this went on until he felt he had something to teach teachers.

Q: So you were a facilitator?

Tyler: That's what an administrator should be: a person who helps make possible what others dream and hope they can do. I might name a good many others I tried to help; for example, Herb Thelan. I found him teaching chemistry in the university high school in Oakland and again I had him, before he taught anything, observe what was going on in teaching. He became interested in the interaction of students and teachers. He said he wanted to work on that, so I set up a laboratory in which interactions in the classroom could be observed and recorded; a place in the laboratory school where he could study different groups of students. We didn't have videotape in those days but we had audiotape and we had ways of looking through one-way mirrors and so on. So he began to have a chance to do what he had discovered to be interesting.

Q: I'm moving through your life too rapidly. I was about to take you to 1953, when you became Director of the Center for Advanced Studies.

Tyler: But you may want to understand that during the war I was also Director of the Examinations Staff to develop educational testing for the armed forces. The GED Test was developed there, guided by Everett Lindquist of the University of Iowa.

We originally developed GED so that young people who were returning from military service after the second world war would have a chance to demonstrate what they'd learned and get some credit for it.

"Kids have to learn to take responsibility and take the consequences when they make a mistake; that's the way they learn."

Q: You were also instrumental—you and Frank Chase—in beginning regional labs in our country.

Tyler: Yes, in 1964 Lyndon Johnson set up a task force headed by John Gardner to see what needed to be done in education. I was responsible for writing the section on laboratories, the substance of which was included in the Elementary and Secondary Education Act of 1965. We viewed laboratories as the "middlemen" between research and schools. We already had the R and D Centers in which educational research and development was supported. What we needed was a way by which the consumers—the schools—could identify problems they had and seek help from research of the past as well as the present. The laboratories were to represent the consumers, but the laboratories that were actually funded were, with some exceptions, oriented toward the producers of research rather than the consumers. We still lack "middlemen" in most regions.

Q: From 1953 to 1963 you were Director of the Center for Advanced Studies. What were the Center's major contributions during that decade before you began work on National Assessment?

Tyler: Providing an opportunity for very able behavioral scientists to spend time thinking and studying when they were not responsible for teaching and other services based on their previous work. At the Center they could think about what they needed next and get ideas for future development.

Q: So once again you nurtured people so they could do good things in education and research.

Tyler: Well, nurture is a term that depends on how suppliant you think they are. And, of course, don't forget the basic political principle that has guided many pressure groups in seeking government funds—when a sow is suckling a pig, the sow enjoys it as much as the pig.

Q: I like that one. Tell me, when you look back on a career that has already had so many pinnacles . . .

Tyler: I don't think there are pinnacles.

Q: Would you buy tiny hills?

Tyler: I don't think of them that way at all. I was just doing what seemed important at the time.

Q: Just plodding along with Ralph Tyler. Is there something that gives you a special sense of personal accomplishment?

Tyler: I never thought of it in those terms.

Q: If you don't think about accomplishments in a personal sense, what about as contributions to education?

Tyler: I thought they were useful, but I never tried to examine them.

Q: You don't rank order?

Tyler: No, I certainly don't.

Q: Okay. But you've often been referred to in the literature as the father . . .

Tyler: I invented the term "evaluation" when applied to educational procedures; so if naming the child, as the godfather names babies, makes you father, then I am. And when it began to be a cliché and evaluation meant so many different things to different people, I began using the term "assessment."

Q: Well, that's what I wanted to ask: the amount of paternal responsibility you take for this offspring that is credited to you.

Tyler: You can't take responsibility for what other people do, so the only thing you can do when anything becomes a cliché is to get a new word.

Q: And that's "assessment"?

Tyler: Right now its assessment, but that will become a cliche too because many people quickly catch on to forms and labels without understanding the substance of something.

Q: Speaking of labels, there are a growing number in evaluation. I think Michael Scriven said that, at one count, there were over 50 evaluation models. We have at least two major professional evaluation organizations; we have a number of evaluation journals, and several sets of standards. Do you think this is progress?

Tyler: Probably not. It depends on whether evaluation has become so popular that it's a fad and is likely to fade. However, there will be people who really are concerned with finding out what is going on in our educational program and want to understand it. That's what science is about—trying to find out what's really going on.

Q: If you were to run a major project tomorrow, would you hire someone called an evaluator to work with you on the project?

Tyler: It depends on whether the person could do what needed to be done.

Q: What kind of a job description would that be?

Tyler: Evaluation is a very broad term—what is it that needs to be done?

Q: Let's talk about the need for educational statespersons and how to get them.

Tyler: You might want to talk first about why some situations produce more statesmen than others. Amos advanced a theory in his book of the Bible that in periods of affluence (he described vividly how women flaunted their jewelry), people were no longer interested in God because they could satisfy their wants easily. The great ethical period for the Jews was in their Babylonian captivity. The general theory, which is hard to refute because it seems to fit so many historic periods, is that the human being is both an animal that, like other animals, depends upon various physical things—food, for example—and is greatly attracted to material possessions but also is capable of immense efforts to attain goals that are nonmaterial: concern for others, unselfishness, altruism, and so on. In times when it's easy to satisfy the material wants, people generally become greatly attached to material things. In difficult times, when the physical gratifications are not easily obtained, more time is spent in seeking nonmaterial goals.

John Dewey pointed out that people are problem solvers. They're not just cows that chew their cud after a nice meal in the pasture. People have been able to meet new environmental problems when other organisms perished because they couldn't adapt. This suggests that the environment in which people will continue to develop is one where goals require effort and problems must be solved.

Now, that's a theory of history that may be useful in this connection. Look back at the times we've had people we call statesmen. For example, in the case of Horace Mann, it was when there was a great expansion in the elementary school system of Massachusetts. They didn't have enough teachers, and he had to solve the problem of how to educate teachers, so he invented the normal schools. But during the periods before that, when there wasn't a great expansion and when there weren't problems of educating teachers, they didn't have any demand for persons to lead them in new ways.

Q: If times are getting bad, are we about to see the emergence of some new statesmen?

Tyler: The times ahead are likely to be austere, but that does not mean they necessarily will be bad for education or for people who care about serving others. Those are things that can become better during periods of austerity.

Q: So the funding hiatus in education might in fact help us?

Tyler: It's probably going to produce better education.

Q: What are the major problems of American education K–12?

Tyler: We are still struggling with reaching all the children of the whole population. The civil rights movement has made us conscious of a lack of adequate service for various minority groups. That's still with us, and it is likely to be with us for some time because of the increased number of illegitimate children born to teenage mothers who won't be able to provide a background for their children unless their grandparents bring them up. We're going to have a lot of children coming in who do not have the background in the home that we've been accustomed to, so that's certainly a problem—the education of so-called disadvantaged children.

The second problem we've got to work on more effectively is the transition of youth into constructive adult life, which means being able to move easily from school to work, being able to accept and carry on effectively the responsibilities of citizenship, of all aspects of adult life. We have continually tried to keep youth off the labor market, and we've continually tried to lengthen their period of childhood without allow-

ing them to gradually assume more responsibilities. Kids have to learn to take responsibility and take the consequences when they make a mistake; that's the way they learn.

A third problem, greatly related to it, is the problem of rebuilding the total educational environment for children. What's happened with changes in the home; with mothers' employment? What's happened with television taking the place of more constructive recreation? We've got to rebuild that environment because the demands for education are far greater than can be met in the limited time available in school.

Why don't we stop with those three. I could add some more if you wish; they're enough to keep us busy and happy for some time.

Q: Thank you, I've enjoyed it.

Tyler: Now, fine, can we make a date for a later time . . .

Q: Sure . . .

Tyler: And a different place . . . ☐

[1]Roger Farr, "Is Johnny's/Mary's Reading Getting Worse?" *Educational Leadership* 34 (April 1977): 521–527.

This article is adapted from "An Interview with Ralph Tyler," by Jeri Ridings Nowakowski, Occasional Paper Series, The Evaluation Center, Western Michigan University, Kalamazoo.

Educational Leadership 44 (May 1987): 39-43

On School Improvement in Pittsburgh: A Conversation with Richard Wallace

Pittsburgh is widely recognized as a school district on the move. What do you do to get these things to happen?

We have a set of priorities, established by our board in 1981, that have energized the district. A good example is our Schenley High School Teacher Center. When we started planning it, I pulled together a group of people from all levels. I typically do this for several reasons: I want a cross section of people to begin thinking through a problem, and while we're doing that I look for people who have ideas, who have ambition, who are willing to take risks.

When you called the group together did you already have such a center in mind?

Yes. In fact, I had recommended it to the board, in a two-paragraph memo. When they asked how much it would cost, I said I really didn't know; probably between a million and a million and a half a year, but I couldn't tell them more until I had worked out details. Naturally they said they'd be more comfortable if I handed them a more definitive plan, so that's how we got started. I asked people in the district about potential talent; I got the names of a lot of people, including

In 1981, Richard C. Wallace, Jr., Pittsburgh's Superintendent, initiated a broad program of educational reform to improve quality of instruction, educational performance of students, and the professional workplace for educators.

"One of the most important things we've done is to turn around student achievement and significantly narrow the gap in black/white achievement. There is still a gap—about 18–20 percent—but when we started it was 35–40 percent."

Judy Johnston, now director of the center, and I convened a group of about 16. We worked together over a period of five or six months developing the proposal. Each of them, by the way, was also on a satellite committee. We had 200 teachers all told involved in the planning.

Whose idea was it to organize that way?

I guess it was mine. I firmly believe that if something is going to work you've got to involve the people who will be implementing it. We presented the plans to the board, they adopted them unanimously, and we got planning money from the Ford Foundation. The person I felt had the most leadership potential was Judy Johnston, so she was appointed director.

How did you go about getting money for something like the Schenley center? For most school districts that would seem impossible.

Well, it was a little difficult. We got a one-year $120,000 planning grant from the Ford Foundation. Once the board agreed to go ahead with it, we thanked the 200-member teacher steering committee and convened another group of 75 teachers to do detailed planning with Judy when she was appointed director. Then, during the course of that year I went to a committee of local foundation people and told them, "Our board is making a very substantial commitment to improve the quality of education in the city, and you need to demonstrate that you appreciate what they are doing. I want to sell you endowed chairs. I want you to support the resident teachers at Schenley by paying half their salaries." They said they didn't like that idea, so I asked what they would be willing to do. We spent four to five months deciding how we would seek funding.

Then they did a very smart thing. They convinced me to compile a kind of shopping list of potential support activities and sponsors for Schenley. One committee member said, "We'll put up the first $25,000 to hire a part-time development director who will go around to all these foundations and do the fund raising you don't have time to do." We were able to raise over $1.4 million from local foundations to support Schenley.

How do you get a board of education to approve such a project?

In our case it grew out of a comprehensive needs assessment. Probably the smartest thing I ever did when I arrived in Pittsburgh in September of 1980 was to get Bill Cooley and Bill Bickel [of the University of Pittsburgh] to work with me, because at that time I had only one evaluation staff member, who managed testing. We conducted a very broad-based needs assessment, surveying samples of public school and private school parents, community leaders, and every level of employee in the district. We got huge amounts of data in the fall of 1980, and then in January 1981 we presented the results to the board. I reminded board members that they had been part of the data pool, and I said, "This is what people in this city say are the problems of the district. Now what do *you* think are the problems? I want you to identify priorities for me to go to work on." I did that for two reasons. One, for self-protection; I recognized that their concerns about the schools were so diverse that there was no hope of my succeeding unless I could focus their attention on a few achievable priorities. Second, the board had been bad-

ly divided over desegregation when I arrived, so I felt they had to be unified some way.

So the board voted their priorities. The top priority was improving student achievement, the second was improving the quality of personnel evaluation, and the third was managing enrollment decline. It was very apparent that we had to close three high schools and a number of elementary and middle schools. After spending about nine months talking about school closings, I said, "I think you have a unique opportunity here. You've got to close at least three high schools, but if you do you're going to lose 100–150 relatively young veteran teachers (teachers with 7 to 15 years' experience) that I don't think you can afford to lose. And how can you achieve your top priority of improving academic achievement with staff who haven't been back to graduate school in probably 15 to 20 years? Here's an opportunity to take one of the high schools that is slated for closing and make it a clinical center for staff revitalization. If we do this, everybody in the district will know what we expect of them instructionally." So the board members said, "Let's go."

You're saying the board supported the plan partly because the need had been carefully established.

Yes. They didn't know exactly what they were supporting, obviously, and most of the staff didn't either. I did, because I had experienced it before. As a student and as a junior faculty member, I had been in the Harvard-Lexington and Harvard-Boston programs back in the mid-60s. When I was director of elementary and middle schools in Holliston, Massachusetts, we had the opportunity to open a new middle school. I got some federal funds and made it a condition of employment (that was in the days before collective bargaining) that to teach in that middle school you had to go through a clinical summer training program similar to the Harvard programs.

Both of those experiences paved the way for Schenley, but the Holliston program, like Harvard-Lexington, had been held during the summer. Not only was the Schenley program to be

in a fully operating school during the regular academic year; it was to be at the *high school* level (the Harvard-Lexington program was for elementary and junior high).

Schenley is completing that first big four-year effort and moving into a new phase, isn't it?

Yes. We're considering a proposal to provide the Schenley training program to high school teachers from suburban communities in Allegheny County.

We're also working on ways to disseminate the "spirit of Schenley" to all high schools in the district. We call them "Centers of Excellence." We'd like to see each high school develop, demonstrate, and disseminate its own unique instructional, organizational, or pupil service technique to improve pupil performance, and share it with other schools. The Schenley faculty, for example, plans to concentrate on personalizing instruction for students and on interdisciplinary teaching.

That sounds like a very ambitious agenda. Can it really happen?

Absolutely. We have created such a powerful group of professionals at Schenley that they believe they can do anything—and they can.

What makes them so powerful?

Well, we've put them in a highly professional environment, and we've given them an opportunity to develop their individual talents to the fullest. Whenever one of them has come up with an idea, we've found ways to support it, so they believe they can make a difference.

You say when they come up with an idea you support it. Surely people have bad ideas now and then.

Well, bad ideas don't work, so you don't continue them.

But you don't shut them off earlier?

No, because you never know what's going to work.

I understand that you typically have lots of things going on at any one time in Pittsburgh. Why?

You've got to have many things going on simultaneously because you don't know which ones are going to work. If you put all your eggs in one

> "We've established that virtually every youngster can master the basic fundamentals of learning—but that's not education. At this point, we are defining the educated person as a person who can respond, both orally and in writing, to higher-order questions that deal with concepts, generalizations, and themes coming out of the academic disciplines."

"We've now got a system . . . that's simple, workable, and clearly effective. We call it MAP: Monitoring Achievement in Pittsburgh."

basket, you increase your likelihood of failing. There are lots of things to be done in schools. The more ideas you are trying out, the more people you have involved, the greater the likelihood of creative solutions to problems.

You seem to be saying that it's perfectly okay if some things *don't* work.

Oh sure.

But there are people who say that our schools shouldn't be laboratories where we test untried ideas. They say we should know whether something works before we use it.

We'd never make progress if we played the game that way. We have to guarantee parents that at a minimum, their kids will be educated, and I think we have to take all the appropriate safeguards—which is why we typically pilot-test programs very carefully before we implement them throughout the district.

Say a little more about that minimum guarantee.

One of the most important things we've done is to turn around student achievement and significantly narrow the gap in black/white achievement. There is still a gap—about 18–20 percent—but when we started it was 35–40 percent. Both groups of students are now above national norms, by the way. On the average, white students in the elementary schools have gone from about the 60th to the 80th percentile on standardized tests, and black kids have gone from about the 36th to the 60th. We think it's quite dramatic—and it demonstrates what the process I call "achievement monitoring" can do. I've been working on the idea professionally for about 25 years, and I think I've made all the mistakes one can make. We've now got a system in Pittsburgh that's simple, workable, and clearly effective. We call it MAP: Monitoring Achievement in Pittsburgh.

How does it operate?

Let me tell you how we started, because again you'll get the notion of participation, which is so important. When I'd been in Pittsburgh just a couple of months, I made an assumption that student achievement was going to be the board's top priority. I had done a lot of work over the years in developing achievement monitoring programs; in fact one that my colleagues and I developed in Fitchburg, Massachusetts, was validated for statewide dissemination. Here's how it works: we pull together a group of teachers—English, math, science, and so forth—and we ask them to tell us the 20 most important learning outcomes in their academic disciplines at each grade level. We ask for 20—not 220—because I've learned over the years that teachers can manage effectively only about 20 objectives a year, give or take a few. Once we have achieved reasonable consensus among that group, we ask all the other teachers whether or not they agree with their colleagues that these are the most important learning outcomes in math or whatever, so we involve everybody. And the rule is that if you do not agree, you must provide a constructive alternative. When we have consensus on what the most important learning outcomes are, we dismiss that group and convene another group. We say to them, "Your colleagues say these are the most important learning outcomes. Your job is to develop what you're willing to accept as evidence that these outcomes have been achieved."

So it's not technicians who develop the test items?

No, the teachers do it. Once again we send the materials out for everybody to agree or disagree with and bring back the data. Then we dismiss that group and call in another group of teachers and say, "Okay, your colleagues say that these are the outcomes, these are the measures; now you take a look at the instructional materials you have and tell us whether these materials are adequate to the task that's been laid out. If not, we want you to find materials that will help teachers teach to these objectives."

Then we call in representatives from the three groups of teachers who have participated in this multi-tiered process and ask them to develop a plan for implementing the program, including teacher training. Well, in that process, we've involved an awful lot of people. It usually takes a year to a year and a half to go through this entire process for one subject. Now, I knew I could do math very quickly because I had done it a number of times in the past, so we were able to crank up the system within six months and get the math program operating in all the schools, grades one to eight, by September of 1981. Math is relatively easy. Writing, grammar, composition are much more difficult—and reading is the most complex. We now have monitoring systems in all those subjects. On top of that, we have added critical thinking.

We test kids on multiple occasions during the year. We test them on *all* objectives on all occasions, whether they've had instruction on the objectives or not: thus we are constantly foreshadowing for the kids what we expect them to learn. And we test them using one item per objective, because we don't want the test to consume too much instructional time. We give computer printouts to the teachers, but also to the kids to take home to their parents, so everybody knows where everybody is at any given point in time. The kids and the teachers know what's expected of them.

Is this process so complicated and expensive that smaller districts just couldn't do it?

No, it isn't. I did it in a small district in Massachusetts, and the cost at that time was less than $2 per student per year for any academic subject.

What about the security problems involved in having only one item per objective?

That's not important. Being able to divide fractions is being able to divide fractions. We expect teachers to teach to the objectives. There's no point in cheating, anyhow, because the real criterion performance is on the California Achievement Test.

In this and other things you seem to have an idea in mind for where things might lead when you start something. Many times you're thinking two or three years beyond where you are now.

Yes. Let me give you an example. We're now working on what we call our "syllabus-driven" examination program. We've been building up to this for six years. We've established that virtually every youngster can master the basic fundamentals of learning—but that's not education. At this point, we are defining the educated person as a person who can respond, both orally and in writing, to higher-order questions that deal with concepts, generalizations, and themes coming out of the academic disciplines. We expect to model our questions after the advanced placement examination systems, with one very fundamental difference: these exams will be for all kids. Also, rather than administering the test just once and making a pass/fail judgment about the youngster, we will test quarterly. As in our achievement monitoring program for skills, we will be constantly communicating to the students what we expect them to learn.

We did a feasibility study on the examination system a year or so ago in a world cultures course that's taught to every tenth-grader. We found that all kids can move constructively in the direction of mastery. So we're now in the process of developing a brief syllabus, four to five pages in length, that will lay out for the kids what it is that we expect them to learn by the end of tenth-grade English or eleventh-grade U.S. history. We'll give them examples of how they will be tested—sample multiple-choice questions and sample essay questions—so they will understand what the expectations are.

This, by the way, reflects a very strong bias of mine: you figure out what your goals ought to be, you move immediately to criterion outcomes, and then you look at how you get from here to there. Eventually our syllabus-driven examination system will be the way we judge how well our kids are being educated.□

Richard C. Wallace, Jr., is Superintendent, Pittsburgh Public Schools, 341 S. Bellfield, Ave., Pittsburgh, PA 15213. **Ron Brandt** is Executive Editor of the Association for Supervision and Curriculum Development.

Educational Leadership 41 (Oct. 1983): 42-44

Arthur Wise by Al Way

On Standards and Public Policy: A Conversation with Arthur Wise

Ron Brandt

Arthur Wise, Senior Social Scientist at the Rand Corporation, Washington, D.C., criticized the tendency of courts and legislatures to bureaucratize schools in his 1979 book, *Legislated Learning*. In this interview Wise, a consultant to the ASCD task force that investigated the Florida legislature's new graduation requirements, argues that public officials are still using the wrong approach in their efforts to improve education.

RON BRANDT

The Commission on Excellence recommends higher graduation requirements, more stringent standards, more homework. What will be the results if those recommendations are followed?

Well, to some degree American education has become soft, so we must have higher standards—intelligently applied. We have gone too far in allowing students to choose electives and we have not expected as much in the way of homework and hard work as we should. But when state policymakers get into the act, there is a tendency for them to try to translate their goals and aspirations into something more concrete by passing legislation.

For example, in the middle and late 1970s, many of the states adopted minimum competency testing. As some of us predicted, that led to an overemphasis on basic skills and preparation for tests. The failure of minimum competency testing to improve education should have taught legislators something, but it probably did not.

You've been opposed to minimum competency testing from the beginning.

It's too simplistic. Its only effect could have been to cause the state to become a more active determiner of educational policy and practice than it should be. You may recall that many of the states said they would start with tests in basic reading and arithmetic but that they planned eventually to cover the entire high school program. In other words, there would be a statewide test for graduation that would in effect determine the high school curriculum. Fortunately, we haven't seen that happen, and while minimum competency testing remains on the books, people are paying less and less attention to it, in part because policymakers have recognized the limitations of that approach as we face the obviously growing demand for a more highly educated citizenry.

Is there a difference between minimum competency testing mandated for a whole state and tests used at the local level to check whether students are learning what they should?

Tests are a necessary part of good school management. What bothered me about the minimum competency testing movement is that if it were taken seriously, it would have led to the creation of a state-level bureaucracy that would not only have planned the tests, but would slowly have gotten into the management and design of the curriculum.

And even though testing is necessary, I think standardized testing is overemphasized in this country. Instead of teaching children reading and history in a way that will help them gain appreciation for those subjects, we teach them so as to ensure that they will do well on the tests.

How did we get to be so dependent on testing?

It arises partly because we no longer trust teachers to tell how well students have learned. It used to be that teachers' grades were accepted as an accurate statement of students' learning. Schools continue to have report cards, of course, but they've also been developing external mechanisms to check on teachers, and teachers recognize that.

Tests are part of a wide-ranging set of forces that are undermining the teacher's role and making teaching less attractive, which in turn causes fewer talented people to choose teaching as a career. And that brings us full circle. Having intervened repeatedly in the last decade or two to try to improve the quality of education, policymakers may have made things worse, which in fact will result in even poorer teachers than we have now. That is the real crisis in education.

You're saying that policymakers have actually contributed to the crisis.

I believe that at the root of people's lack of confidence in education is their perception of the quality of people staffing our schools. And the regulatory efforts of the last decade and a half that I explored in *Legislated Learning*[1] were attempts to control what was being done in classrooms, even though in fact very little could be done. For the last decade we have had pretty much a static teaching force. American education couldn't be reformed by changing either the nature of the people going into teaching or their preparation experiences. The steps that were taken—regulation, legislation—made the role of the classroom teacher more bureaucratic. And according to research I am conducting with Linda Darling-Hammond, my colleague here at the Rand Corporation, teachers are unhappy about it, especially the best qualified ones. Those with more degrees and those with degrees in the academic disciplines are the most likely to chafe under these restrictions.

So some of them may quit teaching and it will be hard to find people of their caliber to take their place?

Complicating the situation is that in three or four years there will probably be a shortage of teachers, for demographic reasons. And of course research shows that over the last decade or so the average measured ability of people entering teaching has been declining. So not only will we probably have an *abso-*

Ron Brandt is Executive Editor of Educational Leadership.

"If the public has evidence that academically talented people *are* becoming teachers, they will begin to develop confidence in the schools and may be willing to leave teachers relatively alone to practice their profession."

lute shortage of teachers, but we almost certainly will have a shortage of people whom the public would regard as highly qualified. Now, having high measured academic ability does not ensure that a person will be a good teacher, but in the public's mind, especially now, there is a close association. So if they know that academically inferior people are becoming teachers, they will not have confidence in the schools.

Conversely, if the public has evidence that academically talented people *are* becoming teachers, they will begin to develop confidence in the schools and may be willing to leave teachers relatively alone to practice their profession. That, it seems to me, is the key to solving many of the problems that beset American education.

Are there some ways that legislators and other policymakers can do a better job of foreseeing the results of their actions?

Well, there is an approach we use at the Rand Corporation called "policy analysis." Typically, you either look back at policies enacted by governments and try to trace their effects, or you try to predict the consequences of policies being considered. These two classes of activities—retrospective and prospective policy analysis—are rather closely related. To analyze possible effects of policies currently under consideration, you try to apply lessons learned from the application of other policies in the past.

Policymakers haven't displayed a lot of interest in policy analysis in recent years; indeed, there is almost a disdain for it. The Commission on Excellence, for example, did not betray any great understanding of the findings of educational research or of policy analysis. Their report seems to have been written

by thoughtful people, but they did not take a lot of time to try to understand the full implications of what they were saying.

What's an example of successful use of policy analysis in the public sector?

Policy analysis is only one ingredient in policy making. Policymakers are driven more by a desire to gain credit for having done something about a problem as by any other motivation. I'm not suggesting they are deceitful or cynical, but that political careers—even bureaucratic careers—are made by proposing new things. You get credit for raising people's hopes about your ability to solve a problem shortly down the road. Nobody in the political arena gets credit for saying he or she is going to solve a problem 10 or 15 years from now. It has to be within the next three years. When you're trying to have rapid impact, you may have a beneficial effect, but you may not. And I'd have to say that much of what has been tried over the last 15 years has missed.

If legislation trying to force higher standards won't work, what is a more appropriate strategy for policymakers?

Most of the policies tried in recent years, particularly at the state level, have cost very little or nothing. They were regulatory initiatives. The result was what could have been expected: pay little, get little. I'm afraid that what is needed is going to cost money. Teacher salaries, for example, have been declining in recent years in real terms. We have a long way to go to make beginning and average salaries of teachers somewhat competitive with the alternatives available to able people.

Besides that, I think that frankly we're going to have to lure people into teach-

ing. College education these days is very expensive, so you could get young people to think about teaching by offering financial assistance—scholarships, fellowships, loans—either for teaching generally or for teaching in specified fields.

Paradoxically, some things that need to occur may not be all that expensive. In some cases we have evolved rather elaborate bureaucracies in our school systems that are costly and tend to deprofessionalize the work of classroom teachers. If you have central administrators doing all the planning and decision making, you downgrade the role of the classroom teacher. One of the ways to make teaching more attractive is to delegate some of the responsibilities that have gravitated upward in the bureaucracy. That is, I think that teachers—while remaining classroom teachers—must be freed part of the time to do the important work of inducting new teachers into the school system, of helping evaluate their peers, of planning the curriculum, of providing inservice workshops, and so on.

A final comment on higher standards?

The road from standards to standardized testing to standardized teaching to standardized students is a short one. We must keep from going all the way down that road. We have to find a way to establish high standards and expectations, and communicate them to the people who need to know and use them, without the rigidities I've seen associated with much educational policymaking.□

[1]Arthur E. Wise, *Legislated Learning: The Bureaucratization of the American Classroom* (Berkeley: University of California Press, 1979).